L.Y.

TOWARD
A THEORY OF
EUROCOMMUNISM

Toward a Theory of Eurocommunism

THE RELATIONSHIP OF EUROCOMMUNISM TO EUROSOCIALISM

Armen Antonian

CONTRIBUTIONS IN POLITICAL SCIENCE, NUMBER 166

GREENWOOD PRESS
New York • Westport, Connecticut • London

Library of Congress Cataloging-in-Publication Data

Antonian, Armen, 1954–
    Toward a theory of Eurocommunism.

    (Contributions in political science, ISSN 0147–1066;
no. 166)
    Bibliography: p.
    Includes index.
    1. Communism—Europe. 2. Socialism—Europe.
I. Title. II. Series.
HX239.A58 1987   335.43′094   86–19395
ISBN 0–313–25295–5 (lib. bdg. : alk. paper)

Library of Congress Catalog Card Number: 86–19395
ISBN: 0–313–25295–5
ISSN: 0147–1066

First published in 1987

Greenwood Press, Inc.
88 Post Road West, Westport, Connecticut 06881

Printed in the United States of America

The paper used in this book complies with the
Permanent Paper Standard issued by the National
Information Standards Organization (Z39.48–1984).

10 9 8 7 6 5 4 3 2 1

Contents

Abbreviations

CERES	Centre d'Etudes, de Recherches et d'Education Socialistes
CGIL	Confederazione Generale Italiana del Lavoro
CGT	Confédération Générale du Travail
Comintern	Communist International
CPSU	Communist Party, Soviet Union
DC	Democrazia Cristiana
FGDS	Fédération de la Gauche Démocratique et Socialiste
PCE	Partido Communista Español
PDF	Parti Communiste Français
PDI	Partito Communista Italiano
PS	Parti Socialiste Français
PSI	Partito Socialista Italiano
SFIO	Section Française de l'Internationale Ouvrière

Acknowledgments ___

The principal guiding force behind the development of this work was Professor Irwin Wall. I was fortunate to be able to call on Professor Wall's extensive knowledge of international Communism and on his expertise on the French Communist Party. His keen criticisms kept this admittedly "free" thinker in line, and yet, like a true teacher, Professor Wall allowed me the latitude to produce what I hope is a significant work. I believe that our "experiment" at the University of California, Riverside of allowing a graduate student in political science to cross disciplines and work with a professor of history proved to be fruitful.

I am also grateful to the University of California, Riverside for providing me with financial assistance in the form of a Humanities Research Grant and the Chancellor's Patent Fund.

I received generous hospitality and assistance from the Combredet family in Paris, especially Nicole Combredet and the late Agnes Combredet. There are many others who were especially accommodating to me in France and many along the way who took the time and effort to help me in countless other ways. I am similarly indebted to those who granted me interviews in France and Italy and shared their invaluable personal observations.

My own family, Arden, Sarkis, and Mariam Antonian, and my uncles, Sarkis and Bedros Antonian, stood behind me throughout the duration of the study.

Virginia Bustamante provided expert preparation of the text.

TOWARD
A THEORY OF
EUROCOMMUNISM

1

Toward a Theory of Eurocommunism ____

In June 1976, the Italian Communist Party (PCI) polled a remarkable 34 percent of the vote in the parliamentary elections. The PCI's strategy of a peaceful and gradual "Italian road to socialism," carefully cultivated after World War II, was on the verge of success. The PCI, as it developed into the largest nonruling Communist Party, had by the force of its own example commanded the attention of political observers. It had been, after all, the party of the noted Marxist theoretician Antonio Gramsci, who developed the concept of a gradual transition to socialism ("war of position") in the Western democracies, and of Palmiro Togliatti, who, as secretary of the PCI, fostered the notion of polycentrism, or multiple centers of power in international Communism, challenging the dominance of the Soviet Communist Party (CPSU).

However, the PCI, on its own in the international Communist movement, was considered a "freak." Italian Communism seemed to exist uniquely in the political vacuum of Italian politics. A confluence of political events in Western Europe in the mid–1970s changed this perception by altering the PCI's seeming isolation. The Spanish Communist Party (PCE) won its hard-fought battle for legalization in Spain after the death of Francisco Franco. The PCE portrayed itself as a champion of democracy, and its electoral prospects looked bright as it became legalized in April 1977. Meanwhile, in France, the left was enjoying a phenomenal period of unity; Socialists and Communists had polled 49 percent in the second round of the 1974 French presidential elections, and they had developed a programmatic accord (the Common Program) for a future government.

As the French Communist Party (PCF), despite its strong Stalinist heritage, signed a joint declaration with the PCI boldly endorsing "bourgeois" democracy in November 1975, enough new elements had emerged within Western European Communism to force observers to reconsider the role of nonruling Communist parties in the Western democracies. *Eurocommunism* was the word used to embrace and to describe this confluence of events, political strategies, and ideological modifications. *Eurocommunism* was tossed to and fro; from journalists to academicians to politicians, in order to explain the new twists in Western European Communism in the 1970s.

As academic research began to uncover the strategies of the principal Western Communist parties, it posed anew the question of whether Communist parties could be taken at their word with regard to their liberal democratic intentions or whether they had merely adopted a new, clever strategy of penetration or infiltration of Western institutions, and as scholars began to shed some light on Eurocommunism, so too, did they begin to dilute the term by using *Eurocommunism* to describe any deviation in international Communism.

It was little wonder, then, after an avalanche of literature on Eurocommunism, written from various perspectives in the discipline of political science as well as from the historian's point of view, that scholars began asking if the term really meant anything at all. Eurocommunism, now an apparent figment of the journalistic imagination, seemed to disappear from political discourse as quickly as it had surfaced, with scarcely an afterthought. Works written on the subject of Eurocommunism from the 1979–1982 period virtually apologized for adding yet another piece to the already burgeoning literature on the subject. Authors justified their contributions by pointing out that they intended to approach Eurocommunism from a different angle or to cover a different aspect of the topic.[1] Fortunately, this state of affairs did not endure; *Eurocommunism* has indeed become embedded in political discourse even though it remains a nebulous term.[2]

The tone for a more cautious approach to Eurocommunism was set by Jean Revel in a January 1978 article in *Foreign Affairs*, in which he criticized American scholars for paying too much attention to Eurocommunism and, in doing so, unwittingly giving it a credence it did not deserve (for Revel, Eurocommunism did not exist). After the failure of the "union of the left" in the legislative elections in France in March 1978 and the May 1978 kidnapping and murder of the leader of the ruling Christian Democratic Party, Aldo Moro, by the Italian Red Brigades, the PCI's ambitions for gaining cabinet posts in the government suffered a setback (Moro was a symbol of compromise with the PCI within his party), and the immediacy of the Eurocommunist movement and its overall strength substantially declined. In June 1979, the PCI experienced significant losses in parliamentary elections, which hinted that its dramatic electoral rise in the mid–1970s had peaked. In the same vein, the PCE, after the June 1977 parliamentary elections in

Spain, was not as strong electorally as many had anticipated; the PCE attained only 10 percent of the vote. Furthermore, as Georges Lavau pointed out with some merit, much of what was supposed to be new about Eurocommunism consisted of ideas that had, in fact, been previously expressed in some form by the three major Communist parties in the Eurocommunist equation: the French, the Italian, and the Spanish.[3] Perhaps Eurocommunism was not something novel after all.

Eurocommunism was buried even before it had ever been defined. One of the most striking aspects of the literature on Eurocommunism is the paucity of definitions of the subject. Certain observers have attempted to explain their reticence in defining Eurocommunism by pointing to its transitory or ephemeral character. Thus, for Peter Lange and Maurizio Vannicelli, Eurocommunism was an uneven process of change that could be seen to occur in fits and starts.[4] Annie Kriegel saw it as a "temptation," a temptation for the Western Communist parties to escape from the ruins of Stalinism.[5] But, if Eurocommunism is a process in which the Western Communist parties, in adopting a liberal posture, are attempting to escape the negative images of their past, where is this process going and what are its elements? What can the observer look for in order to ascertain whether or not it is genuine? Whether Eurocommunism is an embryonic political movement or an ideology, it cannot be expected to exist in the real world in any clear-cut form. A definition of Eurocommunism remains important, however inchoately it may have first appeared, or, if such be the case, however rapidly it may have disappeared.

Temporary or even permanent setbacks of the aforementioned Communist parties cannot justify avoiding a categorization of Eurocommunism. There have been many movements and ideologies that have never had a great political impact or been the basis of a government but are nonetheless a part of general political discourse and have defined characteristics. Anarchism is one prime example.

Another reason for the inadequacy of the literature on Eurocommunism, a reason that is instrumental in explaining why Eurocommunism still has no concrete definition, is the mode in which it has been studied. Eurocommunism has been principally studied either in the realm of international relations or from the perspective of comparative politics, the latter approach mostly from the angle of the study of a single Communist Party. The first mode of analysis has been unable to pose many relevant questions since it has been too bound up with strategic emphasis on international policy. The second mode of analysis has been employed in too narrow a fashion to draw general conclusions. Insofar as Eurocommunism is a new concept, an unfolding ideology, or a new political movement, it may be adequately classified if it is looked at historically and addressed from the point of view of political theory. In this way, the political specificity of Eurocommunism may be determined. For example, different approaches of the Eurocommunist parties to NATO or the European Community do not necessarily mean that a coherent Eurocommunist position does not exist, as had been suggested in the literature on Eurocommunism. It is quite possible for two political parties with the same ideological basis and the same political goals to have differing opinions on a host of contemporary issues. Rarely does an ideology or political orientation provide a blueprint for all such issues.

The fact that Eurocommunism has not yet received a clear-cut or satisfactory definition does not mean that certain building blocks or elements for such a definition have not been uncovered by the early writings on the subject. However, while many elements of Eurocommunism have been pinpointed, the concept of Eurocommunism has also been *misused* in political discourse, a misuse that has tended to dilute the term, already somewhat vague, by making it a catchall phrase and thus sapping its power and utility as a tool of analysis. Eurocommunism at first was a concept, an analytical category imposed on social practice by the observer to better organize and understand reality.[6] For this be done effectively, the term must have some defined limits.

Eurocommunism is a recent phenomenon. Lange and Vannicelli noted that Eurocommunism was a concept of the 1970s.[7] Thus, any use of the concept to explain events in earlier periods of international Communism must be done cautiously. *Eurocommunism* is a political label attached to *nonruling* Communist parties. To use the word to also describe orientations of the Communist parties of Eastern Europe can be misleading. That the Romanian and Yugoslavian Communist parties have similar positions on international affairs on some points with the Italian Party does not, in itself, warrant the usage of the term *Eurocommunism* to describe these parties jointly.

The term *Eurocommunism* implies a European orientation. One of Kriegel's possible scenarios for the development of Eurocommunism was precisely that it could be a revolutionary strategy for the conquest of power on a regional level. Eurocommunism could then be seen as a regional Communism distinct from an international or a national Communism.[8] However, this is not the case. Lange and Vannicelli noted that Eurocommunism should not be so much associated with Europe as it should be associated with industrial democracy.[9] The former chairman of the PCE, Santiago Carrillo, stated that the policy and theoretical formulations that justify Eurocommunism are "valid for all developed capitalist countries."[10] Manuel Azcarate, a member of the Political Bureau of the PCE in the 1970s and then leader for the PCE on foreign relations, noted that Eurocommunism is a "current of ideas," a "political force," and a new "strategy" for the transformation of *"advanced indus-trial societies"* to a new conception of socialist society.[11]

Why not use the word *Eurocommunism* to describe the orientations of Eastern European Communist parties? The positions of Eurocom-munism regarding the separation of the party and the state, the need for the plurality of political parties, the acceptance of basic freedoms, and at least the *pretense* of not trying to dominate a ruling political coalition are propositions that ruling Communist parties cannot ac-cept; these are formulas that threaten to undermine their basis of power. What the Eurocommunist parties propose as elements in their model of socialism have little to do with the "socialism" in the East. Thus, H. T. Willetts argued, "What seems undeniable is that these pronouncements [various statements of the PCI, PCE, and PCF in the 1975–77 period associated with Eurocommunism] have opened up an ideological rift far wider and deeper than that between the USSR and Yugoslavia ... or than that between the USSR and China."[12] This is why the Soviet journal *New Times* was so vehement in its criticism of Carrillo's 1977 book *Eurocommunism and the State*, when Carrillo hinted, however timidly, that while still respecting the historical ex-perience of the Russian Revolution, Eurocommunism could be a spe-cific model of socialism. In the *New Times* article and for the Soviets generally, "Communism, real scientific Communism, is unique."[13] Vernon Aspaturian noted, in reference to this article, that if Eurocom-munism could not be assimilated into the Soviet experience, it would be on a collision course with the Leninist brand of Communism.[14] The U.S.S.R. has always been opposed to socialist models based on anything other than the Soviet experience that could, by their force of attraction, take on universal qualities.[15] Jean Elleinstein, the principal PCF his-torian in the 1970s, has argued that the PCF failed to explore the theoretical implications of its "Eurocommunist" pronouncements to the party's own detriment. If democracy is both a means and the aim of socialism, then it is impossible for the PCF not to be critical of "those societies calling themselves socialist."[16] The real power of the Eurocommunist tendency lay precisely in its potential to negate the Communist experience stemming from 1917. The novelty of Eurocom-munism is that it has always contained ideological elements that ul-timately projected outside the Communist movement as it has been traditionally understood. Eurocommunism does not hark back to a "golden past" of Communism before the death of Lenin or before the banishment of Trotsky by Stalin. Thus, it should really have come as no surprise that after 1981, the concept of Eurocommunism could be merged, for some, with the larger European left.

Eurocommunism, if taken to the limit, is Communism negating its past history. Can this be done? The majority of observers are naturally skeptical and point to the history of international Communism to justify their skepticism. Thus, G. R. Urban noted that Eurocommunism "is a freak which must end in Social Democracy or revert back to some form of Leninism. In the first case it will cease to be Communist, in the second it will no longer be 'Euro.' "[17] Kriegel addressed the implications of Eurocommunism when she wrote, "At issue is whether an established and fully developed party with well-defined characteristics will be able to dismantle itself, right down to the essential core that has enabled it to survive for so long, and then rebuild itself out of a new concept of politics around a new essential core."[18] Kriegel also concluded that this was impossible since she denied that any third way between Communism or social democracy was possible. Roy Godson hesitated to use the term *Eurocommunism* at all because it implied that Western Communist parties have a type of Communism "diverging radically" from the U.S.S.R. and Eastern Europe. The subtle departure from orthodoxy made by the Western European Communist parties, according to Godson, did not warrant the usage of a "new political category."[19] Thus, several observers already have had a pretty fair idea of what Eurocommunism *implied* but have refused to explore or denied this *possibility*. What are the elements that prevent the Western Communist parties from breaking with Moscow, and conversely, what factors push them into taking distance from the Soviet Union?

Eurocommunism, *if* it lives up to its pretensions, cannot cover the same political space as orthodox Communism in the contemporary world. The reason that this antinomy with orthodox Communism was not immediately apparent was that Eurocommunism was first mentioned, and continues to be mentioned, only with regard to parties once tied to the Communist International. We shall see later that the ideology of Eurocommunism is also pertinent to Socialist parties that have broken with social democracy, with the Socialist Party in France as the leading example. If Eurocommunism does not take root in the contemporary West, then it cannot be said to exist as a *movement*.

However, Eurocommunism's demise as a political movement would not detract from it as an ideology. In fact, the Italian Communist Party has, at every critical juncture, steadily continued to expand its "Eurocommunist" policies to the point that it announced, after the Polish coup in December 1981, that the revolutionary period that began in 1917 was exhausted, and that further progress in the U.S.S.R. and Eastern Europe was in doubt.[20] With this position, the PCI has really fulfilled its Eurocommunist pretensions, even though certain aspects of its evolution remain to be completed. While it is not possible for a Communist Party in power to embrace Eurocommunism, since this would mean that it would willingly abolish the class privileges of its members embodied in the apparatus of the party state, it is possible for a nonruling party to give up its *relative privileges* as an embryonic new class (Milovan Djilas's term), since it continues to exist, vis-à-vis the larger society, in a subaltern position. Nonruling Communist parties are not firmly ensconced in positions of society-wide power and therefore are capable of changing their attitudes toward power and society, although not without immense difficulty.

By deriving the factors that prompted the emergence of Eurocommunism in some nonruling Communist parties, we can better understand its political position. Lange and Vannicelli cited in this regard (1) the decline if not the collapse of the Soviet myth, (2) the breakup of the international Communist movement, (3) the realization that close attachment to the U.S.S.R. is an obstacle to winning national power, and (4) the existence of détente, which provided greater space to maneuver for nonruling Communist parties.[21] Richard Lowenthal added that the Western European Communist parties are given a choice of either following the masses of their members and followers who are becoming integrated into democracy or risking becoming sterile sects.[22] Lowenthal also pointed out, paradoxically, that the influence of the Western Communist parties in the 1970s can be attributed to the Western economic crisis.[23] Thus, a combination of the strength of Western democracy with the weaknesses of its economic structures provided a contradictory impetus to Eurocommunism in the 1970s.

Eurocommunism has repudiated the CPSU's leading role over the whole or any component of the community of ruling and nonruling Communist parties. It has rejected Marxist-Leninist orthodoxy in ideology, politics, economics, and culture, and it denies the universal applicability of the revolutionary experience or "model" represented by the countries of "scientific socialism." Eurocommunism implies the right of the various Communist parties to manage their own political destiny, and it accepts the constitutional guarantees of liberal democracy and the various political freedoms.[24]

However, Eurocommunism differs in kind from Togliatti's notion of unity in diversity or polycentrism in the international Communist movement. Unlike Togliatti's notion of polycentrism, Eurocommunism has, from the outset, contained elements that go beyond the Communist movement itself, at least as it has been constituted since 1917. National Communism, which allowed each Communist party some autonomy as long as it acknowledged the priority of the Soviet experience, did not challenge the basis of single-party rule that provides the political basis of existing Communist societies.

Eurocommunism renounces violent revolution and the dictatorship of the proletariat while acknowledging the reversibility of Communist

power (something a ruling Communist Party cannot do). For Elleinstein, Eurocommunism has meant (1) a radically new conception for
the Western Communist parties of the relation of socialism and democracy, (2) complete independence from the U.S.S.R., and (3) a major
internal democratization of the "Eurocommunist" Communist parties.[25] One of the reasons given by Georges Lavau for the PCF's Eurocommunism in the mid–1970s was what he called the "Gulag effect"
(in reference to Solzhenitsyn's book on the atrocities of Stalinism) and
the need of the PCF to escape its negative fallout.[26]

Little was left of Eurocommunism as a movement in Western Europe
after 1982. The PCI and some minor parties (the PCF had turned away
from Eurocommunism after the 1978 legislative elections in France)
crystallized and merged with the notion of Euroleft. This was always
implied in Eurocommunism as the PCI and the PCE, though not wanting to break with Moscow principally for reasons of party cohesiveness,
had to nonetheless prepare the way. Carrillo in *Mundo Obrero* as early
as April 1976 had noted, after using the phrase "international *revolutionary* [not "Communist"] movement": "This internationalism has
today a task, particularly in the developed capitalist countries, to tran-
scend the schism produced in the workers' movement by the October
Revolution and to create conditions for co-operation and understanding
among all the socialist forces. This *new internationalism* has today a
new component: the co-operation of the Christian forces which support
a departure from capitalist society."[27] The iron was in the fire, ready
to be forged if need be. Heinz Timmerman was quick to take notice
of this potentiality in stating, "If it should prove true in the long term
that 'the nondogmatic,' leftist-Socialist trend within the Italian Communist party could gain dominant influence, then the possibility can
no longer be excluded that at some time in the future similar or
converging programmatic proposals may be jointly put forward by
Democractic Socialists, progressive bourgeois forces, and Eurocommunists."[28]

The notion of the Euroleft was given concrete expression at the PCI's
Fifteenth Congress in 1979. Here the "new conception of internationalism" was seen to open "a process which tends toward the overcoming
of historical divergences and to a *unitary recomposition* of the working
class movement of Western Europe." Enrico Berlinguer, the PCI chairman, linked this "reunification" to a "la terza via," which would be
connected to a "third phase" in the history of the working-class movement. The first phase was dominated by the social democratic parties
of the Second International and the second phase by the Communist
parties spawned by the October Revolution.[29] Berlinguer gave credence
to this conception by meeting the head of the French Socialist Party
(PS), Lionel Jospin, in Paris in March 1982, stating that the concept of

the Euroleft was always contained in the concept of Eurocommunism.[30] Jospin, not wanting to be outflanked on the left by his new partner, noted, "We are a Socialist Party, *not a Social Democratic one.*" Jospin indicated that inasmuch as his party wanted to break with capitalism in a "progressive movement" and not merely run it better, the notion of a "third road" was interesting to the PS as well.[31]

The Eurocommunism that originated in the Western European Communist parties was a response to the declining aura of Soviet-style Communism. However, the reason it appeared to take root in the mid–1970s was that the social systems in the West were also undergoing a crisis that provided a *potential* opening for a new kind of antisystem party. Thus, there has never really been a question of the social democratization of Western Communist parties even though after 1975, with the PCF-PCI communiqué as an example, the Eurocommunist parties had adopted the position of social democracy with regard to political democracy. Eurocommunism then, is, a variety of democratic socialism. It does, however, explicitly retain the goal of socialism as something to be achieved, marking it off from (post-Bernsteinian) social democracy. It also differs from social democracy in the extent of its nationalization policies. This was also the case with the leftist Socialist Party in France, which prompted Maurice Duverger to label the French Socialist Project a "Socialism of a Third Kind."[32]

Eurocommunism seeks to merge means and ends, that is, it professes to strive for a democratic change to a democratic socialism. Thus, Kriegel writes that Eurocommunism's higher, more comprehensive ambition is "to make up for . . . the Communist movement's inability to integrate freedom into the socialist goal right from the start."[33] Even though Eurocommunists are not social democrats, they have more in common doctrinally with Eduard Bernstein and Karl Kautsky, the theoreticians of social democracy, than they do with Lenin. This has caused John Kautsky to remark, "it is not only in their words but in their policies of peaceful participation in electoral, parliamentary and coalition politics in the pursuit of reformist and gradualist goals that the Eurocommunist parties of Western Europe have in recent years been far more Kautskyist than Leninist."[34] Azcarate has noted that "obviously the answers of an Italian Eurocommunist to the problem of today are more closely related to those of a leftist Socialist than to those of a traditional communist."[35]

Eurocommunism has disavowed any pretense at a minority seizure of power both theoretically and practically. Bourgeois democracy is no longer seen as "bourgeois" but merely as democracy. Eurocommunism implies the withering away of Leninism and a transition, in theory, to a vision of an economically, and socially radical, pluralistic parliamentary democracy.[36] Aspaturian suggested that if Eurocommunism

meant anything at all, it was the stripping away of the Leninist component of Marxism-Leninism and residual Stalinist elements mingled
with Leninism.[37] It is not surprising, then, that in December 1981,
Berlinguer announced that the road to Socialism in the West definitely
cannot be based on Lenin.[38] This gets at the heart of the matter. For
Western Communist parties to really change, they must repudiate Leninist doctrine, a doctrine that contains all the elements of the Communist experience: the minority seizure of power, contempt for
democracy and autonomous institutions, the concept of democratic
centralism in the party, and with it the notion of the party state. The
Eurocommunist parties must conclude that the Soviet Union and the
societies of Eastern Europe are *not* socialist societies. When they argue
that democracy is a universal criterion for socialism, they must accept
as well the logical conclusion that the U.S.S.R. is not socialist. Fernando Claudin has argued that if socialism with democracy were impossible in 1917, Eurocommunism must argue that socialism was then
also an impossible historical task.[39] The Eurocommunists reject any
single "model" of socialism in an obvious reaction to the domination
of the Soviet experience in international Communism. Thus, they are
hesitant to propose their own "model." But there is no choice here.
Eurocommunism must conclude by agreeing with Kautsky that socialism without democracy is unthinkable.[40]

The Western Communist parties are faced with the dilemma outlined by Robert Legvold: "Western European Communist parties are
increasingly compelled to judge the Soviet Union critically in order to
enhance their legitimacy, they, on the other hand, are equally compelled to guard a basic loyalty to it in order to maintain their integ-
rity."[41] The latter consideration, the fear of a loss of cohesion in the
nonruling Communist parties, has prevented them from breaking with
the Soviet Union unless compelled to do so by the course of events.
Other inhibiting factors are (1) historical ties to the Soviet Union, (2)
normal ambiguities in the evolution away from old habits and patterns
of thought, and (3) a psychological reluctance to break totally from
what one has been.[42] Binding financial ties of Western Communist
parties with Eastern Europe and the threat that Moscow might cut off
a recalcitrant party are other relevant factors. These are all significant
deterrents. Still, the bottom line remains whether or not a mass party
such as the PCI or the PCF would risk its own marginalization in order
to remain aligned with the Soviet Union. So far the PCI has not done
so, while the PCF has. As we will see, the reasons for the PCF's self-
destructive behavior and turning away from Eurocommunism after
1978 are quite complex. While the PCF and the PCI built much of their
strength in the past around the aura of the Soviet model, today their
real strength comes from their hundreds of thousands of party members

and their millions of voters, not from the Soviet Union, which has become a liability.

Eurocommunism is not another variety of Communism like Titoism, Maoism, or Castroism but rather *another* communism, a communism that was originally merged imperceptibly with socialism and radicalism before 1917. Eurocommunists still cling to categories and patterns of thought stemming from their Communist past, but these are increasingly residual. On the other hand, while Eurocommunism has no relevance to ruling Communist parties, it may be associated with leftist Socialist parties such as the French Socialist Party, which has rejected the reformist aspect of the social democratic experience and which loosely harbors the vision of a classless society. *Le Projet socialiste* for the French Socialist Party in the 1980s invoked in a favorable light the century-and-a-half-old notion of a classless society that seeks to eliminate the exploitation of man by man and rests on a profound transformation of capitalist economic structures and relations of production.[43] Eurocommunists and leftist Socialists still sound different in today's Europe if one listens to their discourse. However, they are *saying the same thing*! They occupy the same political space and have largely the same goals. Of course, a Eurocommunist is likely to be more fervent in the underpinnings of his views and more confident of his final vision of a classless society. But the Eurocommunist project is none other than an attempt to salvage Marx's original problematic of socialism, which meant the self-emancipation of the proletariat, a project similar to the search for a "lost socialism" proposed by the CERES (Center for Socialist Studies, Research, and Education) group in the Socialist Party of France. Inasmuch as it embodies individuals and political parties, Eurocommunism is a political movement. Inasmuch as it exists only as a vision, an unattained reality, it is an ideology.

NOTES

1. For example, see the preface to one of the better books on Eurocommunism, edited by Peter Lange and Maurizio Vannicelli and entitled *The Communist Parties of Italy, France, and Spain* (London: George Allen & Unwin, 1981).

2. Recent works on Eurocommunism have conveyed a renewed, positive attitude in the study of the subject. See Howard Machin, ed., *National Communism in Western Europe: A Third Way for Socialism?* (London: Methuen, 1983); Lawrence L. Whetten, ed., *The Present State of Communist Internationalism* (Lexington, Mass.: Lexington Books, 1983).

3. Georges Lavau, "Eurocommunism: Four Years On," *European Journal of Political Research* 7 (December 1979): 360.

4. Lange and Vannicelli, p. 9.

5. Annie Kriegel, *Eurocommunism: A New Kind of Communism?* (Stanford, Calif.: Hoover Institution Press, 1978), p. xi.

6. Ronald Tiersky, in Rudolf L. Tokes, ed., *Eurocommunism and Détente* (New York: New York University Press, 1978), p. 143.

7. Lange and Vannicelli, p. 3.

8. Kriegel, p. 9.

9. Lange and Vannicelli, p. 3.

10. Santiago Carrillo, *Eurocommunism and the State* (Westport, Conn.: Lawrence Hill & Co., 1978), p. 8.

11. Manuel Azcarate, in Richard Kindersley, ed., *In Search of Eurocommunism* (New York: St. Martin's Press, 1981), p. 23.

12. H. T. Willetts, in Kindersley, *In Search of Eurocommunism*, p. 3.

13. Kriegel, p. 70.

14. Vernon V. Aspaturian, In Vernon V. Aspaturian, Jiri Valenta, and David D. Burke, eds., *Eurocommunism between East and West* (Bloomington: Indiana University Press, 1980), p. 8.

15. Lilly Marcou, *L'U.R.S.S. vue de gauche* (Paris: Presses Universitaires de France, 1982), p. 160.

16. Jean Elleinstein, in Kindersley, *In Search of Eurocommunism*, p. 71. The PCF never adopted a critical view of the U.S.S.R.; it maintained that the societies of Eastern European Communism maintained a "positive balance sheet."

17. G. R. Urban, *Eurocommunism* (New York: Universe Books, 1978), p. 8.

18. Kriegel, p. 2.

19. Roy Godson and Stephen Hasseler, *Eurocommunism* (New York: St. Martin's Press, 1978), p. 4.

20. *Revolution*, February 12–18, 1982. See also *Communist Affairs* (October 1982).

21. Lange and Vannicelli, p. 15.

22. Richard Lowenthal, in William Griffith, ed., *The European Left: Italy, France, and Spain* (Lexington, Mass.: Lexington Books, 1979), p. 240.

23. Ibid.

24. Rudolph L. Tokes, *Eurocommunism and Détente*, p. 2.

25. Elleinstein, in Kindersley, *In Search of Eurocommunism*, p. 67.

26. Georges Lavau, *A Quoi Sert le Parti communiste francais?* (Paris: Librairie Arthéme Fayard, 1981), pp. 348–85.

27. Santiago Carrillo, in Lange and Vannicelli, *The Communist Parties of Italy, France, and Spain*, p. 275.

28. Heinz Timmerman, in Griffith, *The European Left: Italy, France, and Spain*, p. 191.

29. Enrico Berlinguer, Grant Amyot, *The Italian Communist Party* (New York: St. Martin's Press, 1981) p. 227.

30. *Le Monde*, March 31, 1982.

31. *L'Unité*, April 30, 1982.

32. *Le Monde*, December 24, 1982.

33. Kriegel, p. 16.

34. John Kautsky, "Karl Kautsky and Eurocommunism," *Studies in Comparative Communism* 14 (Spring 1981): 7.

35. Manuel Azcarate, in Lawrence L. Whetten, ed., *The Present State of Communist Internationalism* (Lexington, Mass.: Lexington Books, 1983), p. 108.

36. William E. Griffith, in Tokes, *Eurocommunism and Détente*, pp. 385–86.

37. Aspaturian, p. 10.

38. *Le Monde*, December 17, 1981.

39. Fernando Claudin, *Eurocommunism and Socialism* (London: New Left Books, 1978), p. 61.

40. Karl Kautsky, *The Dictatorship of the Proletariat* (Manchester: National Labour Press, 1920), p. 5.

41. Robert Legvold, in Tokes, *Eurocommunism and Détente*, pp. 346–47.

42. Ibid., p. 346.

43. Parti Socialiste Français, *Le Projet socialiste pour la France des années 80* (Paris: Club Socialiste du Livre, 1980), p. 9.

2

The Russian
Revolution Revisited _

To understand Eurocommunism as either a political ideology or a movement, some notion of the political ideology and movement from which it first emerged, that is, orthodox or Leninist Communism, must be developed. Communism, in conventional political discourse, was seen as a result of the Russian Revolution of 1917, from which several subvarieties—Titoism, Maoism, and so on—subsequently developed. *Eurocommunism* was a term initially and primarily associated with political parties once tied to the now defunct Communist International. At the outset of the investigation, we must attempt to reconstruct defining features of the Russian Revolution and the Communist experience that have had a major impact on the Western European nonruling Communist parties. This will be accomplished by covering key aspects of the debate between the Second and the Third Internationals involving the great historical figures of Karl Kautsky, V. I. Lenin, Leon Trotsky, and Rosa Luxemburg. In this debate, we will attempt to point out positions that may be directly or indirectly linked to Eurocommunism. Finally, contemporary criticism of the U.S.S.R. based primarily on the pioneering analysis of Eastern European dissidents will be synthesized as a basis for Eurocommunist theory.

The Russian Revolution was to have been the event that precipitated the beginning of the socialist epoch. Such a process would mean, in Marx's view, the beginning of the "regeneration" of mankind, which he claimed had been progressively stripped of its human attributes in the "prehistory" of human society. It was to mark the beginning of the transition to Communism, to the self-regulated society, where the "realm of necessity" would become the "realm of freedom" and where the agelong exploitation of man by man would be eliminated. It was this communist vision of Marx that the Bolsheviks appropriated and used as an ethical principle to capture the awakening aspirations of early–20th-century Russian society. To this day, Communists claim to seek the realization of this vision, and the Communist parties in power cannot assure their rule over society without continually propounding it.

The foremost attribute of the Communist ideology, then, as it has existed since 1917, is that the Russian Revolution must be regarded as the beginning of a socialist epoch leading to Communism. It is secondary whether individual Communists or Communist parties have subsequently maintained that the Russian Revolution has degenerated into this or that form. It is the recognition of the Bolshevik Revolution as a socialist revolution that distinguishes the Communist ideology.

Probably the most overriding factor in the emergence and spread of the brand of Communism originating from the Russian Revolution was the prevailing belief throughout the gamut of the left parties in Europe after World War I that revolution was at hand. A second elevating factor was the perceived black mark against the Second International for its acquiescence to the First World War. It is only with these factors in mind that one can understand how a relatively insignificant wing of social democracy, the Russian Bolsheviks, considered somewhat arbitrary in their political formulations by Marxism in the West, could eventually become the linchpins of the Communist movement. The bottom line was this: the Bolsheviks had made a revolution, and in an era of "moribund" capitalism, such a revolution was seen to mark the beginning of the socialist epoch. After all, didn't the revolution embody the movements of the most downtrodden classes of society? Weren't both the aristocracy and the capitalist class eliminated from Russian society? Those who gave affirmative answers to these questions, wanting to believe that a new era had dawned, were swept away by the Bolshevik logic.

According to Franz Borkenau, the first fifteen years of the Communist International were based on the notion of impending revolution, sure to occur if only a reliable Communist Party modeled on the Russians' were constituted to combat socialist betrayal.[1] Borkenau wrote, "The basic conviction of Communism is that it needs only a truly 'Bolshevik' party applying the appropriate tactics, in order to win."[2] It was only in stipulating the notion of an impending revolution in the West that the Bolsheviks were able to remain within the political framework of social democracy. The two principal Bolshevik theoreticians, Lenin and Trotsky, always intended the socialist revolution in Russia as a prelude to the European revolution. To have done otherwise would have been to deny the validity of Marx's stipulations regarding the necessity of certain preliminary developmental stages before the possibility of achieving a socialist society. Even with this theory of

permanent revolution, Trotsky never overlooked the factor of inadequate backward economic and social conditions in Russia as potentially
inhibiting the development of a socialist society. As for Lenin, while
he often hinted, in the wake of the Bolshevik success, at the universal
applicability of Bolshevik tactics and the historical inevitability of
many primary and secondary factors of the Russian Revolution, in *Left-
Wing Communism*, he still argued that after revolution in the West,
Russia would remain backward in development.[3]

The prevailing view of the proximity of social revolution was also
manifest in the social democracy in the West. Kautsky and Eduard
Bernstein, two of the standard bearers of social democracy, in their
own ways, were no more impervious to this notion than the Russian
Bolsheviks. If the left revolutionaries saw revolution behind every
strike or rebellion, the parliamentary wing of social democracy tended
to see every new piece of social legislation as further proof of the
mounting influence of the working class via the growth of democracy.
Indeed, some social democrats were cautious about the overall pre-
paredness of the proletariat to take political leadership in the democratic state. Bernstein, for example, warned of the prevailing low level
of development of productive forces in society. Nonetheless, the social
democrats as a group tended to see the socialist revolution as impending via waves of democracy initiated by the class action of the proletarian parties. Kautsky did not begin to modify his view with regard
to the rapidity of the socialist revolution until 1925 in his *Labour
Revolution*.[4] But wasn't Marx himself susceptible to utopian formulations in extrapolating from the political realities of the nineteenth
century? Kautsky indicated that with all his acuteness, Marx often
unduly translated into reality what he foresaw at the level of theory.[5]
Bernstein argued that Marx overestimated the pace of capitalist development when jumping from his theoretical writings in *Capital* to
actual capitalist development in the nineteenth century.[6]

The Bolsheviks saw their revolution as an outgrowth of the greater
European revolution, on the crest of the communist impulse that originated in the West. Lenin was always quick to cite the Russian Revolution as a continuation of the Paris Commune, and he held up as an
ideal the Commune's program, which called for the abolition of a
standing army and for having elected officials subject to recall while
being paid the wages of workmen. But the analogy of the Russian
Revolution to the Paris Commune was incongruous. The Paris Commune was timid in its use of force against perceived exploiters; the
Bolsheviks were not. Kautsky pointed out that in the Paris Commune,
all shades of socialist parties took part, that is, the entire proletariat,
whereas in the Russian Revolution, one socialist party gained power
in fighting against the other socialist parties, excluding them from the

ruling executive.[7] For Lenin, the first phase of socialist revolution meant only to juxtapose the principal adversaries in society, making the working classes and not the proprietary classes the dictatorial power. Thus, the Leninist conception of social revolution initially does not eliminate but actually intensifies class-based power or class politics. Stalin built upon this later, arguing that the class struggle in Russia intensified in the 1920s and 1930s.

But did the Russian Revolution fulfill even what Lenin wanted: to place the majority in the position of dictatorship? Until the Bolsheviks seized power, they had been vociferously calling for a Constitutional Assembly. Once in power, elections were held based on earlier lists of candidates when the Bolshevik presence throughout the country was not as great. As a result, the Bolsheviks received only a quarter of the votes. Lenin and Trotsky pointed out that the news of the revolution had not yet spread into many areas of Russia, which explained the low score for the Bolsheviks. Lenin pointed out that a possible resolution to this situation would be new elections. But he also hinted that if this did not occur, the Constitutional Assembly, the newly suspected place of "counterrevolution," could not be tolerated by the "Soviet power." As is well known, the Assembly was forcibly dissolved by the Bolsheviks.

Rosa Luxemburg pointed out that the resolution to the Bolshevik dilemma would have been to call for new elections. She believed that Lenin and Trotsky's decision to shut down the Constitutional Assembly would contribute to the general constriction of political life in the country, creating a situation in which the right of suffrage would have no practical significance. Luxemburg felt that this could only mean that life in the soviets and every other public institution would inevitably dry up, leaving the bureaucracy as the sole active force.[8] Luxemburg, arguing in this vein much like the liberal philosopher J. S. Mill, saw freedom for only one party as no freedom at all, real freedom being always freedom for the one who thinks differently. She considered such freedom important not because of any "fanatical conception of justice, [but because] this has been practically demonstrated."[9] Luxemburg believed the Bolshevik dictatorship would become a dictatorship of a few active politicians. Martial law would lead to arbitrariness and the degradation of society.[10]

Luxemburg's views, despite her strong concerns regarding the maintenance of democratic rights and institutions, still fell within the Bolshevik framework in important ways. Unlike Kautsky, she chose to view the Russian Revolution as potentially a socialist revolution. She did so also on the presupposition that revolution was on the agenda in Europe, which would quickly surpass the political and economic development in Russia, allowing support to be channeled to the Russian Revolution from the West. She was so caught up with the idea of revolution in Europe that she chided the German proletariat for its "unripeness" and its "inability to fulfill its historic tasks."[11] Again, the promise of a European revolution seemed to hold the key. With a European revolution, the Russian Revolution would prevail as a socialist revolution or at least would not be construed as a utopian endeavor. What if, on the other hand, no European revolution was forthcoming? This scenario was not addressed by the Bolsheviks and their supporters. But this was precisely what took place. Thus, Boris Souvarine wrote, "Contrary to their programme, the Bolsheviks had undertaken to introduce Socialism—that is Communism—without any transition.... Driven by the desperate necessities of civil war and by the mystical-romantic strain inherited from anarchism, they destroyed all private enterprise, though they could not replace it by popular initiative."[12] The Bolshevik situation, then, came to resemble what Marx himself called "crude communism."

Luxemburg accepted the arguments of Lenin and Trotsky, believing that the choice in Russia was between a Bolshevik Revolution and reaction. For Luxemburg to argue, as Kautsky did, that the conditions for a socialist revolution were not ripe in Russia was to betray oneself.[13] She argued that the revolution must take energetic "socialist" measures based on the dictatorship of a class, rather than the dictatorship of the party. But she did not stop at this point. She attacked the Bolsheviks for their early land policy with regard to the peasantry, which stated, "Go and take the land for yourselves," pointing out that this policy would create a new, stronger bourgeois class in the countryside. But what could have been the alternative? Such a development in agriculture could only have been avoided by the methods of dictatorship.

Kautsky, on the other hand, concluded that the revolution in Russia had initially brought in its train only what was achieved in France in 1789 and later in Germany, namely, the beginnings of capitalist development.[14] What Kautsky later came close to but did not actually see was that the Bolshevik Revolution brought into being a new social form, Communism, which represented neither a capitalist society nor a socialist one. Kautsky, in 1925 in *The Labour Revolution*, saw the Russian situation as one where socialists with socialist phraseology were completing the bourgeois revolution. By 1931, he saw the Communist Party as the bearer of a counterrevolution in the Bonapartist sense, destined to fail: "This wild experiment can only end in a disastrous collapse."[15] It was Boris Souvarine who accurately conceptualized the outcome of the Russian Revolution when he wrote, "Therefore the over-eager prophets of a Thermidor, still more of a Brumaire, have now plenty of leisure to meditate on the *unique char-*

acter, which they mistook, of the Russian Revolution."[16] Souvarine concluded, "But Stalin's new opponents were not yet aware of the transition of the Party into a social class interested in the preservation of the status quo and passively solid for the leaders, nor of the degeneration of the regime into the dictatorship of the Bolshevik caste over the working class."[17]

Besides open disdain for the parliamentary institutions, what else distinguished the Bolsheviks? One other noted feature was their general disregard for independent trade unionism. Lenin wrote, "Trade-unionist politics of the working class is precisely bourgeois politics of the working class."[18] Such reasoning was based on the view that the working class, if left to its own initiative, could only produce a trade union consciousness. From this basis, Lenin justified the need for a revolutionary party as a vanguard leading this same working class. Lenin's notion of the party followed in this pattern. Publishing houses, bookshops, libraries, and so on, must all be under party control. This control devolves upon the elite of the Central Committee. It was on the key issues relating to the constitution of the Communist Party that Luxemburg and Lenin had major differences. The particular conception and role of the party is one of the central characteristics of Leninism and therefore Communism. For Lenin, the party would break up if it were not able to keep strict discipline. As time went on, Lenin no longer spoke only in terms of Russian prerevolutionary conditions under the czar but rather posed the question of party discipline in universally applicable absolute terms. Luxemburg recognized this change, noting that Leninist centralism was not even appropriate to Russian conditions.[19] Luxemburg remarked that in "One Step Forward, Two Steps Backward," Lenin outlined "a most pitiless centralism."[20]

Luxemburg argued that Lenin's thesis on the party, giving the Central Committee unmitigated powers and complete discretion over the party's local committees, would lead to a situation in which the Central Committee would be the only thinking element in the party. Luxemburg contended that unlike that of other political movements, social democratic organization depended upon the direct and independent action of the masses.[21] According to Luxemburg, Lenin's perception of this difference was inadequate. She argued that the difference between democracy and Blanquism, for Lenin, was that a class-conscious section of the proletariat takes over the function of a handful of conspirators.[22] Revolution still begins and *ends* with the actions of the few.

Luxemburg quoted Lenin as defining a revolutionary social democrat as a "Jacobin joined to the organization of the proletariat, which has become conscious of its class interests."[23] Luxemburg maintained, to the contrary, the social democracy is not joined to the proletariat but rather is, itself, the proletariat. Such a view is comparable to Marx's own statement in the *Communist Manifesto* about the role of a Communist Party. Concerning the relation of the party to the working class as a whole, Marx stated, (1) "The Communists do not form a separate party opposed to other working-class parties; (2) They have no interests separate and apart from those of the proletariat as a whole; (3) They do not set up sectarian principles of their own, by which to shape and mold the proletarian movement."[24]

Another major defining feature of the Russian Revolution was the spontaneous development of the soviets, the localized, multifaceted organizations of peasants and workers functioning as interest and support groups. For Lenin and the Bolsheviks, these organizations represented new state bodies, and for Lenin in particular they embodied a "higher form" of social institution, a higher form of democracy, meaning they had transcended parliamentary institutions, making them obsolete. In other words, Lenin did not see the soviets as autonomous forms of direct democracy, accentuating and complementing representative democracy, but rather, he saw them as state bodies capable of *replacing* representative bodies. Kautsky, quick to perceive the danger of the Bolshevik policy toward the soviets, pointed out that the Bolsheviks had made an organ of a class (soviets) into an organ of government. He concluded that it was therefore appropriate that they had ceased calling themselves "social democrats" in favor of calling themselves "Communists."[25] But Kautsky also argued, on the other hand, that compared to the party and trade union organizations of countries more advanced than Russia, the soviets did not represent a higher form of proletarian organization but were instead developed at the spur of the moment to provide what was lacking in Russian society.[26]

Kautsky, like Bernstein, placed the concerns of the level of industrial development and maturity of the proletarian class in the forefront of any question concerning the transition to socialism. Thus, unlike Luxemburg, Kautsky did not sanction the implementation of "socialist" policies whenever the proletariat temporarily had the power to do so. Kautsky did not question the legitimacy of the Bolshevik Revolution itself. But neither did he accept the argument of Trotsky, echoed by Luxemburg, that the choice was between a revolutionary movement leading to socialism and slipping back to reaction. Whereas Lenin felt no qualms about taking socialist measures based on a political alliance of workers and peasants under Russian conditions, Kautsky felt otherwise. Kautsky felt that the interests of the Russian peasantry with its slogans of "Liberty and Freedom" would come into conflict with the Bolsheviks, once the Bolsheviks began to initiate "socialist" measures. Unlike the Bolsheviks, and more consistently than Luxemburg, Kautsky held firm to Marxian socialism in indicating that socialism as a means to the emancipation of the proletariat without democracy was unthinkable.[27] This is also the principal contention of Eurocommunism.

Kautsky was adamant in his criticism of the attitude of the Bolsheviks toward representative institutions and democracy. He condemned as erroneous the assertions of the Third International that parliamentarianism and democracy were essentially bourgeois institutions. Kautsky denied that democracy with universal suffrage meant domination of the bourgeoisie, pointing out that previous bourgeois revolutions had not immediately introduced universal suffrage.

In Kautsky's view, the proletariat could have no single political party because of its broad, variegated class structure. For only one party, the Communist Party, to be in power in Russia, could only mean, for Kautsky, the dictatorship of one part of the proletariat over the others.[28] Following in the Marxian framework, just as a class can split into various parties, a party may consist of the members of various classes; parties and classes are not seen as necessarily coterminous.[29] Thus, the same class interest may be represented in a variety of ways, and the representatives of the same class may be divided into different parties. This view became the basis of the PCI strategy of "historic compromise" in the 1970s.

Kautsky concluded that the Bolsheviks had established a dictatorship of a party within the proletariat.[30] Some sixty years later, militants at the base of the Communist Party of Poland in Lodz echoed these remarks of Kautsky by stating, "The dictatorship of the proletariat should not be a dictatorship *against* the proletariat."[31] It is significant that those Communist parties that are influenced by Eurocommunism have indicated that they do not intend to govern alone as sole proprietors of the state.

But the political foresight of Kautsky was most evident in his consideration of what the Russian Revolution meant to the European labor movement. Kautsky was one of the first who began to distinguish European socialism from "Communism" and thus may be considered a forebear of Eurocommunism. He saw the task of European socialism as one of warding off the moral catastrophe of Communism, stemming from a particular method of socialism (Bolshevism). He cautioned that the failure of Communism could lead to the denigration of the idea of socialism in general. For Kautsky, European socialism had to therefore distinguish between the Bolshevik methods and Marxist methods.[32] An underlying motivation of much of Eurocommunism has been the growing realization of the unpalatable nature of the Eastern European regimes to most Western constituencies. Such a sensitivity has been more and more tied to a notion, often vague, that there is something *fundamentally* wrong in these countries.

The Bolshevik who later became most identified with criticism of the Russian Revolution was Trotsky. However, Trotsky never took his criticism to the point of repudiating the Russian Revolution as a socialist revolution, and given his special role in this revolution, perhaps it would be expecting too much for him do have done so. Trotsky instead viewed the "deviations" of Stalinism as a possible prelude to the resurgence of capitalism. Nonetheless, by 1939, when writing on the Nazi-Soviet pact, Trotsky came very close to posing the question that can provide a rich and useful framework for understanding the nature of Soviet society and, ipso facto, Communism. Trotsky wrote at that time, "either the Stalin regime is an abhorrent relapse in the process of transforming a bourgeois society into a Socialist society, or the Stalin regime is the *first stage of a new exploiting society*."[33] If, indeed, the second prognosis were correct, "[the] bureaucracy will become a new exploiting class." Trotsky, at this point, no longer regarded the Soviet Union as "halfway between capitalism and socialism," as he tended to do at other times. Rather, he allowed for the possibility of a "new exploiting society" as having been the outcome of the Russian Revolution.[34] The idea of the uniqueness of Communism as a social form later worked its way through East European dissidents such as Milovan Djilas and Michael Voslensky and has taken root in Eurocommunist circles.

How was Trotsky's Bolshevism still inhibiting his analysis? For Trotsky, it was still the "Stalin regime" that was an "abhorrent relapse"; it was a degenerated bureaucracy that prevented the "workers' state" from coming into being. It was not the regime of Lenin and Trotsky, it was not the party of Lenin and Trotsky that was pinpointed as the problem, because the regime of Lenin and Trotsky supposedly entailed the active participation of the workers through the soviets (why the soviets lost their power was explained by Luxemburg and Kautsky). The Bolshevik Party was always the party of factions for Trotsky, true to democratic centralism, while under Stalin the party was marked by bureaucratic centralism. Was there really no "organic" relationship between democratic centralism and bureaucratic centralism in the development of the Bolshevik Party?

Nonetheless, Trotsky introduced *The Revolution Betrayed* with this sober formulation: "If you remember that the task of socialism is to create a classless society based upon solidarity and the harmonious satisfaction of all needs, there is not yet, in this fundamental sense, a hint of socialism in the Soviet Union."[35] After discussing economic policy in the 1920s in the Soviet Union, Trotsky wrote, "Thinking people saw plainly that a revolution in the forms of property does not solve the problems of socialism, but only raises it."[36]

Trotsky saw that the bureaucracy, by not allowing the working class in active participation in daily life, would lead to a society of economic stagnation. In Trotsky's view, the Soviet state did not die away because of material want and cultural backwardness. At this point, Trotsky quoted Marx on the consequences of a communism under conditions of general deprivation and stated that the Russian Revolution was a catalyst in producing a situation where the "struggle for individual existence" took on an "unheardof ferocity."[37] Trotsky now had come to see the Bolshevik experience as the application of socialist methods for presocialist problems, but he believed that Soviet forms of property in a country like America would indeed represent the first stage of socialism. Here Trotsky came close to pronouncing a socialist revolution under Russian conditions impossible, although he never really adopted this position. He did point out in retrospect that Lenin had underestimated the tenacity of the state bureaucracy.[38]

Trotsky, in commenting on the structure of the Soviet system, argued that while the means of production belonged to the state, the state belonged to the bureaucracy.[39] The social organs in Soviet society did not represent their respective sectional interests because they were made to duplicate the hierarchical structure of the party, meaning the last word regarding their operation was held by the party, a party that itself was now seen as linked to the overall bureaucracy. In other words, basic social institutions had become mere caricatures.

The weakness of Trotsky's arguments were again that the chain of causation went back into the state bureaucracy, not to the party and its upper echelons. Trotsky wrote, "The denigration of the party became both cause and consequence of the bureaucratization of the state."[40] But more telling in this regard was the following statement: "From the first days of the Soviet regime the counterweight to bureaucratism was the party. If the bureaucracy managed the state, still the party controlled the bureaucracy."[41] When Stalin consummated the merger of the two, according to Trotsky, he did the bureaucracy a service by assuring its rule.

Why did Trotsky stop short of seeing the Soviet regime as another form of class society at this point? Trotsky remained uncertain of the ultimate course of Soviet society, although he saw the October Revolution as having been betrayed. But it had not yet been overthrown, according to Trotsky, and the privileges of the bureaucracy were seen as an abuse of power rather than as part of the logic of the Bolshevik institutions themselves.[42] Trotsky believed that for the bureaucracy to solidify its class rule, the collapse of the planned economy and the abolition of state property would be necessary.[43] But why kill the goose that lays the golden eggs? To do away with state property would be to do away with the privilege of what Milovan Djilas came to call the Communist party class, which stands high above society.

A "EUROCOMMUNIST" VIEW OF THE U.S.S.R.

What has constituted the secret of the Communist social system, what has given it its dynamism? Communism has been a response specific to underdeveloped societies where the class that should "lead" society, the bourgeoisie, was unable to do so because of a combination of political and economic factors of both internal and external origin. The Communist system, then, has been a way to meet the challenge of industrialization in a world that is already partially industrialized and where remaining preindustrial is tantamount to remaining backward. Rudolf Bahro wrote, "Its task [the Bolshevik Revolution] was not yet that of Socialism, no matter how resolutely the Bolsheviks believed in this, but rather the development of Russia on a non-capitalist road."[44]

The Communist revolutions, via the party apparatus, brought into being a new class, a class first of all of the revolutionaries themselves. For Milovan Djilas, it was the party that created the class.[45] Souvarine wrote, "The Party was superimposed on the State like a lid of the same shape on a pyramid."[46] The key to the anatomy of the Communist system is seen at its root: the dominating role of a vanguard party maintained through democratic centralism. Thus, the logic of Leninism inevitably became the modus operandi of the Communist parties, and Leninism naturally became the state ideology of Communism.

For Djilas, the new class should be understood as a modernizing one, formed by the party and initially accepted by society to meet the challenge of modernization that the previous dominant class had failed to achieve. Lenin was adamant with regard to the imperative of economic development or modernization: "The decisive thing is the organization of the strictest and countrywide accounting and control of production and distribution of goods."[47] Continuing in this vein Lenin wrote, "In the last analysis, productivity of labour is the most important, the principal thing for the victory of the new social system."[48]

According to Michael Voslensky, the new class was formed in three stages. First, the organization of professional revolutionaries, that is, the embryo of the new class, was formed. Second, with the taking of power, the organization of revolutionaries diversified as the party was flooded by an army of careerists. The old-guard Leninists remained at the top, but the inferior levels of the party were then controlled by the "Nomenklatura," who became the privileged executors of the state. The third stage saw the liquidation of the old guard by the Nomenklatura.[49] Djilas wrote, "The new class may be said to be made up of those who have special privileges and economic preference because of the administrative monopoly they hold."[50] Voslensky made this important distinction: the bourgeoisie in capitalism is the possessing class and for that reason the ruling class; the Nomenklatura in Communist society is the ruling class and for that reason the possessing class. The Nomenklatura, unlike the Western bourgeoisie, derives its power, in the first instance, from its *political power*.[51] In this way the Nomenklatura becomes the collective owner of the state property.[52] In the same vein, Bahro wrote, "Unusual therefore as it might seem at first sight, exploitation in our [Soviet] system is a *political* [Bahro's emphasis] phenomenon, a phenomenon of the distribution of political power."[53] Djilas wrote, "Communist political bureaucracy uses, enjoys, and disposes of nationalized property.... The class administers and distributes in the name of the nation and society."[54]

Although the Nomenklatura cannot buy and sell its part of the social property, it can be sure of obtaining the proceeds therefrom in a manner analogous to that of a shareholder. The Nomenklatura constitutes the exploiting class in Soviet society; it appropriates the social surplus product via the state and disposes of it as it wishes.[55] Souvarine remarked, "For the individual appropriation of surplus value is substituted a collective appropriation by the State, a deduction made for the parasitic consumption of functionaries.... The bureaucracy takes an undue part of the produce, corresponding more or less to the old capitalist profit, of the subjugated classes, which it submits to an inexorable sweating system."[56] It was not surprising, then, that one of the principal targets of Solidarity's draft program for its National Conference in 1981 in Poland was to restrict unjustified material privileges by members of the party, especially privileges linked to the exercise of power.[57]

The new class cannot flaunt its wealth, as the bourgeoisie in the West does, but this has not prevented it from consuming a disproportionate share of the social product. Djilas pointed out that the "new class" arose from the proletariat and depends upon the working strata for new recruits. As such, it is violently anticapitalist in its makeup.[58] This characteristic has seduced many people into thinking that Communist societies must indeed be socialist. However, the secret to the Communist anticapitalist stance is that the Communist regimes were brought into being by the downtrodden classes of society against the previous property holders with the communist vision that originated in the West as a moral and ideological rallying point. Once consolidated in power, the new class had to maintain a corresponding ideology. The following remark of Djilas is even more telling: "To divest Communists of ownership rights would be to abolish them as a class."[59] So the Communist party class and the capitalist class, despite the fact that both are dominant classes, are nonetheless at loggerheads with each other on the issue of property, which is one of the central although not exclusive locations of power. To the Communist bureaucrat, any notion of private property is tolerated only as a necessary evil, since the power of his class is derived from state property. To the capitalist, of course, the relationship is reversed. The different basis of power between the dominant classes in the East and the West provides the major stimulus for their mutual antagonisms.

The new class feels insecure as long as there are any owners of property other than itself.[60] This remark of Djilas explains the constant drive in Communist societies to place all the means of production of society under the control of the state even if this means bringing about unnecessary economic dislocation. Kautsky highlighted general insecurity in production predicated on the Communist economic form in the *Labour Revolution* pointing to the Bolshevik frenzy of abolishing all existing private property irrespective of the economic consequences.[61]

A feature of Communist societies abundantly outlined by liberal theory is the absence of any truly autonomous institutions from the central authority, that is, from the Communist Party. The character of the Communist party class is unlike any previous dominant class in its degree of cohesiveness. This may seem dubious at first glance, since the interparty struggles for power in Communist societies frequently take on violent dimensions. But it is precisely the imperative for the unity of the class as a whole that produces such violent confrontations.

The Communist societies have created another proletariat, one that does not exchange its labor power for capital, but a proletariat nonetheless. Bahro stated, "The abolition of private property in the means of production has in no way meant their immediate transformation into the property of the people. Rather, the whole society stands property-less against its state machine."[62] The working classes in Communism have no control over the decision-making processes in production, no control over the makeup and disposal of the means of production or of the product, and no means to combine autonomously with their fellow workers. The working classes are also excluded from exercising any control over political institutions.

While it is true that there is no buying and selling of labor power in the Communist countries, the appendage of the worker to the processes of production, as dictated by the dominant class, is no less severe than under capitalism. What is primary in Marx's classification of the proletariat is not simply the question of ownership of the means of production in the formal sense, nor necessarily being bought or sold on the market, but rather being totally divorced from directing one's conditions of existence. In Communism, it is the state that owns the means of production, but it is the party, through the system of Nomenklatura, which owns the state. Thus, the usage of the notion of class to describe the party is warranted since the party ultimately derives its wealth, by the way of its monopoly of political power, from its *control of the means of production.*

Eurocommunism as a political movement stemming originally from Communist parties once tied to the Communist International must deny the existence of socialism in the U.S.S.R. for it to be a viable force in the Western world. The historical significance of the Bolshevik Revolution must be separated from the present role of the Soviet Union.[63] Eurocommunism as an ideology, in order to be plausible and coherent, would have to go further by denying the validity of the Russian Revolution as a socialist revolution. Eurocommunist theory would have to side with Kautsky over Lenin.

The Eurocommunist view of the U.S.S.R. cannot be based on the critical positions of Trotsky since his criticisms never really got to the basis of the new class; Trotsky did not see that it was the nature of the party itself and the methods used in the seizure of power that created the party state. It is the Leninist party, welded together by democratic centralism, that is the key issue in this regard.

Theoretically, the major critical thrust of Eurocommunism must be directed at Lenin. Concerning the suppression of political life and the establishment of the one-party state in the course of the Russian Revolution, Eurocommunism must line up with Luxemburg and Kautsky in maintaining that political democracy is essential to socialism and, conversely, that the concept of socialism cannot be applied to situations where democracy does not exist. Thus, Eurocommunist ideology must ultimately side with Kautsky by denying the possibility of establishing socialism in Russia in 1917. In doing so, it is natural that Eurocommunism embrace the original Marxian problematic of socialism resting on the preexistence of a large proletariat in a developed industrial society.

Eurocommunism remains a form of communism. Eurocommunist ideology retains the vision of a classless society harking back to Marx. In order for Eurocommunist parties to maintain this vision and have a chance of remaining a viable political force in contemporary Europe, however, they must hold that Lenin and the Bolsheviks falsely appropriated this vision and, following in the manner of Souvarine and Kautsky, must deny the continuity of Bolshevism with Marxism in the West.

NOTES

1. Franz Borkenau, *World Communism: A History of the Communist International* (Ann Arbor: University of Michigan Press, 1962), p. 176.

2. Ibid., p. 413.

3. V. I. Lenin, *The Lenin Anthology*, Robert C. Tucker, ed., (New York: W. W. Norton & Co.), 1975, p. 551.

4. Karl Kautsky, *The Labour Revolution* (New York: The Dial Press, 1925).

5. Ibid., p. 16.

6. Eduard Bernstein, *Evolutionary Socialism* (New York: Schocken Books, 1978), p. xxiv.

7. Karl Kautsky, *The Dictatorship of the Proletariat* (Manchester: National Labour Press, 1920), p. 1.

8. Rosa Luxemburg, *The Russian Revolution and Leninism or Marxism?*, Bertram D. Wolfe, ed., (Ann Arbor: University of Michigan Press, 1961), pp. 62–63, 71.

9. Ibid., p. 69.

10. Ibid., pp. 72, 74.

11. Rosa Luxemburg, *Rosa Luxemburg Speaks*, Mary-Alice Waters, ed. (New York: Pathfinder Press, 1970), p. 368.

12. Boris Souvarine, *Stalin* (New York: Longmans, Green & Co., 1939), p. 274.

13. Luxemburg, *Rosa Luxemburg Speaks*, p. 76.

14. Kautsky, *Dictatorship of the Proletariat*, p. 116.

15. Karl Kautsky, *Bolshevism at a Deadlock* (London: George Allen & Unwin, 1931), pp. 27–28.

16. Souvarine, p. 284.

17. Ibid., p. 400.

18. V. I. Lenin, *What Is to Be Done* (New York: International Publishers, 1969), p. 83.

19. Luxemburg, *The Russian Revolution and Leninism or Marxism?*, pp. 100–102.

20. Ibid., p. 85.

21. Ibid., pp. 85–86.

22. Ibid.

23. Ibid., p. 89.

24. Karl Marx, *The Marx-Engels Reader*, Robert C. Tucker, ed., (New York: W. W. Norton & Co., 1977), p. 345.

25. Kautsky, *Dictatorship of the Proletariat*, p. 74.

26. Karl Kautsky, *Terrorism and Communism* (London: National Labour Press, 1920), p. 68.

27. Kautsky, *Dictatorship of the Proletariat*, p. 5.

28. Ibid., pp. 45–46.

29. Ibid., p. 31.

30. Ibid., p. 85.

31. *Le Monde*, December 2, 1980.

32. Kautsky, *Terrorism and Communism*, p. 207.

33. Leon Trotsky, *The Basic Writings of Trotsky*, Irving Howe, ed., (New York: Schocken Books, 1976), p. 313.

34. Leon Trotsky, *The Revolution Betrayed* (New York: International Publishers, 1970), p. 255.

35. Ibid., p. 3.

36. Ibid., p. 26.

---

37. Ibid., pp. 55–56.

38. Ibid., p. 58.

39. Ibid., p. 249.

40. Ibid., p. 94.

41. Ibid., p. 279.

42. Ibid., pp. 250, 257.

43. Ibid., p. 218.

44. Rudolf Bahro, *The Alternative in Eastern Europe* (London: Verso, 1981), p. 50.

45. Milovan Djilas, *The New Class* (New York: Frederick A. Praeger, 1957), p. 40.

46. Souvarine, p. 287.

47. Lenin, *The Lenin Anthology*, p. 447.

48. Ibid., p. 483.

49. Michael Voslensky, *La Nomenklatura* (Paris: Pierre Belfond, 1980), p. 91. Voslensky defines the "Nomenklatura" simply as the class of administrators. But he distinguishes them from mere functionaries in noting that the "Nomenklaturists" are not merely privileged executors of the state but also masters of the state. He later calls the Nomenklatura the collective owner of the state property and the exploiting class in Soviet society. However, the term implies still more: membership in the Communist Party, the correct class background, a certain kind of demeanor, a certain choice of words in discourse, etc. Thus, the class of Nomenklaturists may be compared to its counterpart in the West, to the bourgeoisie. In its own way, the Nomenklatura provides the "flavor" of Communist society.

50. Djilas, p. 39.

51. Voslensky, pp. 100–101.

52. Ibid., p. 146.

53. Bahro, p. 97.

54. Djilas, pp. 44–45.

55. Voslensky, pp. 146–47, 154–55.

56. Souvarine, p. 564.

57. National Negotiating Committee of Solidarity Draft Program, *Socialist Review* 58 (September–October 1981).

58. Djilas, p. 41.

59. Ibid., p. 45.

60. Ibid., p. 56.

61. Kautsky, *The Labour Revolution*, pp. 85–87.

62. Bahro, p. 11.

63. Manuel Azcarate, in Lawrence L. Whetten, ed., *The Present State of Communist Internationalism* (Lexington, Mass., Lexington Books, 1983), p. 105.

3

Communism as a Political Movement in the West (1919–1956)

The Communist parties of Western Europe came into existence predicated on the twenty-one points outlined by Lenin for acceptance into the Third International (Comintern). The essential points included that the whole press of every party be under the control of the Central Committee, that all "reformists" and "centrists" be removed from party positions, that the party maintain a complementary underground machinery, that Communist parties work within trade unions to overthrow "reformist" leaders, that the party's Central Committee strictly control its elected parliamentary group, that periodic purges of the party be conducted, that obligatory support be given any Soviet republic, and that national Communist parties be subordinate to the decisions of World Congresses and the Executive Committee of the Comintern.

In the post–World War II period, allegiance to international Communism came to involve a few basic tenets, and the various controversies among the Communist parties usually centered around slightly different interpretations thereof. These tenets propounded "fundamental laws" for the building of socialism while maintaining a coherence in international Communism based upon the guiding Soviet experience. Their main features included (1) carrying out a socialist revolution in one form or another, (2) founding the dictatorship of the proletariat [in one form or another], (3) the foundation of a Marxist-Leninist party, and (4) the abolition of capitalist property.[1] These laws were combined with the notion of proletarian internationalism, which meant an unquestioned support for the Soviet Union.

Several of these tenets are important in relation to the subsequent issues raised by Eurocommunism. On the one hand, even within Communist orthodoxy, earlier beliefs that the dictatorship of the proletariat would necessarily have to duplicate the Soviet model were progressively eroded. The so-called people's democracies represented, for international Communism, another way to attain this goal. Thus, when the Eurocommunist parties began to drop the term *dictatorship of the proletariat* in the 1970s, this did not, strictly speaking, indicate a turn away from orthodoxy. On the other hand, it was an important symbolic gesture, taking on both political and psychological dimensions.

Since the form of a transition to socialism came to be conceived by Eurocommunists in the context of a multiparty system with the full range of individual freedoms guaranteed, the traditional Communist claim to "vanguardism" became eroded. Although the acknowledgment of multiple parties, a peaceful transition to socialism via parliamentary institutions, and the like may also be found in orthodox Communist strategies, especially since 1956, this has always been within a framework where the Communist Party *must be* the dominant force.

Point 3 of the "fundamental laws," in particular, is most important to Communist identity. A Communist Party can no longer be a Communist Party if it does not hold to the Leninist conception of party organization because it is this party structure, in conjunction with the overall Communist ideology, which was instrumental in producing the new form of class society that was labeled "socialism." Even in the nonruling Communist parties, it was the mechanism of democratic centralism that maintained a privileged group in power within the party, which, in appropriate conditions, could become the driving force of a new class. It is the organization and role of the party and its potential role in society that gives Communism its most defining characteristic. The question of democratic centralism in the party necessarily becomes a key issue in establishing the Eurocommunist claim to a liberal identity.

The other major factor that has played a role in the altercations among Communist parties in the postwar period is the notion of proletarian internationalism. Since the formation of the Comintern, this notion had been developed to assure an unquestionable obedience to the Soviet Communist Party. In terms of developing a theory of Eurocommunism, this theme is relatively unimportant, since a national Communism, one that disregards supposedly international commitments for those of national priorities (China, Yugoslavia, etc.), is not incompatible with Leninist Communism per se. Nonetheless, certain features pertaining to the national Communist movements that provided greater autonomy for individual Communist parties later opened the door for Eurocommunism.

A balance sheet of Orthodox Communism may be used to provide a guide for measuring the authenticity or specificity of Eurocommunism. The points of reference that have bound the various ruling Communist parties of the world together even after their many splits are (1) the Leninist character of the party, (2) the acceptance of the Bolshevik Revolution as a socialist revolution, (3) the view that the Communist Party must be the head of any political grouping associated with defining and defending the interests of the working class, (4) that all other parties of the left are inferior to Communist parties due to their class collaborationist character, (5) that in a socialist society, a Communist Party must be hegemonic, (6) that for socialism to be realized, the state *must* own and control *all of* society's major productive enterprises, and (7) that the U.S.S.R. is a socialist society.

The central themes binding these various points revolve around Leninism, democratic centralism within the party, and the proposition that, whatever the social characteristics of a particular society, the Communist Party must be its dominant group. These are the characteristics that precisely define as well the configurations of the new party class. A ruling Communist Party will not renounce them without being forced to by popular pressure, since such a renunciation would be tantamount to giving up its basis of power as a class.

A major event in international Communism bearing on the emergence of Eurocommunism was the impact of the Khrushchev speech at the Twentieth Congress of the CPSU in 1956 concerning the Stalin personality cult. The effect of this speech was to open the eyes of many party members of the Western Communist parties for the first time to actual Soviet realities and to challenge lingering utopian views regarding Soviet society. There was now a crack in the edifice of the Soviet system.

Nonetheless, traditional Communism was able to weather the storm of 1956 and emerge temporarily rejuvenated. The purge of the police apparatus in the CPSU was an absolute necessity for the continued viability of the party and for the consolidation of the power of the new class. Michael Voslensky argued that the sole point of contention between the class of Nomenklaturists and the Stalinist methods that had served to solidify the power of the party in crucial periods was that Stalin did not guarantee the Nomenklatura's inalienability or permanence of position.[2] For this reason, even the most privileged members of the party class lived in fear. The need of the party class for this purge, therefore, was so great that whatever risks it incurred were discounted as a chance that had to be taken.

The Khrushchev thesis of 1956 stated that with a capitalist encirclement in the 1920s, and an intense class struggle combined with Trotskyist, opportunist, and bourgeois tendencies within the party, conditions were set for the Stalinist pattern. Stalin was given too much credit for the party's successes, and this went to his head. After all, hadn't Lenin warned of the peculiarities of Stalin before he died? Stalin falsely argued that the class struggle became more violent under socialism, even after the exploiting classes had been liquidated. Purging the "antiparty" elements by Stalinist methods established the very resilience of Soviet democracy.

Khrushchev went on to sanction different paths to socialism (people's democracies) predicated on the differing historical, social, and economic conditions of the country in question. He acknowledged the legitimacy of the Yugoslav model and pointed to the possibility of a peaceful transition to socialism based on a scenario of transforming parliamentary bourgeois democracy into a "genuine" democracy.

The limits of the Soviet concessions became quickly apparent. Khrushchev stated at the Twenty-first Congress of the CPSU in 1959, "The Yugoslav revisionists minimize the Party's role and in effect reject Leninist doctrine that the Party is the guiding force in the struggle for Socialism."[3] Khrushchev maintained at the Twenty-second Congress in 1961, "In life there is only a single, Leninist course toward the construction of Socialism and Communism."[4] As in the 1957 joint declaration of communist Parties, which was not signed by the Yugoslavs, "basic laws" in the building of socialism were upheld, albeit now in the context of a variety of national peculiarities and traditions, which somehow were to be taken into account.

Some of the subsequent debates in the PCI involving the Khrushchev revelations bear on the later development of Eurocommunism. PCI leader Palmiro Togliatti, in his report to the Central Committee for the party's Eighth Congress in 1956, noted that the Soviet explanation of the cult of the individual (Stalin) did not really get to the bottom of the "errors," even "serious errors," committed in the Soviet Union. Togliatti rejected any prospects for a centralized organization for international Communism, calling instead for bilateral relations between parties.[5] However, he pointed out that the U.S.S.R. was still the axis, the greatest force of the socialist world. Policy measures in the U.S.S.R. would not be slavishly followed although the fundamental objectives of the PCI and CPSU remained the same.

Mario Alicata, a member of the PCI Political Bureau and editor of L'Unità, the party newspaper, pointed out divergences in his party regarding the Twenty-second Congress of the CPSU in 1961 in the wake of Khrushchev's 1956 speech. He said that the problem with Khrushchev's earlier pronouncements at the CPSU's Twentieth Congress was the lack of connection made between socialism and democracy and the fact that only one road to socialism was authorized.[6] Giorgio Napolitano, a member of the PCI's Central Committee, suggested that there must be something more systematic to Stalinism than what the Soviets admitted, and asked, "What concrete organizational forms of party and state, what theoretical, political, and cultural directions were at the basis of the deformations and errors?"[7] Gian Carlo Pajetta, a member of the PCI Political Bureau, stated flatly that it was not enough to point to the limits of bourgeois democracy and simply juxtapose it with socialist democracy to prove the latter's superiority.[8] Five years after Khrushchev's speech, the PCI exhibited a boldness in its views concerning the development of the U.S.S.R. that would eventually lead, in the 1970s and 1980s, to a rift large enough to spawn a distinct ideology, namely, Eurocommunism.

The PCF, on the other hand, though not acknowledging that it knew of the existence of Khrushchev's secret speech (the party admitted in 1977 that its leaders were indeed made privy to this speech) did *also* condemn the purported errors of Stalin. The PCF called for a Marxist analysis of the matter since the purported Soviet explanations for these errors were unsatisfactory.[9] This was, however, an empty proposition. The PCF condemned the conclusions of the PCI's Eighth Congress. Philippe Robrieux noted that one could not even mention the word *crime* in the PCF in reference to Stalin without oneself being investigated.[10] Khrushchev's report was not published, and its authenticity was discounted. According to Robrieux, *L'Humanité* did not mention the word *crime* with regard to events in the Soviet Union until 1961.[11]

Developments in world Communism from World War II until the Czech invasion of 1968 have been described by Alexander Dallin as follows: "What has been taking place (rival power bases, Moscow, Peking, Belgrade) is not a clear-cut division into two rival Communist camps, but a trend toward diversity and multiplicity of positions and policies—in brief, toward the crystallization of varieties of Communist experience."[12] H. T. Willetts noted that a modus vivendi had been reached between the U.S.S.R. and the Western Communist parties after 1956, with the CPSU grudgingly allowing some leeway for the national conditions of these parties while maintaining the need for proletarian internationalism, the need for a common ideology, and the recognition of basic modalities of the Soviet model as integral to the Communist experience.[13] The debates among Communist parties centered on the degree of their allowable differences with regard to the guiding Soviet model. The PCI, for example, while disagreeing with the policy changes of the Chinese Communists, refused openly to condemn the Chinese Party after the Sino-Soviet split. While the questions posed by Eurocommunism do not fall within this framework of polycentrism in international Communism, the germs of Eurocommunism were nonetheless evident.

THE PCF AND THE PCI AFTER THE SECOND WORLD WAR

After the war, the Communist parties of Italy and France participated in the development of republican constitutions in their countries, and they participated in their respective governments. In a very real sense, they were setting the parameters for their future political action by acting within the confines of Western democracy. This may already be perceived as a move back to pre-Bolshevik communism, to a tradition that saw the achievement of socialism as a completion of liberal and democratic principles. The two parties had, in effect, already given up the pretense of using war to precipitate armed struggle or of instigating a violent seizure of power. In other words, the PCF and the PCI had already admitted in their actions that the Bolshevik strategy was not applicable to their political situation. From here, it was a matter of time before the party's theoretical formulations would catch up to their practical activities, which, in this case, sensed the appropriate strategy for survival and perhaps eventual success. Of course, the two parties in question were still far from Eurocommunism, remaining closely bound to the Soviet Union. But the stage was set for a possible historical reversal.

The Italian Communists planned, even before the end of the war, to attempt to constitute themselves as a national rather than a strictly class party. This followed from Antonio Gramsci's thesis on the need to form a historical bloc that would become socially and culturally hegemonic before actual governmental power was attained. Following Gramsci, the PCI would attempt to present the sectional demands of the working class in the light of the national interest rather than channeling the national interest into working-class sectional demands.[14] While Gramsci's view of the "war of position" was marked with the emblem of Leninism, predicated on a situation of dual power, with the new power bloc being an embryonic state, it is also clear that his conception of the party had strayed from the strict vanguardism advocated by Lenin. Gramsci's notion of "war of position," distinct from a "war of maneuver" or a sudden assault on the state, authorized a political gradualism in the transition to socialism that the PCI was eager to adopt. By following the strategy of Gramsci instead of that of Lenin, the Italian Communist Party became a mass party. These differences did not constitute enough of a rift to speak of a break with Leninist Communism. However, that they were not insignificant is evident in comparing the PCI and the PCF as they have evolved since World War II. The PCI has improved upon its strategy to the point where its presence is felt in nearly every region of Italy. The PCF, in conceiving of its role mostly in terms of a working-class party in the strict sense, has never really moved beyond its narrow economic-corporatist confines. The PCF's strategy and conception of its role in French society have always contained built-in limits to a broader success.

The resiliency of the Italian strategy did not become immediately evident, however. The Communist parties of Italy and France were forced out of their governments in 1947. By the early 1950s, they had been substantially isolated from general political life. With reference to the PCI, Donald Blackmer noted that PCI behavior in the postwar period rested on an often uneasy balance involving the development and maintenance of the PCI itself, the search for political alliances for the "Italian Road to Socialism," and the maintenance of a close line to the U.S.S.R.[15] However, the strategic choices made between 1943 and 1948—the drive for national unity, the openness to political alliances, the cultivation of the twin notions of a mass party and a party of government, the party program of progressive democracy instead of immediate socialism, and so on—remained basic to PCI policy.

With the PCF, the developments toward isolationism were particularly pronounced. The PCF had been formed at the Congress of Tours in 1921 when the pro-Bolsheviks managed to capture two-thirds of the socialist mandates. Nonetheless, as the left divided into socialist and Communist groupings, the party's influence in France was minimal. It underwent a series of purges as part of a gradual process of Bolshevization. The PCF religiously followed the Comintern's strategy of class against class initiated in 1928, which targeted the social democrats as a dangerous wing of the bourgeoisie.[16] A volte-face occurred in 1934, first led by the independent-minded Jacques Doriot, who was later expelled by the party for his actions aimed at bringing about unity of the left. The theme of unity of the left was then taken up by the leadership of the party on its own terms, which culminated in a pact of unity of action with the socialist Section Française de l'International Ouvriére (SFIO) in July 1934.[17] As the Comintern officially acknowledged the strategy of "popular front" in 1935, the PCF was on its way toward implanting itself in French social life. The PCF vote doubled from 1932 to 1936. Although it refused ministers in the Socialist government in 1936, it had attained the status of a party at the national level. It was during this period that the PCF began to implant itself in the trade union movement.[18]

The period of the Nazi-Soviet pact from 1939 to 1941 all but obliterated party gains as the PCF was ordered by the Comintern to acquiesce in the German occupation of France. The party even applied to German occupation authorities for legal status. However, with the German invasion of the Soviet Union in 1941, matters quickly changed as the PCF became free to play a national and patriotic role in the resistance. The PCF emerged as the largest party in France after the war. However, with its stay in government short-lived and increasingly at odds with the Socialists, the PCF and its audience, by the 1950s, had been hermetically sealed off from the rest of French society, serving to create the phenomenon of the countersociety referred to by Annie

Kriegel. With the PCF and its large bloc of supporters ensconced in its own countersociety, the right was content to rule its half of France in the name of the nation.

NOTES

1. Jacques Duclos, in Alexander Dallin, ed., *Diversity in International Communism* (New York: Columbia University Press, 1963), p. 498.

2. Michael Voslensky, *La Nomenklatura* (Paris: Pierre Belfond, 1980), p. 115.

3. Nikita Khrushchev, in Dieter Dux, ed., *Ideology in Conflict: Communist Political Theory* (Princeton, N. J.: P. Van Nostrand Company, 1963), pp. 31–32.

4. Ibid., p. 93.

5. Palmiro Togliatti, in Peter Lange and Maurizio Vannicelli, eds., *The Communist Parties of Italy, France, and Spain* (London: George Allen & Unwin, 1981), p. 220.

6. Mario Alicata, in Dallin, *Diversity in International Communism*, pp. 436–37.

7. Giorgio Napolitano, ibid., p. 438.

8. Gian Carlo Pajetta, ibid., p. 440.

9. In Lange and Vannicelli, pp. 242–43.

10. Philippe Robrieux, *Histoire intérieur du parti communiste, 1972–1982*, vol. 3 (Paris: Fayard, 1982), p. 238.

11. Ibid.

12. Alexander Dallin, in Dallin, *Diversity in International Communism*, p. xxvii.

13. H. T. Willetts, in Richard Kindersley, ed., *In Search of Eurocommunism* (New York: St. Martin's Press, 1981), p. 3.

14. P. Allum, *The Italian Communist Party since 1945* (Occasional Publication No. 2 of the University of Reading Graduate School of Contemporary European Studies, 1970), p. 7.

15. In Donald L. M. Blackmer and Sidney Tarrow, eds., *Communism in Italy and France* (Princeton N. J.: Princeton University Press, 1975), p. 23.

16. Donald R. Brower, *The New Jacobins* (Ithaca, N. Y.: Cornell University Press, 1968), p. 15.

17. Danielle Tartakowsky, *Une Histoire du PCF* (Paris: Presses Universitaires de France, 1982), pp. 32–33.

18. Georges Lavau, *A quoi sert Le Parti Communiste Français?* (Paris: Librairie Arthéme Fayard, 1981), pp. 70–71.

4

The PCF and the Long March Out of the Ghetto (1958–1972)

In the first years of the Fifth Republic, the PCF tried to organize "all republicans" against the regime of "personal power"; it wished to reinstate a regime whose primary power rested on a National Assembly similar to the postwar regime of the Fourth Republic.[1] The party had begun its "long march" out of the political ghetto. It was seeking to attain once again the status of a party of government.

At the PCF's Fifteenth Congress in 1959, the party for the first time made tangible proposals for the transition to socialism.[2] The PCF's success of liberalization culminated in its proclamation of the goal of a "socialism in French colors" at the Twenty-second Party Congress in 1976. Yet much of the PCF overture toward the Socialists before 1962 represented more of a political ploy, to demonstrate the "bad faith" of the Socialists, than a distinct change in the party's attitudes and political direction.[3]

Annie Kriegel believes that from 1958 to 1962, the party was still an opposing force without really seeking to be an alternative to Gaullist power.[4] Nonetheless, the PCF, by attempting to construct a basis for joint action at the level of a common program with a Socialist Party was, in fact, embarking on a novel path, unprecedented in Europe.[5] The novelty of this strategy was obscured at the outset because it was couched in the old terminology of the Popular Front. Furthermore, significant strategic and ideological differences still existed between the two major poles of the French left prohibiting any easy alignment. And Gaullism had yet to show its vulnerability, as it would do later in May 1968.

Waldeck Rochet, who was to assume the party leadership after the death of Party Secretary Maurice Thorez in 1964, allowed for the possibility of a multiparty alignment during the transition to socialism

in an address at the Sixteenth Congress in 1962.[6] However, this statement, even taken at face value, provided little opening to potential
political partners. The PCF still had a long way to go before it would
acknowledge that it would submit to being turned out of power once
it had been in office; the party accepted this only in the 1970s.

While the PCF was the best-organized political force in France, isolated in the countersociety it was a sterile force.[7] The PCF therefore
began to push for its reintegration into French political life: sometimes
consciously and sometimes in spite of itself, that is, as a reluctant
follower of important events. The reason for this dichotomy was that
its reintegration into the French political system could mean not only
the potential fruits of political power but also the possible dangers of
getting lost on the way, thus compromising PCF identity and its comfortable position in the countersociety. The danger of a loss in identity
cannot be taken lightly for a party cut so thoroughly in the traditional
Communist mold. Irwin Wall has noted, "The PCF has never been
willing to abandon its organizational specificity as the price for such
[national] integration."[8]

The early attempts at a rapprochement between the two major poles
of the French left were, then, quite timid and generally couched in
terminology emanating from the past. Rochet mentioned at a Central
Committee meeting in 1962 that the existence of the Atlantic Pact
and the Common Market were no longer considered by the PCF to be
major obstacles preventing the unity of action between Socialists and
Communists.[9] The form of the constitution of 1958, however, remained a stumbling block to left unity. The PCF, by 1964, was the
only major oppositional party to propose a new constitution. This position did not change until the major programmatic accord with the
Fédération de la Gauche Démocratique et Socialiste (FGDS) in February
of 1968, when the PCF no longer demanded the abolition of the constitution of 1958 as a prerequisite for any general political agreement
with the Socialists.[10]

At the PCF's Sixteenth Congress in 1962, democracy was proclaimed
an essential step in the struggle for socialism, and a distinction was
made between a democratic program and a socialist program.[11] Later,
in the 1970s, the contours surrounding the democratic program and
the socialist program would become blurred, if not indistinguishable.

The PCF's new slogan of "advanced democracy" was adopted in the
party resolution at the Seventeenth Congress in 1964 and was contrasted with the Gaullist regime of "personal power." The PCF also
called for an alliance with the SFIO against the "antisocial policies of
the monopolies."[12] The Seventeenth Congress also mentioned the possibility of opening a different road to socialism than that of 1917, but
one conceivable only because of the existence of the "socialist" bloc
as a counterweight to U.S. imperialism.[13] This juxtaposition merely

followed the positions of the Twentieth Congress of the CPSU, which authorized the existence of a peaceful road to socialism.

The Seventeenth Congress dropped the notion of a "parti unique" under socialism. Such a terminological change could have had a double meaning. It was probably interpreted by the bulk of French Communists to follow the prescription of the "people's democracies," in which several parties and a variety of associations existed on paper but enjoyed no real autonomy from the Communist Party in practice. Only later, under a different set of circumstances in the 1970s, would the notion really become "Eurocommunist."

The Seventeenth Congress discounted the postulate of an acting minority seizing power in the name of the majority and tended to put aside but not remove altogether the principle of violence. The dictatorship of the proletariat would be brief in France and less violent, presumably, than in 1917.[14]

The PCF moved officially back into the political arena in 1965 with its support of François Mitterrand in the presidential election. The PCF indicated that the policy of unity between Socialists and Communists had become a "fundamental" policy objective.[15] Although a common program was not then drawn up between the PCF and the SFIO, the 1965 Mitterrand campaign was really the first time there had been the semblance of a united left in France since the immediate postwar period.[16]

Some members of the PCF wanted the party to run its own candidate in 1965. This was overruled by Waldeck Rochet, who argued that the other parties of the left would not support a PCF presidential candidate under the political and social conditions that were then present in France. What was important to Rochet and the PCF in 1965 was that Mitterrand had refused the option of searching for political alliances on the right, sealing the failure of Gaston Defferre's initiative for a center-left coalition.[17] The Mitterrand candidacy of 1965 was, then, a forerunner of the victory of the French left in 1981. With the running of a single candidate in 1965, the contours of an internal party struggle between party traditionalists and the future Eurocommunists within the PCF, a battle that emerged often in the 1970s with greater and greater éclat, was already discernible. The reemergence of the French left in the 1960s was spectacular even though it was not accompanied by any significant theoretical revision. Mitterrand forced de Gaulle into a runoff, losing only on the second ballot with 44.8 percent to de Gaulle's 55.2 percent of the vote.

THE MAY EVENTS: THE "OTHER HALF" OF FRANCE AWAKENS

In February 1968, the PCF and the FGDS signed a joint declaration outlining common goals that may now be seen as a prelude to the historic Common Program between the PCF and the revamped Socialist Party in June 1972. The document authorized the nationalization of key sectors of the economy: those seen to create the principal riches of the nation, as well as sectors deemed a "monopoly" and enterprises that relied primarily on state contracts.[18] The program was comprised of three categories: institutions and defense of liberties, economic and social problems, and foreign policy. Where there were disagreements between the two parties, the positions of both sides were stated. The program reflected postwar social democratic orientations based on the economic abundance of the 1960s; it was not a radical program with socialism as a goal.

By 1968, unity among the French left had become more than an occasional affair. Communists, Socialists, and radicals signed an electoral accord in December of 1966 for the legislative elections of 1967, and the PCF-FGDS declaration of 1968, while not a common program for government, was a tangible result of ongoing negotiations on the left. Yet these various initiatives during the 1960s by the parties of the left did not prepare them, in a serious way, for a possible run at political power. This became evident during the student-worker uprisings of May–June 1968, which abruptly raised the stakes of the political battle in France, demonstrating the vulnerability of the right-wing majority. What had occurred in fits and starts since the period of the Algerian War in the late 1950s, suddenly appeared in striking form with the mass movements of May 1968. France now aspired to change. But the parties of the left, at that time, had little that was innovative to offer.[19] Thus, the street demonstrations of students and workers could only move in a void and act out the revolutionary movements of earlier periods, ultimately making for a farcical situation labeled by Raymond Aron a "psychodrama."[20] Aron wrote, "The development of the May Crisis was reminiscent of some of the revolutionary adventures of the nineteenth century. Paris . . . rehearsed once again the Great Revolution."[21] The events of May, taken more seriously by Michel Rocard, constituted a movement originating in the West, but which lived in the language and representation of Communist experiences of third world agrarian countries.[22] For Rocard, the contradictory nature of the May movement was evident in the fact that it entailed a strong liberational and antihierarchic thrust, yet this sensitivity was most prevalent in ultraleft groups of Leninist ideology, producing a strange contradiction between the cultural experience of May 1968 and its political expression. The extreme left, according to Rocard, neither could nor wanted to pose the question of power; the left neither could nor wanted to translate the aspirations of May 1968 into practical political policy.[23]

This strange scenario served to mask the real balance of political power in France then and in the decade of the 1970s. The imbalance between right and left was further accentuated by the total defeat of the left parties in the special elections of June 1968, leading many observers to subsequently misread the events of the 1970s by underestimating the real power of the left. In retrospect, since 1968, it would be only a matter of time before the "other half" of France attained political power. The period from 1968 to 1981 was a period in which the predominance of the left at the street level and, in significant ways, on the cultural and moral fronts, was translated into institutional power. The events of May 1968, then, held the key to French politics throughout the 1970s. The psychological victory registered by the contingent of social forces in May 1968 that the left came to represent became an institutional victory in 1981 with the election of François Mitterrand as the president of France.

The May events also illustrated the inability of street action to change the nature of an industrial society by forcing a sudden confrontation of social forces. Thus the PCF opposed the maximalist propositions of the students, epitomized by student activist Daniel Cohn-Bendit's statement that from May 27 to May 30 "nobody held political power in France," and happened to find its tactical position justified. The party's intent was to abide by "le cadre de la legalité républicaine."[24] This, however, does not obscure the party's lack of understanding of the extent of the protest and its overt disdain for the students. Embarrassingly, the PCF went all out to condemn the students as "Maoists, Trotskyists and pseudorevolutionaries serving the interests of Gaullism" in Georges Marchais's article in L'Humanité, May 3. The PCF did not want to see a major social movement unleashed that was out of its control.

If the May events were directly responsible for producing the collapse of the SFIO, which had been discredited by its penchant for the center-left, and was stigmatized as "class collaborationist" in the eyes of many left advocates, the position of the PCF was no less put into question. The May events not only decimated postwar social democracy in France; they also exposed the inadequacy of Soviet-style Communism. In the aftermath of the May events, the PCF had no more claim to be the inheritor of the popular slogan coined in the May movement, "autogestion" or self-management, than the SFIO. But sooner or later, there was bound to be at least one inheritor.

A race would ensue to capture the thrust of May 1968 pitting the two great poles of the French left against each other, a race that, due to what had now become the burden of its Stalinist legacy, the PCF did not win. What the May events had shown was that the PCF could no longer afford to be a party that was "not like the others." The full effect of the May events on PCF identity, in serving to undermine the basis of its former vision, that of the Soviet model of society, only became fully evident much later.

The PCF had been the major force of the French left after the war as a consequence of its political adroitness and militancy, but also by default as the Socialists conceded their left flank by participation in center-left governments. The PCF's constant militancy had been sufficient to overcome its lack of concrete proposals for power. From 1968, it would have to be a serious oppositional party in order to maintain its ground. The political stakes in France had become real. There was a weakness in governmental power.

THE CZECH EVENTS—A WARNING FROM THE EAST

The second major event of 1968, and the second time in the postwar period that the Western Communist parties were jolted into the realization that their historical ties to the Soviet Union could become a major liability to their ambitions in domestic politics, was the invasion of Czechoslovakia by the Warsaw Pact countries. The first such warning had been delivered by Khrushchev in his 1956 speech. With the Czech invasion, the PCF, for the first time, spoke out against the CPSU on a major event. Fernando Claudin remarked that for credibility, the Western Communist parties had to come out against the Czech invasion, because what the Czechs were trying to do resembled the Western parties' own political formulas for socialism.[25]

During the Czech events, the Czechoslovakian Communist Party began to allow greater autonomy for social organizations in the political system, noting that state power should not be monopolized by one or several parties. This movement, nonetheless, contained built-in limits since it originated from above, within the party, something that was not the case a dozen years later in Poland. Thus, the Action Program of the Czech Communist Party stated, "We exclude the possibility that socialist democracy would develop in our country at the present time by forming an oppositional political party which would be outside the National Front, as this would result in a revival of a struggle for power."[26]

The Western Communist parties, in opposing the Soviet invasion as an infringement on the right of each Communist Party to choose its own path of development, were, in effect, relying on a radical interpretation of the "unity in diversity" formula outlined by Khrushchev in 1956, giving it an interpretation that was never really acknowledged by the CPSU. The CPSU version of self-determination or national roads to socialism never diminished the importance of the universal example of the Soviet model. Thus, the criticisms by the Western Communist parties of the Soviet invasion of Czechoslovakia fell into a void and did not really amount to anything new. As Claudin concluded, "None of the parties that had dared to resist Moscow was able to break the umbilical cord that linked them to Eastern socialism and take their criticisms to their logical conclusion."[27] Indeed, the Western Communist parties had developed neither the ideological tools nor the political will power to make such a move. The PCF, in particular, first disavowed and then disapproved of the invasion of Czechoslovakia by Warsaw Pact troops. Rochet had been actively involved in negotiations between Khrushchev and Alexander Dubček, the secretary of the Czechoslovakian Communist Party, during the political turmoil and was left out on a limb by the Soviet actions. However, the party later backtracked on its position of disapproval, not wishing to press the matter against the CPSU.

THE AFTERMATH OF MAY 1968

By December 1968, the PCF was back on its unitary path, renewing the pursuit of a common program with the Socialists. It published a document labeled the Manifesto of Champigny, which highlighted its concept of an "advanced democracy" as a steppingstone to socialism. The Manifesto of Champigny offered a more sophisticated version of the concept of a gradual transition to socialism, but one that, nonetheless, had not completely eliminated the old terminology and categories of traditional Communism. François Hincker saw the Manifesto of Champigny as the culmination of the "new course" of the PCF that resulted from the Waldeck Rochet era. This course was seen to have embodied five major notions: (1) state monopoly capitalism, (2) the alliance of the working class and the intellectuals (called for at the Central Committee meeting at Argenteuil of March 1966), (3) the first stages of the union of the left, (4) the reprobation of the Soviet intervention in Czechoslovakia, and (5) the new form of party discussion embodied in the use of assembly debates.[28]

The PCF's "state monopoly capitalism" thesis regarding the French economy was made more explicit by the Manifesto of Champigny. The PCF called for the alliance of all strata who were seen as victims of "monopoly power," now said to comprise the immense majority of the population. The Gaullist power of the monopolies was to be replaced by an "advanced democracy," one penetrating both the political and the economic sphere and opening the road to socialism.[29] The May events were cited in acknowledging the role of the intellectuals in class struggle. Small and medium-sized firms were to exist for a long period of time under socialism, and more than one party was authorized to exist. However, only parties that affirmed the Socialist regime and respected its laws could participate in political life. This was meant, for all intents and purposes, that only "Socialist" parties by PCF definition would be authorized in advanced democracy. The socialist power still sounded conspicuously like the dictatorship of the proletariat; power would be concerned principally with those who might undermine it.

In the 1969 presidential election, the PCF ran its own candidate, Jacques Duclos, who obtained a respectable 21.3 percent of the vote on the first round. Meanwhile, the political parties of the non-Communist left were in complete disarray. In the elections of June 1968, just after the May events, the FGDS had dropped to 16.5 percent of the vote. In November 1968, Mitterrand ended his association with the FGDS. In the 1969 presidential election, Gaston Defferre received only 5 percent of the vote for the SFIO. This produced the strange scenario of a centrist and a right-wing candidate facing off on the second ballot, a situation that was stunning to the strong left-wing constituency in France. In France, such a runoff did not accurately reflect the real balance of political forces.

The fate of Political Bureau member Roger Garaudy at the PCF's Nineteenth Congress in 1970 was particularly revealing regarding the rigid internal structure of the PCF based on democratic centralism, and it provides insight into what the "Eurocommunists" in the 1970s were up against in attempting to redefine the PCF's political orientations. In a move unprecedented in PCF history, Garaudy was allowed to express his minority position at the Congress. Garaudy's challenge to PCF dogma defined the "working class" in broad terms, ostensibly more similar to Marx; the working class comprised all who have only their labor power to sell, whether manual or intellectual laborers, and who also created surplus value.[30] This definition of the working class was broader than what the PCF had been employing and broader than the definition used in traditional Communism, which focused only on the industrial working class. For Garaudy, no unique model of socialism existed.[31] This assertion was a radical interpretation of the notion of separate roads to socialism. For Garaudy, where the working class was educated and constituted a majority of the population, it would not be necessary to conduct affairs in a high-handed manner, something that had come to be the norm with democratic centralism. In this way, Garaudy went on to challenge the Leninist notion that consciousness had to be brought to the working class from without.[32]

Marchais criticized Garaudy's Gramscian notion of a "new historic bloc" of social forces, yet in the text of the document for the Congress, he accepted much of Garaudy's analysis without acknowledgment. Where Garaudy had gone too far was in challenging the necessity for democratic centralism in the labor movement. This represented a challenge to the leadership of the PCF. The PCF leadership allowed Garaudy to speak only so that he could discredit himself in the eyes of the party. It knew that Garaudy's propositions would be construed as out of touch with the delegates' sensitivities.

The Congress's resolutions went on to cite thirty trusts as dominating the French economy; the nonmonopoly, salaried portion of the population was said to represent 76 percent of the working force. Within this grouping, the role of the working class was seen as instrumental. The party had confidence in the future of the existing socialist systems in the East with its "balance sheet of considerable success."[33]

The PCF seemed to have emerged from the turbulence of 1968 almost unscathed. Its call for unity of the left was more pertinent than ever before. Its future allies were in a definite position of weakness. How could the party not be optimistic? Yet, from this point forward, the weight of the PCF's history and the rigidity of its ideology and organization would prohibit it from making the necessary changes rapidly enough in the direction of what came to be called "Eurocommunism." In retrospect, when the Socialists reconstituted themselves on the left at Epinay in 1971, without the PCF having made necessary changes toward democratic socialism, it was inevitable that the PCF would become the minority party on the left.

The race between Socialists and Communists to capture the aspirations of May 1968, to refine and organize its anticapitalist thrust, was like the story of the tortoise and the hare. The tortoise, the PCF, had an enormous advantage at the outset. But in the end, unlike the fairy tale, it was the hare, the revitalized Socialist Party, that won. The PCF lost all chance at creating an "Italian situation," in which the PCI dominates the left, by not changing when it had the clear advantage. With a rival left Socialist Party on equal terms with it in the 1970s, the PCF, because of the burden of its historical ties to the Soviet Union, was outflanked by the PS. Each time the PCF moved in the Eurocommunist direction and experienced the now insurmountable strength of the PS, the hardliners or "go-it-aloners" (George Ross's term) would point to the change itself as the reason for the growing imbalance on the left. The changes would then be circumscribed, and the party would sink further into an abyss.

NOTES

1. François Borella, *Les Partis politiques dans la France d'aujourd'hui* (Paris: Editions du Seuil, 1973), p. 189.

2. Ronald Tiersky, *French Communism, 1920–1972* (New York: Columbia University Press, 1974), p. 276.

3. Yves Roucaute, *Le PCF et les sommets de l'état: De 1945 a nos jours* (Paris: Presses Universitaires de France, 1981), p. 55.

4. Annie Kriegel, in Donald L. M. Blackmer and Sidney Tarrow, eds., *Com-*

munism in Italy and France (Princeton, N. J.: Princeton University Press, 1975), p. 71.

5. Jean Baudouin, "L'Echec communiste de juin 1981: Recul electoral ou crise hégémonique?," *Pouvoirs* 20 (1982): p. 48.

6. Tiersky, p. 277.

7. Borella, p. 174.

8. Irwin Wall, *French Communism in the Era of Stalin* (Westport, Conn.: Greenwood Press, 1983), p. 228.

9. *Le Monde*, December 15, 1962.

10. Borella, p. 190.

11. Tiersky, p. 231.

12. *Le Monde*, May 15, 1964.

13. Ibid.

14. Ibid.

15. *Le Monde*, July 1, 1965.

16. Borella, p. 157.

17. *Le Monde*, September 25, 1965.

18. *Le Monde*, February 25–26, 1968.

19. Andrew Feenberg, in Carl Boggs and David Plotke, eds., *The Politics of Eurocommunism* (Boston: South End Press, 1980), p. 133.

20. Raymond Aron, *La Révolution introuvable* (Paris: Librairie Arthéme Fayard, 1968), pp. 36–37.

21. Ibid.

22. Michel Rocard, *Parler vrai* (Paris: Editions due Seuil, 1979), p. 97.

23. Ibid., pp. 86, 97–98.

24. *Le Monde*, July 11, 1968.

25. Fernando Claudin, *Eurocommunism and Socialism* (London: New Left Books, 1978), pp. 43–44.

26. In Alexander Dubček, *Czechoslovakia's Blueprint for "Freedom"* (Washington, D. C.: Acropolis Books), 1968, p. 334.

27. Claudin, p. 45.

28. François Hincker, *Le Parti communiste au carrefour* (Paris: Albin Michel, 1981), p. 59.

29. *Le Monde*, December 8–9, 1968.

30. *Le Monde*, February 7, 1970.

31. Ibid.

32. Ibid.

33. *Le Monde*, February 5, 1970.

5

The 1970s and the Return of the French Left

The years between 1969 and 1972 were years of regrouping for the French left. This regrouping naturally centered on the relations between Socialists and Communists and whether or not these two poles of attraction could put forth a credible alternative program for French society. The PCF Central Committee meeting of October 1970 stated that a convergence of analysis on French society was apparent in a number of domains between Socialists and Communists, including the analysis of the state and of a peaceful road to socialism.[1]

The PCF's first joint text with the now realigning Socialists was issued in December 1970. Important differences were still evident between the two groupings. The PCF clung obstinately to the general laws of the construction of socialism founded on Marxism-Leninism and to a positive evaluation of the experience of the Eastern European countries.[2] The PCF defined socialist power as the power of the working class and other strata of the laboring population.[3] While the PCF called for the separation of the party and the state, an unstated reference to and tacit criticism of Eastern European socialism, it sidestepped the issue of what it would do if it were voted out of power. In this same text, the Socialists, in contrast, refused to accept the dictatorship of the proletariat and stipulated that the left must resign if voted out of power.[4] The list of liberties endorsed jointly by the two parties was fairly extensive. Political and economic democracy were viewed as closely bound together, and the taking of power by the left was to be a consequence of a majority movement of the population.[5]

Nonetheless, it was striking that the Socialists signed a document that was so evidently lacking in concessions by the PCF with regard to political democracy. The need for unity of the left was so important in their eyes that it took precedent over other concerns.

THE COMMON PROGRAM

The Common Program aligning Communists and Socialists finally came into being in June 1972. The importance of this event has since been mistakenly downplayed because the victory of the left in the presidential elections in 1981 occurred at a time of PCF-PS disunity. However, any notion of a left victory, let alone a common government, would have been inconceivable without the period of unity from 1972 to 1977 as an antecedent. During this period, ties were established between the two great cultures of the French left (Michel Rocard's term) that went well beyond the party formations themselves.

The Common Program, at the time of its signing, was a monumental event. During the 1970s it became almost a myth, offering a tremendous psychological advantage to the left. François Borella remarked that it represented the first time since the split of the French left at Tours in 1920 that Communists and Socialists had signed a common program for government in an *offensive* mold.[6] It should be recalled that the basis for programmatic action during the Popular Front in the late 1930s was a defensive one, in reaction to the danger of fascism.

The Common Program was heavily influenced by the PCF, which virtually dictated its terms. The text of the Common Program was similar to the PCF's own project, published earlier under the title of "Changer le Cap." The Common Program consisted of four chapters: (1) a better life, (2) changing one's existence, (3) democratizing the economy, and (4) democratizing social institutions. In addition, a section on international affairs was also cut in the PCF mold. Enterprises to be nationalized were to be those engaged in public services, as well as those corporations dependent largely on state contracts. The principal centers of accumulation in the economy, plus the "dynamic" or "advanced" sectors such as computers, would also be targeted for nationalization.[7] The national enterprises were to be managed under the principle of "autogestion" for the PS and under the rubric of "democracy in the enterprise" for the PCF.[8] Nine major groupings or holding companies were to be nationalized, which was pared down from the larger list originally demanded by the PCF.

The PCF now finally accepted the concept of "alternance," that is, it accepted the notion of regular elections as a way for citizens to change existing governmental parties and their policies, and with that, it finally accepted the idea that it could be voted out of power. The right of opposition would be legally guaranteed.[9] The PCF reaffirmed its belief that a left victory could only be the result of a majority movement, thus rejecting any minority path to power. Marchais called the Common Program not a socialist program, but a program of "advanced democracy" opening the way to socialism.[10]

With the signing of the Common Program, the PCF became much more concretely a party of government. But in signing the Common Program had the PCF come to endorse a new form of democratic socialism as well? Certainly many of the postulates later considered "Eurocommunist" were present in the Common Program. Any notion of a minority seizure of power had been both practically and doctrinally repudiated. The PCF would abide by the electoral rules. The concept of a nonsocialist opposition was recognized. Yet it was nonetheless true that the PCF had in important ways maintained its old point of departure. Existing socialism in the East continued to provide an important part of its identity. The party still maintained a strict democratic centralism and a fervent posture of "vanguardism" in relation to its alliances.

THE NEW SOCIALIST PARTY

In terms of the development of Eurocommunism in France, it is important to note that if by 1972 the PCF had begun to make major concessions in the area of political democracy, the PS had moved toward the positions of the PCF in relation to capitalism. Jean Rony viewed the Socialist Congress at Epinay in 1971 as the "anti–Bad Godesberg of French social democracy"; this remark was in reference to the 1958 Congress of the German Social Democratic Party that dropped Marxism from its program, making it an openly reformist party.[11] Mitterrand indicated that the strategy of the union of the left with the PCF put in place at Epinay by the PS intended to win the political terrain lost to the Communists as well as establish the Socialist Party among the new "salariat."[12] In France, Eurocommunism can be linked with aspects of the PS as well as with elements coming from the PCF, although this reference was seldom made, even during the radicalization of the PS in the 1970s. A short survey of the political positions of the principal opposing tendencies inside the PS in the 1970s after the Congress of Epinay allows for this comparison.

For Michel Rocard, who came to the PS in 1974 from a small leftist party, and whose group represented the "right wing" of the party in the 1970s, the Common Program represented the synthesis of the two great cultures of the French left.[13] One of these cultures, which had been dominant for a long period, was seen by Rocard as Jacobin, centralist, statist, nationalist, and protectionist. This culture had, according to Rocard, succeeded in gaining the stamp of Marxism, but it was not its true descendant. On the contrary, in Rocard's view socialism, for Marx, beyond the victory in the class struggle, lay in the disappearance of the state into society, with the organization of production based on the self-determination of the working class. Rocard asserted that this "real" Marxism must be rediscovered as against Ferdinand Lassalle, V. I. Lenin, and Jules Guesde.[14] The other culture, following Rocard's version of Marx, was seen as decentralist, regionalist, and "autogestionnaire."[15] For Rocard, socialism "autogestionnaire" was a way of refusing the "false" alternatives of Communism and social democracy.[16] Although nationalization was not seen as a fundamental principle of socialism, those nationalizations proposed by the Common Program were viewed by Rocard as representing a "privileged tool" in the governmental policy of the left.[17] Risks, economic sanctions, and the market were seen as essential in socialism, to assure efficiency in production.

According to Rocard, the project of the left originated in the years 1968–70 in the West. After years of economic development, a strong social malaise continued to exist; correspondingly, after Prague, the countries of the East were also seen as inadequate in meeting human needs. This twin failure (double échec) forced the French left to face reality (condamneé a la lucidité).[18] Rocard, like Jean-Pierre Chevenement from CERES, saw the heritage of the split at Tours to have weighed heavily on the two families of the French left. Both argued that the PS liberated itself from many of the negative consequences of this split at Epinay, while the PCF, because of an even stronger negative heritage from the past, has not been able to do so.[19]

Chevenement, representing the left wing of the PS, stated in the same vein; "And the problem which was posed by the Socialist Party at Epinay was to understand if it could realize a socialist transformation of Social Democracy, to escape the strong tendencies which have almost always made, in the past, the socialist parties as parties of rupture in theory, but parties of the system in practice."[20] Chevenement, following the position of Jean Longuet in relation to the Socialist/Communist split at Tours in 1920, argued that the inevitable result of the splitting of the labor movement was that each side drifted into its own abyss, producing "a permanent reformist current incapable of making reforms and a revolutionary one incapable of making the revolution."[21] In other words, each side, left to itself, accentuated its own worst characteristics.

For Chevenement, as for Rocard, the Leninist notion of an educating party leading an unconscious mass left no room for the self-development of the people or for the self-organization of the working class, thus excluding the development of Marx's important notion of the self-emancipation of the proletariat.[22] The CERES group, integral to the PS, was no less fervent in its vision of a future society without distinct social classes than the Communist left. Its political/ideological vision was manifest: "It is a question of constructing, apart from the class society emanating from capitalism, a society without classes."[23]

The CERES group was formed in January 1966 and was originally based on three projections: (1) the liberalization of the PCF so that the political gap on the left could be bridged; (2) the potential for revolutionary action in advanced capitalist countries (especially France); and (3) the need for a complete overturn of existing societal structures to avert what was seen as the impending decay of bourgeois society.[24] The CERES group searched for a Socialist strategy whose means would not pervert its ends. It found the notion of autogestion to be the potential key for the resolution of this antinomy. The notion of autogestion would be the basis of a "démarche" or action that sought to establish a society "radically different," where man would not be "mutilated."[25] The vehicle for such action would be an authentic Socialist Party, based on class struggle, but one that avoided reformist and Bolshevik deviations.[26] Such a party would have to establish a "front de classe" that would align the working class in the strict sense—the industrial working class—with portions of other salaried workers, immigrant workers, and small artisans into an antimonopolist bloc.[27]

Pluralism would be the fundamental guarantee against the confiscation of the revolution by a new minority. Such a project was called the "recherche du socialisme perdu" or "search for a lost socialism," referring back to Marx, Engels, August Bebel, Karl Kautsky, Otto Bauer, Rosa Luxemburg, and Antonio Gramsci.[28] In reference to the PS as a whole, it was noteworthy that CERES was instrumental in forming the ideology and economic program for the party at Epinay.

The Socialist Party that signed the Common Program with the PCF in 1972 had distinctly placed itself on the left, rejecting traditional social democracy. Importantly, with regard to the battle between the PCF and the PS for preeminence on the left in the 1970s, this was a development the PCF refused to and quite possibly could not admit. This was so, according to Chevenement, because "56 years after Tours, if the principal justification for the scission, in the eyes of the Communist party is nothing other than its existence as a revolutionary party, it is easy for one to understand that it cannot do without a reformist party alongside it."[29] With the Socialist transformation at Epinay, the PCF lost another of its principal points of reference while in a difficult process of self-reexamination and reflection. Another of its key reference points, identity with the Soviet model, had been increasingly difficult to maintain without qualification since 1968 and would continue to be so throughout the 1970s. Meanwhile, with the signing of the Common Program, the PCF had unavoidably merged its image with that of the PS. The PCF made its first negative reference to the dictatorship of the proletariat at this time in a hint of what was to come. Marchais stated that the term *dictatorship* was a bad one, connoting fascism rather than the party's goal of the broadest form of democracy.[30]

THE BEGINNING OF A SPLIT INSIDE THE PCF

By the time of the PCF's Twentieth Congress in 1972, much of what was to comprise its version of Eurocommunism was already evident without being labeled as such. But it must be kept in mind that most of the PCF's liberal concessions occurred without the party having come to terms with either its past or the implications of its new open course toward governmental power. The Twentieth Congress found the PCF happily casting itself in its usual role of vanguard of the popular union of the left. The party's concept of unity was significantly enlarged to include not only Socialists but also radicals and, eventually, other "republicans."[31] A democratic renaissance, the PCF now admitted, could not be the work of a single party; the equality of rights and duties of the partners of the Common Program were recognized. The Twentieth Congress endorsed the Common Program, in particular its guarantee of individual liberties, freedom of political parties, and respect for universal suffrage. The PCF would no longer look to a foreign model on which to base French socialism.[32] Rocard rightly refers to the Twentieth Congress as the PCF's attempt to enlarge its social basis and meet the challenge of the PS with an "ouverture idéologique."[33] Similar overtures would emerge in more forceful forms in 1974 and again, on shaky ground (with regard to internal party politics), in 1976 with the Twenty-second Congress and Eurocommunism.

At the Twentieth Congress, the PCF flatly declared for the first time that PCF internal party organization, based on democratic centralism, would not be imposed on French society as a whole.[34] The reason why democratic centralism would be implemented *only in the private domain of the party* was not made clear. But the issue was fundamental. Without channeling existing French institutions into the framework of democratic centralism, the party could not hope to establish the "party state" common to the Soviet bloc. The PCF, in effect, was attempting to distance itself from Eastern "socialism," implying that there was something unpalatable about such regimes. Yet when directly addressing the realities of "real, existing socialism," the PCF still remarked that the people's democracies represented unmatched human progress, "un bilan grandiose."[35]

It did not take long for the unity of the left to appear to pay dividends. The March 1973 legislative elections produced a gain for the entire left, but more so for the Socialists than the Communists. This trend continued in 1974 when Mitterrand came tantalizingly close to winning the presidential election. These early dramatic electoral results, first, the overall progression of the left, which meant the PCF was finally close to sharing governmental power, and second, the disproportionate gain for the Socialists, served to sharpen the distinctions among those in the PCF who would eventually embrace the concept of Eurocommunism wholeheartedly and those who felt that the Eurocommunist position threatened the identity of the party by failing to distinguish it sharply enough from the PS. The latter category of hardliners saw the "revolutionary soul" of the party threatened by its new liberal positions; they feared that the PCF would become a mere steppingstone for the PS and Socialist policies, leaving it to be tarnished, for all its efforts, by a social democratic governmental experience. The hardliners' positions were far from homogeneous and comprised several distinct strands of thought. They comprised a number of traditional Leninist intellectuals, but more significantly a powerful layer of party bureaucrats that held access to the party apparatus and had important connections in the leadership itself. This latter contingent of party career bureaucrats could count, as leverage in its battle with the "Eurocommunists," on the support of a significant portion of the workers at the base of the party, workers who still felt largely rejected by the existing bourgeois society, finding refuge in the "golden" image of Soviet "socialism." Importantly, it was precisely this category of workers that traditionally gave the PCF its most unmitigated devotion. A source of strength to the party in the past, this traditional Communist "ouvrieriste" constituency was now a conservative (and sterile) force inhibiting the dynamism of the party. To be sure, the "true" Leninists and the party bureaucrats did not see eye to eye on many key issues. They often regarded each other as warily as Trotsky regarded Stalin, each claiming legitimacy by virtue of a doctrine that could allow only *one* interpretation. Where they held common ground was in their mutual opposition to many of the liberal concessions made by the PCF. The reemergence of a dominant PS was something the hardliners stemming from the party bureaucracy could not countenance. Interestingly enough, the hardliners as a group came not only from pre–1968 generations of PCF devotees and from the party's working-class base but also from some newer members.[36] François Hincker confirmed that there was a new influx of hardliners in the 1970s principally as a result of the worsening economic crisis.[37]

The notion of significant internal splits existing in Communist parties is not a common one. Regarding the PCF, Irwin Wall's book *French Communism in the Era of Stalin* cited party splits in the 1950s as being responsible for numerous otherwise unexplained shifts in party policy. In the 1970s the articles of Patrick Jarreau in *Le Monde* often hinted at party cleavages. High-ranking PCF members themselves give contradictory opinions on this matter. Two of the most highly regarded observers of the PCF, Philippe Robrieux and Annie Kriegel, continued to deny the existence of internal party differences as a source of policy change, preferring instead to explain shifts in party policy as a result of Soviet influence. Since plausible explanations for PCF behavior generally may be derived from changes in the French polity, however, frequent emphasis on the Russian factor is often misplaced. At any rate, purported Russian influence, either through direct pressure on PCF leaders by way of a threat to split the party or by any other means, is even more difficult to document than supposed internal splits in the PCF. Admittedly one can offer only scant documentation of PCF internal splits and the key figures at the summit of the party involved therein. The structure or sociology of party power, however, which tends toward the status quo, and the recent proximate position of the PCF with regard to governmental power, which has forced the party to alter its comfortable, tribunitary role in response to working-class demands, provide contradictory impetus upon party policy.[38] These competing pressures, reflective both of the internal structure of the PCF and of the PCF's changing role in French society, are surely felt by the members themselves, making the notion of party splits plausible. The constant changes in PCF policy in the 1970s are the effect of the PCF's structural ambiguity.

If the PCF indeed felt its vulnerability to the PS after 1973, it rarely acknowledged this openly. Only after the 1978 elections could one find such views openly expressed among Communists. Danielle Tartakowski, a PCF activist and author of *L'Histoire du PCF*, echoing a concern apparently felt by many in the party privately throughout the 1970s, later did state that the situation in France and the conditions for change favored the PS over the PCF.[39]

By all accounts the 1973 results were disappointing to the PCF despite its progression. The party received 21.4 percent of the vote on the first ballot to 19.2 percent for the PS. The PCF expected to gain rapidly from the union of the left, as it had in previous periods of left unity in France dating back to the Popular Front in 1936. According to Hincker, it felt its norm to be around 25 percent.[40] Despite this disappointment, the party continued steadfast on its unitary course. Jean Rony indicated that the only evident area of discord between the PCF and the PS from the time of the signing of the Common Program in 1972 until the autumn of 1974 involved the attitudes of the respective parties with regard to "real, existing Socialism,"[41] Rony pointed out that the only statement by a major party leader against the official unitary policy of the PCF from 1972 to 1974 came from Roland Leroy, the future editor of *L'Humanité*, in the PCF review *La Nouvelle Critique* of June–July 1973. In this issue Leroy welcomed the movement of the PS away from class collaboration but cited the need to reinforce the PCF to assure that this change of the PS would be maintained, since, according to Leroy, the PS could always once again serve as an arm of the bourgeoisie. In Leroy's article the PS was seen, as was the case throughout the 1970s in PCF formulations, as a reflection either of the PCF or of the bourgeoisie.[42] It counted for nothing in itself.

THE 1974 PRESIDENTIAL ELECTION

The events surrounding the 1974 presidential election and its immediate aftermath are especially important in understanding the behavior of the PCF in the 1970s, and they bear specifically on Eurocommunism. It was during this period rather than in 1976 at its Twenty-second (Eurocommunist) Congress that the PCF embraced the union of the left in its most enthusiastic fashion.

During this period the PCF began to search for alternate international alliances by looking to the Social Democratic parties of Europe.[43] Was the PCF ready to say "Adieu" to the Soviet Union in search of a new political basis on which to strive for governmental power in France? The situation was considerably more delicate. The hardliners in the party, while not at center stage, still represented a potent countervailing force on party policy. The PCF did not expect to win the presidential elections on 1974; the leadership was surprised by the narrowness of the result and, as Rony reported, "euphoric."[44] The PCF had not questioned its relationship to the Soviet Union except to discount the Soviet model as necessarily being relevant to French socialism. Yet this was the most fluid period in the party's fifty-year history. Almost anything seemed possible. If the PCF had kept to the strategy of union of the left, the hardliners might well have been eclipsed within the party. Doctrinal concessions could have been made later to justify the PCF's liberal course. François Hincker categorized this period as a critical crossroad for PCF history.[45]

After the first round of voting for the presidential election, the PCF markedly stepped up its campaign for Mitterrand even though Mitterrand did not emphasize the Common Program in his campaign. This omission did not go unnoticed within the PCF among those already recalcitrant to the unitary line. Still, Marchais indicated that the PCF would not demand key ministries in a left government in order to avoid frightening centrist voters. The election revealed the real strength of the French left, which obtained 49 percent on the second ballot. In addition, of particular importance to the PCF, a Socialist candidate with a Communist partner had almost become president of France. A knee-jerk anti-Communism among significant portions of the French electorate appeared to be eroding as a consequence of the new, liberal image propagated by the PCF. Various opinion polls echoed this new reality.

The alliance between Communists and Socialists now seemed to be flourishing. The party decided that the union of the left had to be intensified. Notions of a rupture with capitalism must be avoided; a left government, the PCF declared, would not embark immediately upon constructing socialism.[46] Charles Fiterman, a prominent PCF member and a future minister in Mitterrand's government, remarked in June 1974 that none of the constitutional laws of the Fifth Republic would be challenged by the "advanced democracy" advocated by the PCF.[47] Hincker has since remarked that the June period represented one in which the PCF became more "Italian" than the PCI, when the PCF began to take on the role of a "parti revolutionnaire mais non bolchevik."[48] This may be somewhat of an overestimation, but the June period entailed a remarkable if brief period in PCF history.

After the election, at a Central Committee meeting in June a new slogan, "union et action du peuple de France," was coined. Meanwhile the Paris Federation opened its meetings to the general public ("coeur ouvert") in an effort to do away with the rigid image of the inner workings of the PCF and to remove some of the taboo surrounding the party. Marchais indicated that a left government would have to attain the support of well over 50 percent of the population to assure the acceptance of its program.[49] There was now no limit to the group of people who were seen as victims of big capital or to those who were defined as receptive to the program of the left.

However, this ideological overture was nipped in the bud by the mounting pressure of the hardliners. The poor showing of the party in the partial legislative elections in early October and the renewed strength of the PS enabled the hardliners to tilt the precarious balance inside the party back in the other direction. The Twenty-first Congress, held later in the year, still maintained the language of a political overture with the key slogan of "union of the people of France," but this overture was to become largely formal.[50]

The 1974 presidential elections began to clearly distinguish the factional struggle in the party, highlighting the phenomenon of two Communist strategies existing in the same Communist Party.[51] The political fate of the PCF and the Eurocommunist tendency inside it lay in the balance. The period from June to October 1974 was a trial run, or what Jean Elleinstein called a "dress rehearsal," for the crucial period from March to September 1977, which would lead ultimately to a break between the PCF and the PS.[52]

THE CHANGE IN COURSE (FALL 1974)

It was Roland Leroy, responsible for party intellectuals and soon to be editor of *L'Humanité*, who, according to both Rony and Hincker, led the counterattack of the hardliners, although clearly a majority of the leadership had begun to worry about the developing strength of the PS after the October elections.[53] It was now felt by many in the party leadership that not only were centrist and rightist voters attracted to the PS but some of the PCF's own electorate as well.[54] Leroy was in charge of drawing up the text for the extraordinary Twenty-first Congress called for by the leadership after the narrow defeat of the left in June to meet the new "advanced" political situation. After purposely drawing up a weak text, Leroy then invited criticism of it, but he selected critics from the left of the party only.[55] According to both Hincker and Rony, Leroy's plot did not become apparent until after the partial elections and the communiqué of the Political Bureau on October 7, which emphasized the importance of the PCF in keeping the PS away from "class collaboration."

Robrieux wrote that there was an original resolution for the Twenty-first Congress which contained many of the ideas featured at the Twenty-second Congress held in 1976, but this resolution was not allowed to see the light of day.[56] Robrieux contends that Leroy inexplicably did not begin working on the resolution, leaving it instead to Pierre Juquin. Robrieux believes that it was Marchais, upon returning from his vacation, who put a different accent on the document, reemphasizing the key role of the PCF in the union of the left.[57] Sensing the shift in tide, since dissent had worked its way down to the base of the party, Leroy took quick action. Federal conferences preceding the Twenty-first Congress witnessed a flood of criticism of the PS and the left radicals; suddenly, small and medium-sized enterprises were condemned for fiercely exploiting workers, and the PCF declared itself once again a "parti revolutionnaire" with socialism as its immediate goal.[58] These events caused Rony to remark, "The idyllic phase of the union of the left was over."[59] As for Leroy, he was to get the editorship of *L'Humanité* for his efforts, a post he would thereafter employ to the distinct advantage of the hardliners in the party.

The Twenty-first Congress reflected this internal controversy in the PCF. The Congress still retained the notion of the union of the people in France, which represented a call to intellectuals, small farmers, artisans, small and medium-sized entrepreneurs, military personnel, Christians, and patriotic Gaullists to join the working class in the battle for democratic change. But in concessions to the hardliners, the text of the Twenty-first Congress referred to the working class as the center and motive force of popular action with, of course, the PCF in the vanguard. The Communist Party alone was capable of leading the "struggle for Socialism."[60] In reference to the PS meeting labeled "Assises du Socialisme," held in October 1974, which brought additional strands of the non-Communist left into the PS, Marchais stated that he could not understand those of the left who said they were

Socialists yet did not recognize the legitimacy of "existing Socialism" in the East.[61] On the contrary the PCF judged the existence of socialism in the East as indispensable for the success of the French left; this, despite the fact that the Soviet ambassador had visited Mitterrand's opponent, Valéry Giscard d'Estaing, between the first and second rounds of the presidential election in 1974 in an obvious snub of the left's candidate, causing some consternation in the party. Leroy sounded a timeworn theme: the PCF had a "scientific" definition of socialism that distinguished it from those who employed "utopian" constructions or models.[62] If specifically French conditions were to be taken into account in the construction of socialism, the new society also had to be founded on the "universal principles" of socialism, which meant taking into account the acquired experience of the U.S.S.R.[63]

After the Twenty-first Congress, the PCF was not able to develop even a semblance of a consistent line. First one line, then the other apparently gained the upper hand, neither on a lasting basis. Changes in party orientations were made, but not to the degree that alternate positions were totally excluded. This situation did not imply, however, that the PCF's functioning had become democratic. On the contrary, as Jean Elleinstein remarked, the PCF was never able to take the consequences of its action into account and open up debate in the party, especially on the key issues of the U.S.S.R. and democratic centralism.[64] This was essential for Elleinstein because in signing the Common Program, the party had intrinsically questioned the concept of revolution inherited from Bolshevik and Leninist thought. To then fail to draw the logical ideological conclusions implied by PCF policy necessarily allowed the PS to gain electorally over the PCF since the PS appeared more coherent to the electorate.

The PCF's inability to respond to changing events was not caused by the tension between the two lines in the party per se. The immobility of the PCF was a consequence of a complex set of factors into which the factional struggles were merged. The principal factors leading to PCF paralysis were the heavy burden of the PCF's past, the rigid stamp of democratic centralism impinging on the internal functioning of the party which prevented disagreements from running their course, and a leadership more often than not content to remain ensconced firmly in its relatively privileged position in the countersociety. These factors worked to prohibit the confrontation of ideas in the party necessary for decisive action. There was nothing inevitable about this situation; the PCI opened itself to internal dialogue but did not experience this same fate in Italy. The PS, for its part, had many more factions than the PCF, but this did not prevent its eventual success.

Without question the internal weaknesses of the PCF were exacerbated by the emerging strength of the PS. The leadership of the PCF knew that the signing of the Common Program could stimulate the rise of the PS (although, for the most part, this was not admitted openly) but not to the extent that the PCF would cease to become the largest party of the left. In June 1974, the Central Committee did acknowledge that since socialism was not immediately on the agenda for France, it would be natural that many voters would not be able to distinguish the PS from the PCF, producing a situation in which a fraction of the PCF vote might go to the PS to assure the left's presence on the second round ("vote utile").[65]

The PCF, after the signing of the Common Program, persistently misread its new partner; it failed to realize (or could not realize) that it was not dealing with a traditional Social Democratic Party. This ultimately made the PCF appear as the culprit in the eyes of the electorate when it broke with the PS in September 1977, implying that the PS had taken a turn to the right ("virage à droite"). Such a perception stemmed from the traditional raison d'être for a Communist Party, which was originally created to counteract a collaborationist Socialist Party. Keith Middlemas states, "Obsessed with the threat to its own identity, the PCF seems to have ignored the degree to which Mitterrand had shifted the PS genuinely leftwards."[66]

THE PCF CASTS AN EYE AT THE PCI

The PCF continued its attacks on the Socialists well into the summer of 1975. Its position vis-à-vis the U.S.S.R., however, was somewhat ambivalent. While moving closer to the image of existing socialism in general, the party disseminated a Declaration of Freedoms, which Neil McInnes saw as a disguised attack on the Soviet repression of civil liberties.[67] The text was designed to be a preamble to the French Constitution and contained clauses guaranteeing the right to strike and the prohibiting of arbitrary internment in a medical institution (a clear reference to Soviet practice for political motives). It also came out against merging the party with the state.[68] The publication of this document was undoubtedly a result of what Georges Lavau calls the "Gulag effect."[69] However, the PCF in the 1970s, while often criticizing Soviet treatment of dissidents, never directly allowed for the legitimacy of their (the dissidents') points of grievance.[70] For example, the PCF regretted that Alexander Solzhenitsyn's *Gulag Archipelago* was not published in the U.S.S.R. but denounced the furor created about him as an anti-Soviet campaign.[71]

Events from Portugal and Italy soon forced the PCF into making a strategic choice and allowed the emerging "Eurocommunists" to regain control of the party. According to Rony, the PCF initially used the events in Portugal to reaffirm its view of the counterrevolutionary aspects of Socialist parties. Contrary to the PCI and the PCE, the PCF chose to side with the position of the Portuguese Communist Party, which had supported the extralegal actions of the Portuguese armed forces to seize power. This stance by the PCF damaged its democratic pretensions.

Then, dramatically, came the election results from Italy. The PCI had broken the barrier of 30 percent. The PCF was caught by surprise.[72] Its tactics were clearly wanting in comparison to those of its neighbors to the south. Suddenly, Rony remarked, it became "safe" inside the PCF to write about the PCI.[73] A PCF-PCE joint document was published in July 1975 and a sparkling, "Eurocommunist" communiqué between the PCF and the PCI in November 1975. The notion of Eurocommunism had been launched, although the term was not yet accepted by the Communist parties themselves.

Paradoxically, the 1975 period also witnessed the publication of a book, *L'Union est un combat,* by PCF Political Bureau member Etienne Fajon, in which a Marchais "secret speech" of 1972 was revealed. In this speech to the PCF Central Committee, Marchais expressed reservations that the PS had really changed its right-wing orientations. The existence of this speech again highlights the phenomenon of internal factional disputes within the party, disputes that were instrumental in the many radical turns in the PCF's policies in the 1970s. From the fall of 1974 to the middle of 1975, then, the PCF maintained a somewhat liberal international policy combined with a "hardening" internal policy, especially with regard to the PS. Thus, the phenomenon of a double line has a real sociological basis inside the PCF.

NOTES

1. *Le Monde,* October 16, 1970.
2. François Borella, *Les Partis politiques dans la France d'aujourd'hui* (Paris: Editions du Seuil, 1973), pp. 191–92.
3. *Le Monde,* December 24, 1970.
4. Borella, p. 192.
5. *Le Monde,* December 24, 1970.
6. Borella, p. 147.
7. *Le Monde,* June 28, 1972.
8. *Le Monde,* June 24, 1972.
9. Borella, p. 193.
10. *Le Monde,* June 29, 1972.
11. Jean Rony, *Trente ans du parti* (Paris: Christian Bourgeois, 1978), p. 208.
12. *Le Monde,* June 15, 1971.
13. Michel Rocard, *Parler vrai* (Paris: Editions du Seuil, 1979), p. 66.
14. Ibid., p. 79.
15. Ibid. *Autogestion,* or self-management, is a somewhat elusive principle.

It has often been translated in reference to workers' control of the enterprise, but its meaning in political discourse in France, and in particular with the Socialists, is much broader. Autogestion among the French Socialists implies not only workers' control in the factories but citizens' control in the communes. The notion of citizens' control is connected to the decentralization of decision making. With the French Socialists, autogestion also implies the socialization of key sectors of the economy, which is seen as a necessary element in assuring workers' and citizens' control of society.

16. Ibid., p. 101.

17. Ibid., p. 81.

18. Ibid., p. 111.

19. Ibid., p. 125.

20. Jean-Pierre Chevenement, *Les Socialistes, les communistes et les autres* (Paris: Aubier Montaigne, 1977), p. 265.

21. Ibid., p. 73.

22. Ibid., p. 161.

23. Ibid., p. 243.

24. Michel Charzet and Ghislaine Toutain, *Le CERES: Un Combat pour le socialisme* (Paris: Calmann-Lévy, 1975), p. 12.

25. Ibid., pp. 141, 177.

26. Ibid., pp. 196–7.

27. Ibid., pp. 205–6.

28. Ibid., p. 244.

29. Chevenement, p. 138.

30. In Neil McInnes, *Euro-Communism* (Beverly Hills, Calif.: Sage Publications, 1976), p. 10.

31. *Le Monde*, December 14, 1972.

32. Ibid.

33. Rocard, p. 112.

34. *Le Monde*, December 14, 1972.

35. Ibid.

36. George Ross and Jane Jenson, "Strategies in Conflict: The Twenty-third Congress of the French Communist Party," *Socialist Review* (November–December 1979), p. 75.

37. Interview with François Hincker, April 19, 1982.

38. The notion of the PCF's role as a tribunitary party in the French political system, that is, as a tribune for the most downtrodden members of the working class, has been developed by Georges Lavau. For his latest work on the PCF see *A Quoi Sert Le Parti communiste français?* (Paris: Librairie Arthéme Fayard), 1981.

39. Interview with Danielle Tartakowsky, April 28, 1982.

40. François Hincker, *Le Parti communiste au carrefour* (Paris: Albin Michel, 1981), p. 109.

41. Rony, p. 163.

42. Ibid.

43. Ibid., p. 170.

44. Ibid.

45. For a full development of this thesis see Hincker, *Le Parti communiste au carrefour.*

46. Rony, p. 170.

47. Hincker, p. 127.

48. Ibid., p. 129.

49. *Le Monde*, June 13, 1974.

50. Rocard, p. 112.

51. See Henri Fiszbin, *Les Bouches s'ouvrent* (Paris: Bernard Grasset, 1980), pp. 179, 299.

52. Jean Elleinstein, *Ils vous trompent, Camarades!* (Paris: Belford, 1981), p. 89.

53. Hincker, pp. 134–35; also Rony, pp. 180–82. On the other hand, Philippe Robrieux denies that Leroy has this sort of power in the party. Interview with Philippe Robrieux, May 17, 1982.

54. George Ross, *Workers and Communists in France* (Berkeley: University of California Press, 1982), p. 246.

55. Hincker, pp. 136–37.

56. Philippe Robrieux, *L'Histoire intérieur de parti communiste, 1972–1982*, vol. 3 (Paris: Fayard, 1982), p. 207.

57. Ibid., p. 208.

58. Hincker, pp. 136–37.

59. Rony, p. 181.

60. *Le Monde*, October 26, 1974.

61. *Le Monde*, October 29, 1974.

62. Ibid.

63. Ibid.

64. Elleinstein, p. 80.

65. *Le Monde*, October 24, 1974.

66. Keith Middlemas, *Power and the Party: Changing Faces of Communism in Western Europe* (London: André Deutsch, 1980), p. 119.

67. McInnes, p. 15.

68. Ibid., pp. 15–16.

69. Georges Lavau, *A Quoi Sert Le Parti communiste français?* (Paris: Librairie Arthéme Fayard, 1981), pp. 384–85.

70. Ibid., p. 394.

71. Ross, *Workers and Communists in France*, p. 244.

72. Rony, p. 195.

73. Ibid.

6

The Emergence of Eurocommunism _____

The origin of the word *Eurocommunism* has been traced to many sources. Most have agreed that the term was of journalistic coinage. It can be argued that the PCI had been implementing a strategy that loosely resembled many aspects of Eurocommunism since World War II and in particular since 1956. Yet one cannot meaningfully speak of Eurocommunism existing at that time. Eurocommunism goes much deeper and differs in kind from Palmiro Togliatti's notion of polycentrism. The Eurocommunist strategy may also be deciphered in Antonio Gramsci's notion of a "war of position," although it makes little sense to call Gramsci a Eurocommunist.

In the 1960s, the section of the PCI associated with the position of Giorgio Amendola, in retrospect, can be called Eurocommunist or a direct harbinger of Eurocommunism. This group had sufficiently distinguished itself in a number of areas: it challenged democratic centralism, the legitimacy of the Bolshevik model, and the breach among the European left stemming from 1920–21 with the formation of the Communist International.

In 1961, Amendola proposed to allow the existence of minority and majority factions in the PCI.[1] By the time of Amendola's often-cited November 1964 article in *Rinascita*, the PCI theoretical journal, a coherent position had developed in the PCI, one that took into account the PCI's position in a Western democracy. Amendola argued in this article that the PCI should free itself from the Bolshevik model to fill the political space left open to it in Italy by the failure of social democracy. In the process the party should try to oversome the historic breach on the left stemming from 1920–21.[2] By the time of its Twelfth Congress in 1969, the PCI was already flirting with the notion of a "third way" between Eastern European socialism and social democracy.[3]

Amendola represented a political wing of the PCI, one that was not in the majority to be sure, but one that existed *inside* the party. One of the many examples of the extraordinary adroitness of PCI politics has been in its ability to harbor such dissident factions. Keith Middlemas pointed out that the "new left" did not leave the PCI en masse in the 1960s because of this PCI flexibility.[4] Amendola's positions were expressed in a party that had already developed a subtle policy toward political alliances. The PCI had long since renounced a purely working-class alternative to bourgeois coalitions of government. Even at its early stages, then, the Eurocommunist thrust distinguished itself from previous independent Communist movements that developed after 1917 by not seeking to authenticate itself by going back to verify a lost "Communist" past that had somehow been compromised in the course of the Soviet experience. Instead, Eurocommunism has always contained important elements that projected *outside* of traditional Communism, without, however, dropping Marx's image of a class-less society, the pivot of any communist ideological position. Euro-communism always contained within it the potential for something novel.

Yet the PCI, "going it alone," did not attract the necessary attention to force observers into considering the possibility of another type of communism. The PCI was discounted as an anomaly. When it was joined in its "liberal" approach by the PCE and the PCF in the mid–1970s, however, the term *Eurocommunism* arose as a reference point.

From another angle, the crisis of the Western societies, particularly as it was manifested in France and Italy, created a situation in the 1970s where a political space had emerged suitable for an anticapitalist political formation, one, however, that also recognized the failure and or inapplicability of Eastern European "socialism." When the PCF signed a joint communiqué with the PCI in November 1975 explaining the converging strategies of the two parties, another type of political discourse was in the making, one that aimed at this political reality. The subsequent evolution of the PCF away from Eurocommunist positions did not detract from the overall importance of this communiqué, nor did it alter the set of political factors in France and Italy in the 1970s that encouraged this movement. France voted for a leftist government in 1981 despite the PCF's subsequent antiunitary actions, and Italy is still in a general crisis in the 1980s with the PCI patiently waiting in the wings, ready to gain governmental power.

The PCF-PCI statement was a bold one. For the PCF it served as a springboard for its spectacular Twenty-second Congress in 1976. The two parties maintained that all liberties emanating from the bourgeois revolutions of the Nineteenth century and from the great popular struggles of the Twentieth century, in which the working classes were instrumental, should be guaranteed and developed.[5] Freedom of thought, expression, publication, association, assembly, and movement were specifically supported. Other areas declared of concern by the two parties included the inviolability of private life, maintenance of religious liberties, plurality of political parties, independence of the judicial system, and free alternation in power of political minorities and majorities through elections.[6]

The two parties advocated democracy in industrial enterprises within the framework of free trade unions and a program of the decentralization of the state. They advocated public control of the principal means of production and exchange while acknowledging the existence of small farm property and small and medium-sized enterprises, which, in their view, had a positive role to play in the construction of socialism. Such a statement had "classic" dimensions considering that these were parties once tied to the Leninist Third International. The two parties now indicated not only that they would abide by the rules of "bourgeois" democracy but that they now no longer considered democracy "bourgeois."

In November 1975, the PCF made another spectacular move by rejecting the Soviet-inspired draft for the Conference of European Communist Parties, eventually held in East Berlin in June 1976, on the grounds that it demanded a unified strategy for all parties. In December, after a BBC film on Soviet labor camps was shown on French television, a PCF guest commentator stated, "If things like that exist, we do not approve."[7] Marchais, wishing to make an impression on observers with regard to the PCF's new tenacity vis-à-vis the U.S.S.R., did not attend the CPSU Congress in February. Marchais pointed out that his reasons for not going were due to the divergences the two parties had over socialist democracy and their different evaluations of foreign policy issues.[8]

FRENCH COMMUNISM CHANGES COURSE: THE PCF'S TWENTY-SECOND CONGRESS (1976)

The Twenty-second Congress of the PCF was labeled "historic" by the party, and rightly so. It was a sincere effort by the PCF both to meet the Socialist surge and to respond to the social and political conditions in France since May 1968, which had favored the left. May 1968 not only produced the Socialist Congress at Epinay in 1971; it also was responsible for the Twenty-second Congress of the PCF. In many ways the Twenty-second Congress was more important in terms of an ideological overture by the party than the signing of the Common Program itself. Because of its dominant position on the left the PCF was able to sign the Common Program in 1972 without significantly questioning the ideological basis of the party. Unity of the left was not a new phenomenon; the period of the Popular Front and the Liberation had always been models to emulate, fully sanctioned in the Leninist mold.

With the Twenty-second Congress the party recognized that it had to change in more fundamental ways. The Twenty-second Congress represented more than a shift in line; it was a partial shift in the political geography of the party. The fact that the Twenty-second Congress had to overcome strong resistance in the party and did not fully succeed in taking root should not detract from its importance. As Fiszbin noted, major doctrinal changes in the PCF do not occur as happenstance but only after the most heated debates.[9]

The PCF renewed its challenge to the Socialists and reached out to the French electorate through the Twenty-second Congress. For the first time in its history, the party was on the verge of really becoming a serious party of government, one fully respecting the rules of political democracy. As Alain Duhamel remarked, the PCF had become serious, even at the expense of losing its religiosity.[10] Actually it was because it was losing its religiosity that the PCF was now becoming a serious governmental party. In an important sense it had become a party like the others, although not because it had ceased to propose to radically change the existing society, but because it had given up its goal of molding the institutions of society to correspond to its own party organization, thus ceasing to be a totalitarian threat to society. It now fully respected the rules of democracy.

This is not to way that the PCF had internally changed; it had not become a Eurocommunist party without qualification on the PCI mold. It still maintained democratic centralism in the party. It still wished to be seen as a vanguard party in the mythical sense. It continued to believe in the socialist nature of the U.S.S.R. The changes that did take place were real, however, irrespective of the fact that the PCF later emptied the "content" of the Twenty-second Congress and for all intents and purposes discarded Eurocommunism.

The main objective of the Twenty-second Congress, according to Marchais, was to indicate what type of society the PCF advocated for France.[11] Hence the Twenty-second Congress proposed a "project of society." In doing so the PCF began to define a new identity for itself with the notion of "socialism in French colors," more than fifty years after its inception at the Congress of Tours. This democratic road to socialism was seen to rest on three essential forces, each viewed as a lever for change: the working class as a decisive social force; the union of the people of France, which amalgamated all those whose interests were seen to be opposed to monopoly capital; and the PCF as a vanguard exercising "directing influence" on the popular movement.[12]

At each stage in the movement to socialism, universal suffrage would be the measure of success or failure. The position of the party expressed earlier in the Manifesto of Champigny, which authorized a pacific road to socialism but also argued that the possible violence of the defeated class would be met by violence of the popular forces, was labeled a "double line" in the tribune for discussion in *L'Humanité* before the Twenty-second Congress. The democratic road to socialism was the only road conceivable in France; no violence was acceptable.[13] The PCF placed itself firmly within the framework of a peaceful transition to socialism. At each stage of the transition, the arithmetic and the political majorities were to coincide. The PCF no longer subscribed to the Leninist notion that bourgeois democracy was merely the best form of capitalist dictatorship in which to plan an eventual seizure of power. On the contrary, this democracy, developed by the bourgeoisie and enriched by working-class struggles, even if viewed as inadequate by the party was seen as the point of departure for a peaceful transition to socialism.[14]

One of the outstanding features of the Twenty-second Congress was its assertion that democracy and socialism were inseparable. This notion was vividly stated in a new conference in January 1976, in which Marchais declared that there could be no liberty without a plurality of parties or without free expression.[15] Marchais went on to state that the principles expounded by the party in relation to democratic socialism have a "universal quality." He further noted, "It is clear that we have a divergence with the CPSU on this matter."[16] Nonetheless Marchais claimed that the "serious" response was that the party's democratic road to socialism remained fully loyal to the principles of Marxism-Leninism.[17] The traditional ideological baggage had to be maintained to placate the party hardliners.

The most outstanding feature of the Twenty-second Congress was its rejection of the notion "dictatorship of the proletariat." This possibility was first mentioned on television by Marchais, to the surprise of many French Communists. The word *dictatorship*, Marchais argued, had purely negative connotations. It obscured the democratic socialism that the party wished to construct. The conception of the "proletariat" embodied in the notion of dictatorship of the proletariat was too restrictive to define the working class in contemporary France.[18] The "dictatorship of the proletariat" did not reflect the vast antimonopoly bloc that the party wished to lead.

Etienne Balibar, an associate of the Marxist political philosopher Luis Althusser, led the challenge to this position from the perspective of the "true" Leninists, claiming that if the party dropped the dictatorship of the proletariat it would be denying the existence of the dictatorship of the bourgeoisie and the role of the state apparatus as an instrument of exploitation.[19] Balibar argued that the real reason the term was being rejected was that the regimes of the East were perceived as dictatorships *over* the proletariat and that they had merged the party with the state. For Balibar, these Communist regimes had not yet realized the true dictatorship of the proletariat.

Guy Besse responded to Balibar's comments for the party leadership in the tribune for discussion in *L'Humanité*, noting that the state could not be changed at once; it had to be "democratized" step by step.[20] The state, for Besse, first had to be disconnected from the banking and financial sectors that dominated it. The new socialist power could not prevent any section of the population from voting or from participating in the politics of the country. Besse further characterized Balibar's term *dictatorship over the proletariat*, used to characterize the U.S.S.R., as unfortunate.[21]

The dropping of the dictatorship of the proletariat had an undeniable symbolic significance for the PCF and cannot be taken lightly.[22] Yet the reasons given for its termination were trivial and opportunistic. The notion was seen as outdated or irrelevant; the party did not really question the concept at its root. Didn't the dictatorship of the proletariat produce some undeniable wrongs where it was implemented? Wasn't the notion of a strictly working-class state really the problem itself? Wouldn't the dictatorship of the proletariat be inappropriate under any historical circumstances? All the PCF could offer was that it wanted a democratic socialism of the working class and its allies that would render the dictatorship of the proletariat inappropriate. If the dictatorship of the proletariat was necessary in 1917 with the proletariat in the minority, in contemporary France, where the working class represented 44 percent of the population and where salaried workers together represented 75 percent, the PCI said it was no longer needed.[23]

Marchais, in his address to the Twenty-second Congress, went on to blame the economic crisis in France on the domination of national life by a caste of the powerful and rich. A capitalist was no longer someone who owned a single shop or even several shops. The real bourgeoisie of contemporary France comprised the twenty-five financial and industrial groups that had hegemony over the entire bourgeois class and were hegemonic over the state.[24] This "state monopoly thesis" had existed in one form or another in the PCF since 1958. It viewed "monopoly" capital as having appropriated the levers of political power to maintain profitability with the help of state funds. Still, this phenomenon was not seen to sufficiently offset a general decline in the rate of profit.[25] Yet PCF policies persistently called for exorbitant taxes on the enterprises as if profits were in fact high. The state monopoly thesis argued that growing antagonisms had developed between the monopoly sector and the rest of the nation. An emerging intermediate strata of workers (scientists, technicians, white collar, administrators, and intellectuals) came to share the conditions of the working class, comprising what was called the "salariat." This stratum of workers increasingly had become the target of cost cutting and work reorganization. These economic and sociological developments combined to produce the basis of broad popular movement against the caste of monopolists.[26]

The Twenty-second Congress noted that the socialism that the party wished to construct would be characterized by different forms of social property: national, cooperative, municipal, departmental, and regional. The continuation of small private property was also said to be important to the mixed economy. Nationalized industry would be run with the participation of the state, representatives of the workers, and representatives of consumers. Regions and departments would be given broader decision-making powers.

The party saw the role of the working class as essential but not all-encompassing. The socialist power would be the power of the working class and other categories of manual and intellectual workers. Multiple currents of thought within the governing coalition of the left were legitimate, their existence guaranteed.[27]

The PCF did not give up its attachment to the existing socialist countries that had been so instrumental to its identity; it merely took a certain distance from them. The party reaffirmed its view that there was more than one model of socialism in a more forceful way than in the past. Nevertheless, Marchais's speech to the Twenty-second Congress acknowledged the "success" of the socialist countries.[28]

Certain "general laws of socialism" such as collective ownership of the principal means of production, the exercise of political power, and the directing role of the working class were upheld by the PCF.[29] Were these the general laws of Communism that the CPSU had always proclaimed, or were they the emerging laws of Eurocommunism, exemplified in the PCF's own proclamation that socialism and democracy are intertwined?

EUROCOMMUNISM OUT IN THE OPEN

The PCF, by beginning to define a "socialism in French colors," taking a slightly critical stance vis-à-vis the Soviet Union on the question of political democracy, and beginning to attach itself to the social and political movements stemming from May 1968, became a key element in the emergence of the *movement* of Eurocommunism, which had been a *policy* incubated for many years by the PCI. The PCF began to use the term *Eurocommunism* only at the "Eurocommunist" Madrid

Conference in March 1977, which was also attended by the PCI and the PCE. Meanwhile "Eurocommunist" parties had also taken root in Japan and Australia. In Greece, Sweden, and Great Britain, Eurocommunist formations existed alongside pro-Soviet Communist parties.

The Twenty-fifth Congress of the CPSU in February 1976 became for the first time an open stage for dissension, where the Western Communist parties not only demanded "independence," "sovereignty," and "equality," as was habitual, but also pressed for the full support of individual and collective freedoms, religious and cultural freedoms, and free trade unions to go along with the notion of pluralist democracy.[30] Santiago Carrillo, like Marchais, did not attend, going instead to Rome, where he remarked in an interview that the Soviet regime represented a "primitive stage" of socialism.[31]

The Conference of European Communist Parties in June 1976 in East Berlin saw this trend continue. The concepts of "proletarian internationalism" and a "single Communist strategy" were replaced with "voluntary cooperation and solidarity" based on the "principles of equality and sovereign independence of each party, the non-interference in its internal affairs and the respect for the free choice of different roads in the struggle for social change of a progressive nature and for socialism."[32] A Soviet motion stipulating identical objectives and a common ideology among the Communist parties was rejected.[33] Enrico Berlinguer noted that many Western European Communist parties proposed a socialist society with the "principles of the secular, non-ideological nature of the state and its democratic organization; the plurality of political parties and the possibility of alternation of governmental majorities; the autonomy of trade unions; religious freedom; freedom of expression, of culture and of the arts and sciences."[34] He employed the term *Eurocommunism* for the first time at this conference.

The crowning point of the first general Eurocommunist thrust occurred in early March 1977 when, for the first time, the three major Western Communist parties met in Madrid. Previously, the word *Eurocommunism* had been attached to various bilateral conferences. Now the term had come to convey an idea, a spirit and movement with its own limits, consistencies, and omissions.[35] At this conference Marchais remarked that conditions existed for democratic socialism in certain advanced capitalist countries. If *Eurocommunism* conveyed such a meaning then he agreed with the term.[36]

With the positions expressed by the three parties in Madrid, the prospects for the further evolution of the PCF, and the publishing of Carrillo's *Eurocommunism and the State* in 1977 indicating the new, more open position of the PCE, something unusual seemed to be emerging. Yet the Eurocommunist thrust stalled quickly after it had surfaced, with the defeat of the French left in March 1978 and the breakdown of the Christian Democrat–PCI alliance in Italy following the kidnapping-murder of Aldo Moro. Eurocommunism subsequently was discounted by many observers as either a smokescreen or a limited conjunctural phenomenon. But the Western Communist parties had already gone too far in their democratic assertions to easily revert to Leninist Communism. The Communist parties of Western Europe could either take the "Eurocommunist" leap into the unknown or risk fading away from the European political landscape, as relics of the past.

THE PCF AND EUROCOMMUNISM

The PCF, by denying its attachment to the Soviet model of socialism and moving away from the dictatorship of the proletariat, was losing its "religiosity." This intensified its identity crisis. The PCF's position in French society stood on tenuous ground since the events of May 1968 in France and the Czech invasion of the same year. As soon as the Socialists reconstituted on the left in 1971, the PCF had to face up to its identity crisis in some manner. It was no longer the unchallenged authority on the left in France. It could not longer secure its position as a result of the center-right alignments of the Socialists or alternately from the positive image of the U.S.S.R.

But how could the PCF distinguish itself from the Socialists while effecting a political rapprochement with French society? The PCF had to make a choice: either to really change, which would mean adopting a more radical, definitive Eurocommunism, or to fall back on its 10 to 15 percent hard-core base of working-class support, to wither away in its political ghetto, a mere relic of the past. The more the PCF changed, however, the more it began to resemble the PS. If it did become another PS, what would be the PCF's specificity and raison d'être? A reinvigorated left Socialist Party already existed in France. If the PCF had begun to change sooner, before the PS regrouped, as the PCI had done in Italy, matters might have been more favorable to it.

Still, in 1972, 1974, and again in 1976, the PCF tried to meet the challenge of its new situation in a serious way; it tried to earn its position on the left, which was being eroded by the PS. With Eurocommunism a new possibility existed for the PCF to carve out a relatively autonomous position. But each time, the Eurocommunist thrust in the party came too feebly and too late. More importantly, it was not sustained long enough for the party to reap any political benefits. At the Twenty-second Congress the PCF attempted to designate reference points for its own road to socialism, but as Alain Duhamel pointed out, these could only be constructed negatively, in contrast to the existing Socialist experience.[37] The political positions of the PCF no longer had any continuity. Party policy took on a double character making for totally ineffective politics, setting the stage for the PCF's eventual decline.[38]

NOTES

1. Keith Middlemas, *Power and the Party: Changing Faces of Communism in Western Europe* (London: André Deutsch, 1980), p. 103.

2. Ibid.

3. Ibid., p. 153.

4. Ibid., p. 103.

5. *L'Humanité*, November 18, 1975.

6. Ibid.

7. Neil McInnes, *Euro-Communism* (Beverly Hills, Calif.: Sage Publications, 1976), p. 16.

8. In David E. Albright, ed., *Communism and Political Systems in Western Europe* (Boulder, Colo.: Westview Press, 1979), p. 344.

9. Henri Fiszbin, *Les Bouches s'ouvrent* (Paris: Bernard Grasset, 1980), p. 140.

10. *Le Monde*, June 2, 1976.

11. *L'Humanité*, January 20, 1976.

12. *L'Humanité*, January 26, 1976.

13. *L'Humanité*, January 7, 1976.

14. *L'Humanité*, January 15, 1976.

15. Ibid.

16. Ibid.

17. *L'Humanité*, February 5, 1976.

18. *L'Humanité*, January 5, 1976.

19. *L'Humanité*, January 22, 1976.

20. *L'Humanité*, January , 1976.

21. Ibid.

22. François Hincker, *Le Parti communiste au carrefour* (Paris: Albin Michel, 1981), pp. 100–101.

23. *L'Humanité*, February 5, 1976.

24. Ibid.

25. George Ross and Jane Jenson, "The Uncharted Waters of De-Stalinization: The Uneven Evolution of the Parti Communiste Français," *Politics and Society* 9 (1980): 273.

26. Ibid.

27. *L'Humanité*, February 5, 1976.

28. Ibid.

29. *L'Humanité*, January 20, 1976.

30. In Vernon V. Aspaturian, Jiri Valenta, and David P. Burke, eds., *Eurocommunism between East and West* (Bloomington: Indiana University Press, 1980), pp. 72–73.

31. Santiago Carrillo, in Albright, *Communism and Political Systems in Western Europe*, p. 344.

32. Ibid., p. 74.

33. Ibid., p. 75.

34. Enrico Berlinguer, ibid., p. 351.

35. *Le Monde*, March 5, 1977.

36. Ibid.

37. *Le Monde*, June 2, 1976.

38. It should be noted that the PCF was stagnating and or losing ground electorally at a time when conditions were favorable to the left in France. This was the case even though PCF membership rose in the 1970s. Robrieux cites PCF membership to have risen from 350,000 to 550,000 from 1972 to 1977; Philippe Robrieux, *L'Histoire intérieur du parti communiste, 1972–1982* (Paris: Fayard, 1982), p. 508. Elsewhere, PCF membership figures were shown to rise from 400,000 to 700,000 from the 1960s until the early 1970s; Annie Kriegel, in George Schwab, ed., *Eurocommunism: The Ideological and Political-Theoretical Foundations* (Westport, Conn.: Greenwood Press, 1981), p. 135. In general, PCF membership is difficult to calculate because cards delivered to the federations on which the party bases its total membership do not correspond to the number of cards actually given to and signed by local members. Hence, the PCF's own count is an inflated one.

7

The Splitting of the Union of the Left in France

The splitting of the union of the left in France was probably the single most important event leading to the weakening of Eurocommunism as a political movement. The sectarian, self-destructive behavior of the PCF after 1978, which led to its electoral debacle in the French presidential election of 1981, permanently weakened the Eurocommunist faction of the Euroleft. The breakdown in relations among the left parties in France highlighted the deep gulf that had existed historically between Socialists and Communists in France. The splitting of the left in France, however, initiated by PCF actions, should not obscure the new relationship between the Communist and non-Communist left in Western Europe.

The Eurocommunists who left the PCF after 1978 sharpened and elevated their Eurocommunist discourse, producing a real gulf with Leninist Communism. The PS, for its part, began an independent pursuit of political power much in the fashion of other Socialist parties in Western Europe. For the PCF the 1977–81 period marked a Stalinist reorientation and demonstrated the enormous difficulty in transforming a Leninist Communist party into a Eurocommunist party.

The falling-out between the left parties in France was more an afterthought than a continuation of the great Socialist/Communist schism of 1919, and it has ultimately posed the new relationship of Eurocommunism to Eurosocialism. The two pivots of the Euroleft have since continued to converge politically and ideologically on new foundations. In France the Socialist Party by itself has come to represent *both* sensitivities.

THE PRETEXT OF THE UPDATING OF THE COMMON PROGRAM

The period from the municipal elections of March 1977 to the legislative elections of March 1978 and their immediate aftermath highlighted the political balance of forces between right and left in France in the 1970s as well as the difficulties within the left itself. By 1977 France had a potential political majority of the left, but the parties of the left were still incapable of translating this situation into an electoral victory.

This period also witnessed the reemergence of the PCF hardliners over many aspects of PCF policy and finally something novel, as individual Communists of both Eurocommunist and Leninist inspiration refused to accept "official" analysis of PCF behavior by the party leadership and were willing to take their complaints outside the party into the public arena. After March 1978, the Eurocommunist faction of the PCF increasingly resorted to this course of action in order to be heard.

In the municipal elections of March 1977, the PCF and the PS for the first time appeared united on the first round of a balloting with a common list of candidates. Out of 221 major cities of over 30,000 inhabitants, there were only 15 cases in which unity failed to occur.[1] As a result, the PCF won access to municipalities where it had had no previous presence. A victory for the left in the national elections set for the following year seemed imminent; the French left had never seemed more united. Yet the March 31 meeting of the Central Committee of the PCF began a process that would break the union of the left. How could this change have taken place after an electoral gain for the PCF and in the wake of its Twenty-second Congress?

The Twenty-second Congress occurred only after much political jockeying within the party, and its innovations were implemented as a result of a tenuous majority in the party, led by the group consisting of Marchais, Jean Kanapa, Charles Fiterman, and Paul Laurent, the supposed liberals. Its continued implementation rested on favorable electoral results for the PCF and on written promises regarding the implementation of the Common Program from the PS should the left win.[2] Certain elements in the party did not accept the Twenty-second Congress on any terms. In the period from the Twenty-second Congress until the municipal elections in March 1977 the attack against the principles of the Twenty-second Congress centered around its "revisionist" notion of the state, which no longer corresponded entirely with the notion of a class-based state. This opposition was spearheaded by the "true" Leninists. Such opposition proved to be sterile. With the gains of the Socialists in the municipal elections, however, recalcitrant members in the party bureaucracy had something concrete with which to challenge the party's new orientation. The hardliners reasoned that if the party had indeed gained in an alliance with the Socialists in the municipal elections, it was questionable that it could do so in the legislative elections of the following year, because of the supposed reluctance of Socialist electors to vote Communist in a national election.

Marchais, in his report to the Central Committee on March 31, indicated that "new conditions of the political battle" in reference to the union of the left could allow the Socialists the possibility of reinforcing themselves at PCF expense. This phenomenon would not be fatal, he indicated, provided "what is necessary to be done is done— and it has been done."[3] So far, so good. Marchais continued, however, to say that the election results would have been "even better" if not for a "certain lack of firmness and determination" on the part of the party. The party would address this "lack of vigilance" or "defaut," which "the progess acquired does not mask," to "reinforce the union."[4] Thus, the municipal elections, in which the PCF had gained votes, were perceived as an electoral failure. It is difficult to cite a speech by a party official that is as categorical as that of Marchais's to the Central Committee on March 31 even while camouflaged in the typical Communist "double language." The strict unity of the left, authorized by the Twenty-second Congress and in place in some form since 1972, was challenged.[5]

In the same March 31 speech, Marchais called for the updating of the Common Program. The leadership of the PCF, after viewing the electoral patterns since 1972, had had enough of unity of the left. It would still plan for a victory in 1978, but one in which the PCF and the PS would campaign separately, each on its own identity. To split the union of the left openly, however, could not yet be done. A pretext was needed. The Common Program needed to be updated; this became the pretext.

According to Jean Baudouin, the party had decided that if it could not attain state power via the electoral process it would insist on certain assurances with regard to the implementation of the Common Program.[6] In particular it wanted a more parliamentary regime to be put in place by a government of the left more likely to be susceptible to PCF influence. The PCF also sought to monopolize, beforehand, what Baudouin refers to as the "periphery" of political power, meaning it wished to take control over the enterprises by emphasizing the social measures of the Common Program. The sudden adoption of the term *autogestion* by the PCF in the fall of 1977 was meant in this light.[7]

The Socialists in turn wondered if updating the Common Program would mean actually altering it. Their fears were realized as the months passed. The Socialists had already begun to make their own economic propositions in an attempt to win over some of the French business class and prepare themselves for governing. These propositions reflected the strong position of the PS and only exacerbated the difficulties within the PCF. Wasn't the PS becoming the future party of government with the PCf in its shadow? Not if the PCF could help it. The pretext of actualizing the Common Program would give the PCF a chance to clearly set itself off from the PS while maintaining its course as a governmental party.

The PCF began to launch its campaign for the updating of the Common Program one day after Marchais's March 31 address to the Central Committee. The Socialists, not wanting to appear as the party that was unfaithful to the Common Program, had no other recourse than to accept. A series of events followed that now seem almost comical. On May 10, the PCF presented its own figures on the cost of the Common Program as well as a suitable timetable for its implementation. Seemingly the PCF wished to appear "serious" in the eyes of the public while taking the centerstage away from the PS. Instead the party was embarrassed since the figures were regarded by the bulk of public opinion as unrealistic. The PCF leadership was taken aback. It had wanted to show its originality while also appearing as the best representative of the most downtrodden elements of the population. The negative backlash on the party, however, should not be surprising. There was evidence to suggest that the figures the PCF chose to publish were derived mainly from political criteria and were purposely disseminated before a Mitterrand-Barre television debate in May to embarrass Mitterrand.[8]

Apparently the projected rate of economic growth for France forecast by the PCF was chosen arbitrarily. A 6 percent growth rate was judged too high (being "productionist"). Anything much lower, however, would not allow the party to distinguish itself from the PS, so a 5.9 percent growth rate was chosen.[9] The party feared taking power the following year with the PS currently at 28 percent in the public opinion polls and the PCF at 22 percent. The PCF hoped to frighten the PS into signing a more forceful economic program while benefiting with the electorate in the process.[10] This political charade by the PCF served to obscure an important reality. It obscured the strength of the oppositional French left. Nothing was more revealing in his regard than the context of the ensuing Barre-Mitterrand debate. In this key debate, it was Raymond Barre who was forced to carry the debate onto the terrain of François Mitterrand. Barre, a representative of a majority that had been in power for twenty years, implicitly acknowledged that the central issue of a preelectoral debate was the political program of the opposition.

In mid-May the PCF broke with one of the postulates of the Common Program by supporting France's nuclear deterrent, adopting a Gaullist style in foreign policy that it would take to the extreme in the 1979–81 period. The shift in party policy regarding France's nuclear deterrent, like the abandonment of the dictatorship of the proletariat, appears to have been taken without any discussion within the party, producing some unrest at the base. The PCF dropped a position that it had maintained constantly since the 1950s. At the same time Marchais, when asked on television if Mitterrand was loyal to the Common Program, remained silent, hinting that the PCF did, in fact, have reservations.[11]

By early June it was clear that the Common Program was clearly regarded by Marchais, not Mitterrand, as inadequate. Marchais stated, "It is not possible to go to battle with the Common Program as it is, with its imprecisions and insufficiencies in key domains."[12] He later remarked that the PCF did not want to be put in a position of simply managing the economic crisis of capitalism; to avoid this pitfall it was necessary to update the Common Program.[13]

In the meantime the Socialists were displaying greater self-assurance at their Congress at Nantes in June. As was the case with the Assises du Socialisme in 1974, the PCF was once again chagrined, and it began to noticeably step up its offensive. The French political scientist Maurice Duverger wrote in September that the PCF had abandoned a moderate reading of the Common Program in publishing its own figures May 10 before the Mitterrand-Barre debate. In doing so it took the position of the hardliners in the party, returning to the PCF's base of militant workers.[14] This was evident in the PCF's narrow view of the salary range among workers, which ignored the interests of supervisory workers. Such action was taken, according to Duverger, "under the pretext of updating the Common Program."[15]

Thierry Pfister in *Le Monde* in early September, before the PCF's actual split with the PS, wrote that the PCF leadership had discerned the dangers of the unitary policies with the Socialists after the results of the 1965 and the 1974 presidential elections as well as after the legislative elections of 1973 and therefore worried about being passed electorally by the PS in the approaching legislative elections.[16] The party hoped to avoid this impending situation by again clearly distinguishing itself from the PS. The PCF must become once more the party of the poor and the disinherited. Close to power, it felt the need to "re-anchor itself ideologically" vis-à-vis the PS.[17] The leadership now felt that an unqualified unitary policy in which the PCF was indistinguishable from the PS was a mistake, creating a situation in which Mitterrand could take the lead on all joint policy matters.

It is interesting to scrutinize again the attitudes of the party hardliners. They reasoned that in the past the PCF had remained dominant on the left by fulfilling the role of a revolutionary party, firmly aligned with the Soviet image and as a party of the working class in the strict sense, thereby easily outdistancing discredited Socialist parties. It must be the new unitary policy of the PCF that had allowed the PS to steal the PCF's revolutionary image and regain its political clout. François Hincker pointed out that many in the party used the term *marcher des dupes*, or figuratively, *enterprise of stupidity*, to describe this perception of the PCF having changed its policies for "nothing."[18] The PCF needed to reaffirm that it was not a party like the others, to reestablish its revolutionary credentials at a time when capitalism was becoming increasingly discredited in France, when the road appeared open for the success of a revolutionary project. What this position overlooked was that (1) the Socialists had really changed in the 1970s by moving to the left, (2) relying on the Soviet image was no longer a strength but a weakness of the PCF, and (3) precisely because the left was capable of attaining power, the PCF could no longer play its tribunitary role to the exclusion of other, more general political roles. It was therefore essential for the party to strip itself of much of its old ideological baggage. The hardliners, then, were misreading the political situation in France in the 1970s, and because they succeeded in controlling the party after March 1977, the PCF would pay severely, perhaps irrevocably, by losing its strong position in French politics.

THE PCF'S "COUP DE THÉÂTRE"

The causes of the split between the PCF and the PS over the updating of the Common Program for government hinged on the differences regarding the extent of nationalization of industry, foreign policy, the wage and salary scale for workers, and the basis of the rights of workers in the proposed nationalized industries. Publicly these were the principal points of contention. However, the real differences were principally of a political nature and were not those of economic or policy disagreements, as was generally thought at the time. This was not a split over programmatic substance but rather over electoral politics.

From early June, the PCF and the PS had made known their respective views concerning the extent of the proposed nationalization program. The PCF demanded that the subsidiaries of a nationalized company, even if it were held by the parent company by no more than a 51 percent margin, should still be nationalized, producing a total of about 1,450 enterprises to be nationalized in all France. The PS stipulated that only those subsidiaries which were 100 percent owned by the parent company should be included, which amounted to a total of 100 enterprises.[19] The PCF wanted Peugeot-Citroën completely nationalized; the PS wanted the government to take a majority holding in it.

The PCF favored a more narrow range of income on the salary scale among workers and sought a higher minimum level of income. In addition, the PCF proposed to nationalize the petroleum and iron and steel industries.

The two parties also fought publicly over the future management of nationalized industry. The PS preferred the option of allowing the state to appoint the director-general who was to lead an administrative council comprised of state, employee, and consumer representatives, while the PCF wanted to have the director-general elected by the administrative council itself. Not surprisingly, each option favored the position of the party that backed it. The PCF, stronger in the factories, would attain greater power if the director-general were elected by the entire representative body. The PS would attain more control if the director-general were nominated by the state hierarchy that it would undoubtedly dominate.

Thus, there were indeed noteworthy differences between the two parties. However, many of the PCF figures regarding nationalization have to be taken with caution. The PS proposals would have accomplished most of what the PCF was aimng for in terms of nationalized industry. The PCF's new independent stance in foreign policy was just that, new, and could hardly be used to justify a break. The single legitimate area of dispute between the PS and the PCF was on the issue of control over the enterprises. But for the PCF, this issue took a back seat publicly to the issue of the extent of the nationalization of industry, an area where PCF-PS differences were more apparent than real.

The month of August witnessed nothing more than a political charade with each side attempting to move public opinion in its own direction. The PS, like it or not, had to be a full participant in the affair. The PCF never brandished the threat of a rupture at this time. Marchais stated that there had been progress on negotiations but that on fundamental points there remained "serious divergences" between the two parties.[20] The Political Bureau, on August 18, warned of a scenario in which the left would win power but, owing to the relative weakness of the PCF, real change would not be achieved.[21]

In September the parties of the left held two final series of meetings, which proved unsuccessful in reaching an agreement. The unity of the left based on a Common Program for government no longer existed. Marchais did not mince words after the failure of the discussions. He argued that the PS definitely had begun to change since the municipal elections away from its previous orientations.[22] Marchais pinpointed the purported change in orientation of the PS to correspond with and conceal the PCF's own change in line, in typical Stalinist fashion.

By October the new position of the PCF with regard to the Socialists was clear. Since the beginning of the year the PS was said to have turned to the right. The PS was once again a political recourse for the right when the right's other options to secure the domination of capital failed. Reformism was in the PS's history and its very nature. The union of the left could not be continued without struggle.[23]

The PCF constantly repeated its desire to return once again to the bargaining table with its former partners as the March elections approached. But this was done purely for public relations. At the National Conference of the party in January 1978, Marchais called the union of the left "an essential and permanent composite of the party's strategy."[24] Marchais repeated that the September discussions broke down on the issues of the minimum wage for workers, the extent of the nationalization program, the rate of tax on wealth and capital, the modalities of workers' control in the enterprises, and national defense.

Also in January, pointing to the first sign of reticence by the PCF regarding Eurocommunism, a brochure entitled *Vivre* was not disseminated by the party, although it had already been printed, because it showed a high-ranking PCF official, Pierre Juquin, shaking hands with a Soviet dissident on its cover.[25] Apparently, Gaston Plissonnier, a high-ranking hardliner of the party, led the initiative to suppress the brochure.[26]

Marchais went on television in February 1978, reaffirming that the PCF was the party of the working class, and contrasted this with the notion of the PS as a party that tried to please everyone, a party without a political soul.[27] At this time the PCF coined its campaign slogan that 25 percent of the vote for the PCF in the upcoming legislative elections would be a good score (presumably good enough to keep the PS from turning to the right) but that 21 percent would not be enough. Marchais even wrarned that without at least 25 percent of the vote the PCF would not support the PS on the second ballot. If there was no Common Program, Marchais stated, it was because the PCF was not strong enough to harness the PS, as it had been in 1972. Hence the solution was to vote Communist in sufficient numbers, and then a political accord with the Socialists would follow. The choice before the electorate, according to the PCF leadership, was either to break with austerity by voting for the PCF and truly change French society or to leave capital in place.

Meanwhile, Eurocommunism was not completely on the backburner. The Soviet journal *New Times* was criticized by *L'Humanité* in January for using the PCE international affairs spokesman, Manuel Azcarate, as a scapegoat in attacking Eurocommunism.[28] Jean Kanapa was quoted as saying that this hard attitude of the *New Times* article toward Eurocommunism did not do justice to the richness of the term.[29] The PCF would develop and elaborate its policies in independence. There was no longer a center to the Communist movement, nor were there any more strict dogmas or models to be emulated. The PCF regretted that the Socialist countries could not tolerate public expressions that were opposed to the policy of the Communist Party and to the state. This was actually a concretization of the reference made at the Twenty-second Congress that the PCF had differences vis-à-vis the CPSU on the question of democracy. Kanapa reiterated that the PCF supported pluralism in France. For the PCF socialism and liberty were inseparable.[30]

One of the key figures representing Eurocommunism within the party at that time, Jean Elleinstein, a featured intellectual in the PCF and author of *L'Histoire de l'URSS*, made a speech at the PCF's January National Conference that highlighted the PCF's version of Eurocommunism. Elleinstein stated, "For the first time the question of socialism is clearly and concretely posed in a major western capitalist country."[31] Without seeking to disparage existing socialism, he noted that the "problems we have to resolve in France in the last quarter of the 20th century are radically different."[32] A socialist revolution could only be democratic, peaceful, legal, and gradual.

For Elleinstein, this peaceful path to socialism did not mean duplicating social democracy, but neither was it to be found in the forty five volumes of Lenin. Rather, it was true to Marx and extended and verified the rights of man proclaimed in 1789.[33] Elleinstein went on to cite the French Socialist Jean Jaurès, who, in expounding a view of the gradual, penetrating force of democracy and the working class at the turn of the century, was said to have propounded a strategy that was utopian at the time but was relevant to contemporary France.[34] In this speech Elleinstein was outlining the contours of a more thorough and refined Eurocommunism, giving the concept greater force. The leadership of the PCF, on the other hand, was more interested in using the concept opportunistically as part of its public opinion campaign. It knew that if it gave the concept real substance an inevitable "epreuve de force" among the contending groups in the party would ensue. It succeeded in avoiding this scenario, but only to the party's own detriment.

The PCF continued to develop its ideological reorientation in important areas but had not yet abandoned Eurocommunism. The fact that it had broken the union of the left should not altogether obscure the important new orientations that remained in force. Yet in returning to much of its traditional Communist image and to its "ouvrierism" or penchant for maintaining an image as the "party of the working class," the PCF could not help but undercut its Eurocommunism, rendering it incongruous. Still, the many elements of Eurocommunism that were evident between September 1977 and March 1978 pointed to the fact that the PCF was still serious about a victory for the left and an ensuing governmental stint.

THE BREAKING UP OF FRENCH COMMUNISM

The two major parties of the French left, the PCF and the PS, drew 20.6 percent and 22.8 percent of the vote respectively on the first round of the March 1978 legislative elections. Despite all the bickering on the left before the elections, a day after the first round of balloting an accord was signed between the PS and the PCF. This sudden turnabout amazed many in the PCF who had reluctantly followed the party in the preceding months even while fearful of the potential effects of disunity to the left's electoral totals. This accord seemed to contradict the previous contention of the party leadership that the positions of the PS were inadequate. After the defeat of the left on the second round, an unprecedented stream of open criticism emerged from PCF intellectuals and militants. Democratic centralism could no longer contain interparty tensions by promoting a false facade of unity. Traditional appeals to authority were no longer adequate. A period of French Communism was at a close.

The intellectuals within the PCF were outraged when the Political Bureau of the party, immediately after the failure of the left on the second round, disavowed any responsibility for the result. The party leadership accepted none of the responsibility for what had transpired since March 1977. In April, Marchais, in a diversionary gesture, raised a few eyebrows by announcing that the PCF would no longer expel any of its members for dissidence.[35] He would be given more than a few occasions in the years that followed to test this new rule. The dissenting intellectuals in the aftermath of the statement by the Political Bureau felt that the leadership of the PCF had attempted to absolve itself of all responsibility for the debacle of the left's defeat without any discussion having taken place beforehand. By mid-April the situation had festered to a point where many of them took it upon themselves to express this concern on the pages of nonparty publications. Jean Elleinstein published a series of critical articles in *Le Monde*. This was soon followed by another series of articles by Luis Althusser. The articles by Elleinstein bear especially on Eurocommunism.

Elleinstein's position in these articles went well beyond the simple postulate that there are many acceptable models of socialism, that is, it went beyond the parameters of Palmiro Togliatti's concept of polycentrism. For Elleinstein, the U.S.S.R. had become an "anti-model of Socialism."[36] The socialism that the party sought to achieve did not exist anywhere, least of all the U.S.S.R. It was not possible to say exactly what socialism would be like, but it was possible to say specifically what it would not be like (the Soviet Union).[37] Later Elleinstein recounted that he was urgently summoned to meet with Marchais on May 12, 1978, because Marchais thought the notion of the U.S.S.R. as an anti-model would be scandalous to important sections of the party (read: the hardliners); Elleintein had already gone too far.[38]

In *Le Monde*, Elleinstein remarked that the fact that the PCF carried the same label as the party states that ruled in Eastern Europe was a great handicap to the party.[39] The basis on which the PCF had formed at Tours in 1920 was outdated; the Twentieth Congress of the CPSU had been the first indication in this regard. A new road to socialism was necessary, one that represented neither traditional social democracy nor the Communism stemming from the Comintern. Revolutionary change in France could only be of a long duration. Such a scenario was "radically new," according to Elleinstein, effacing the "myths" that had founded French Communism.[40]

Elleinstein maintained that the PCF had signed the Common Program without taking its full implications into account. This produced a situation that facilitated the strengthening of the PS, since few people could then be convinced that the PCF had really changed.[41] The PCF campaign slogan of "make the rich pay" did not facilitate the party's efforts in assembling the "union of the people of France." Instead, it harked back to old notions of class against class.[42] Neither Elleinstein nor any of the others who spoke out questioned the party's contention that the PS had moved to the right. They did not yet suspect the full extent of the PCF's chicanery in the preceding months.

With Elleinstein's positions, the theoretical basis of another form of French Communism can be discerned: Eurocommunism had been given a more solid foundation in France but only as it emerged *against the PCF*. Jean Kéhayan, who later forced Marchais to break his promise that there be no more expulsions from the party, wrote in *Liberation* that Elleinstein did not go far enough with the term *anti-model* in describing the Soviet Union; Kehayan wrote, "The U.S.S.R. is the antithesis of Socialism."[43] Jacques Fremontier resigned as editor of *Action* in April, calling for the removal of any traces of Leninism in the party. He called for the study of Antonio Gramsci and the removal of the Socialist label from the U.S.S.R.[44] Similar actions multipled and became commonplace after 1980, as the Eurocommunist thrust in authenticating itself was more and more forced out of the party.

In Marchais's report to the Political Bureau in April, the Socialists were said to have returned to the old rut of social democracy, wishing to abide by the policies of capitalism. They had deceived the French electorate at the Congress of Epinay in 1971 with a false leftist phraseology.[45] The PCF was still attached to the union of the left and to the Common Program. The PCF leadership did admit to having been late in denouncing Stalinism after 1956, something that came close to a self-criticism. And interestingly enough, the differences between the CPSU and the PCF were said to have been aggravated since the Twenty-second

Congress.[46] This again points to the fact that the "Russian factor" was *not* responsible for the breaking up of the union of the left.

Marchais also admitted that his secret report to the Central Committee in 1972 regarding the party's continued suspicions of the PS should have been made public at that time rather than in 1975. Failure to do so left the impression for the left audience that once the Common Program had been signed, all had been settled. It was not necessary to redevelop mass struggles at the base to make the union more solid and durable.[47]

The "Paris Affair," centering around the figure of Henri Fiszbin, then head of the PCF's Paris Federation, highlighted the new realities in the PCF after the March elections. The eventual fate of Fiszbin, his resignation from the Paris Federation, efforts to establish an independent line or pressure group within the party around the journal *Rencontres Communistes*, and the eventual exclusion of both Fiszbin and the Rencontres Communistes group were indicative also of much of the fate of Eurocommunism in the PCF.

According to Fiszbin in *Les Bouches s'ouvrent*, there was a strong grassroots opposition to Marchais's pronouncements regarding the PCF's infallibility after the March elections.[48] PCF intellectuals and university members in Aix-en-Provence circulated a petition with 300 signatures in May (the petition would eventually receive over 1,000 signatures) asserting the right of party members to question the leadership. This petition was signed not only by party intellectuals but also by PCF elected officials and party militants.

This broad outburst of discontent was contrary to what the party leadership portrayed. The party leadership depicted the internal opposition to its policies as only intellectual in origin and politically isolated in the party. Fiszbin cited the flood of letters sent to the leadership as evidence of the extent of the discontent.[49] Jean-Marie Argelés, the second in rank in the Paris Federation, resigned after the Central Committee meeting of the PCF in April, resenting the anti-intellectual tone of the meeting. He was then consoled into reconsidering his resignation by his fellow members of the Paris Federation.[50] *Paris-Hebdo*, a PCF weekly, immediately published an account of local party debates after the elections that focused on the failure of the union of the left. But such accounts were quickly forbidden by the party leadership. Similar debates that were to be held in Paris were called off by the leadership of the party.

In December, a debate was organized by the party to let some of the steam out of the intellectual dissent, and 400 intellectuals expressed their grievances to the Political Bureau. These grievances, manifest since the legislative elections, had been further fueled by the censorship of a PCF monthly for intellectuals, *La Nouvelle Critique*, and by the purging of the editorial board and censorship of *France nouvelle*, a Eurocommunist-oriented weekly of the Central Committee. At the debate, the intellectuals struck a note of discontent with the restrictions on the party press and the lack of a frank attitude by the party on "existing socialism." *L'Humanité* gave an accurate and detailed account of this meeting.[51]

The Paris Affair "officially" emerged with the January meeting of the Central Committee in which Gaston Plissonnier unexpectedly began to discuss the Paris Federation. It was suggested by Marchais that the party because of the alleged "errors" of the Paris Federation had lost the elections in Paris.[52] The Paris Federation was condemned for opportunism and for having sought unity with the Socialists at all cost. As the ritual of affirming the various criticisms by members of the Political Bureau occurred, surprisingly, a dissenting voice was sounded. It was the voice of Henri Fiszbin. Seven other secretaries from the Paris Federation followed in suit.

The Paris Federation was seen by the PCF leadership as too unruly, too intense in its debates, too intent on the line of the Twenty-second Congress. The party leadership was affirming its control, paving the way for the Twenty-third Congress. Eurocommunism was to be used now, even more than before, as a trump card and was not to be taken too adamantly.

Fiszbin stuck to his defense of the Paris Federation and soon resigned as its leader. He agreed to cover up the real reasons for his resignation by falsely citing a problem of health, an act he later regretted.[53] In February, several other leaders of the Paris Federation also resigned. It was not until his unprecedented letter of resignation to the Central Committee later in 1979 that Fiszbin began to draw a connection between the Paris Affair and the hesitation of the leadership of the party to implement the policies of the Twenty-second Congress, revealing the phenomenon of a double line.[54]

The outburst of public discontent among party members after the legislative elections was indicative of the growing malaise inside the PCF. But the PCF leadership had won at least a part of its wager: although the left did not win the election, the PCF had managed to keep abreast of the PS. And the PCF, as a party of struggle, could more effectively wait in the opposition than the PS, or so it seemed. However, by the time of the 1981 presidential election, to the surprise of many, it would be the PCF and not the PS that self-destructed.

NOTES

1. *Le Monde*, March 1, 1977.
2. François Hincker, *Le Parti communiste au carrefour* (Paris: Albin Michel, 1981), p. 146.

3. *Le Monde*, April 1, 1977.

4. Ibid.

5. According to an anonymous PCF group, "Jean Fabien," the CPSU sent a secret letter to the PCF leadership in March 1977, pressuring the PCF to break with the Socialists. See *L'Express*, February 8, 1985. However, the feeling here is that in March 1977 and throughout the 1970s, reasons tied to French politics better explained PCF behavior than factors relating to Russian influence.

6. Jean Baudouin, "Le P.C.F.: Retour a l'archaisme?" *Revue Politique et Parlementaire* (November–December 1980), pp. 35–36.

7. Ibid.

8. See Yves Roucaute, *Le PCF et les sommets de l'état: De 1945 à nos jours* (Paris: Presses Universitaires de France, 1981), p. 175.

9. Ibid.

10. Ibid., p. 178.

11. *Le Monde*, April 20, 1977.

12. *Le Monde*, June 7, 1977.

13. *Le Monde*, June 11, 1977.

14. *Le Monde*, September 29, 1977.

15. Ibid.

16. *Le Monde*, September 2, 1977.

17. *Le Monde, September 15, 1977.*

18. *Interview with François Hincker, April 19, 1982.*

19. *Le Monde*, July 9, 1977.

20. *Le Monde*, August 10, 1977.

21. *Le Monde*, August 20, 1977.

22. *Le Monde*, September 24, 1977.

23. *L'Humanité*, October 7, 1977.

24. *L'Humanité*, January 9, 1978.

25. Philippe Robrieux, *L'Histoire intérieur du Parti communiste, 1972–1982*, vol. 3 (Paris: Fayard, 1982), pp.303–4.

26. Irwin Wall, in Richard F. Starr, ed., *Yearbook on International Communism* (Stanford: Hoover Institute Press, 1979), pp. 141–42.

27. *L'Humanité*, February 2, 1978.

28. *L'Humanité*, January 13, 1978.

29. Ibid.

30. Ibid.

31. Jean Elleinstein, in *Cahiers du Communisme* (February–March 1978), p. 69.

32. Ibid.

33. Ibid.

34. Ibid.

35. *Le Monde*, April 5, 1978.

36. *Le Monde*, April 13, 1978.

37. Ibid.

38. Jean Elleinstein, *Ils vous trompent, camarades!* (Paris: Belford, 1981), p. 13.

39. *Le Monde*, April 13, 1978.

40. *Le Monde*, April 14, 1978.
41. Ibid.
42. Ibid.
43. *Le Monde*, April 20, 1978.
44. *Le Monde*, April 21, 1978.
45. *Le Monde*, April 29, 1978.
46. Ibid.
47. *Le Monde*, May 4, 1978.
48. Henri Fiszbin, *Les Bouches s'ouvrent* (Paris: Bernard Grasset, 1980),
p. 57.
49. Ibid.
50. Robrieux, p. 336.
51. Robrieux, pp. 351–52.
52. Fiszbin, p. 83.
53. Ibid., pp. 113–14.
54. Ibid., p. 195.

8

Eurocommunism in Italy and Spain (1976–1979)

ITALIAN EUROCOMMUNISM ON THE VERGE OF POWER

The PCI strategy of creating a mass party based on a gradual penetration of existing institutions combined with a strong cultural presence in society finally began to bear fruit in the 1970s, spearheading what came to be known as Eurocommunism. The emergence of Eurocommunism is too often delineated in evolutionary terms; if such an exposition has any advantage, it is with the example of the PCI. Antonio Gramsci's concept of "war of position," Palmiro Togliatti's notion of polycentrism and questioning of the Soviet system in 1956, the PCI's rapid adjustment to the postwar conditions of Italian society, and Giorgio Amendola's liberal positions in the 1960s together provided a succession of links on the path of a liberal and independent "communism," one that culminated in the notion of Eurocommunism in the 1970s. In the postwar period, the PCI succeeded in broadening its electoral base and popular appeal while remaining an antisystem party—a striking political achievement.

In 1973 PCI chairman Enrico Berlinguer proposed a strategy of "historical compromise" calling for the participation of the PCI in a future government with the principal party of the postwar Italian establishment, the Christian Democratic Party (DC). Berlinguer published an article in the PCI journal, *Rinascita*, entitled "Reflections on the Facts of Chile," drawing conclusions from the failure of Salvador Allende in Chile and arguing that the PCI would need to come to power among a political coalition of parties including parties of the status quo. For Berlinguer, such a coalition would represent an "historic compromise between the working class and organized catholicism."[1] The PCI jus-

tification for the strategy of "historic compromise" was that the DC
was an interclass party with a large working-class base. It was a party
dominated by the interests of capital, but that domination could be
eclipsed by the DC's "popular" elements. In fact, the Italian Communists felt that one of the weaknesses of bourgeois rule in Italy was
that the capitalist class did not have its own political organization.
This situation is vividly expressed in the remarks of Massimo de
Carolis:

The total failure of the center-left coalitions resulted above all from the failure
of the DC, and Italian Catholicism in general, to follow up the new course
with a new culture, which could confront the Socialist culture. Catholic culture shows its weakness by being often divided between, on the one hand, a
passive conservatism unable to respond to developing social trends and, on
the other, a progressivism that rejects western civilization and pursues, in a
utopian way, mankind's ultimate liberation.[2]

De Carolis concluded, "A Catholic populist component of the DC has
always been inclined to converge with the Marxist left in its critique
of capitalist society."[3]

The other major idea behind the PCI's "historic compromise" was
the understanding of the relative weakness of Italy in the world economy and the weaknesses of Italian political institutions. Berlinguer
remarked that in Italy a coalition of Socialist forces would have to go
well beyond the majority in order to be able to accomplish a change
in society.

The PCI was adopting a conciliatory approach toward the Christian
Democrats, a party that had dominated every postwar Italian government since 1947 but that was beginning to experience negative fallout
from ruling over a society beset with rampant clientelism, mounting
terrorism, organized crime, and a weak economy. The DC tried to
reaffirm its leadership of the anti-Communist bloc, established after
1947, by calling for a referendum to appeal the divorce law in May
1974. To everyone's surprise, including that of the PCI, the DC referendum was defeated by 59 to 40 percent. The referendum on divorce
found the DC isolated with only groups of the extreme right as allies.
In this atmosphere, the Italian Socialist Party (PSI) abandoned its alliance strategy of center-left with the DC, leaving a partial opening for
the PCI in the Italian political system and setting the stage for the
elections to the Chamber of Deputies in 1976.

In the elections, the PCI, running on a slogan of "good government"
and projecting itself as "a party of struggle and a party of government,"
polled an extraordinary 34.4 percent of the vote to 38.7 percent for the
DC and only 9.6 percent for the PSI. This contrasted sharply with the

27.2 percent the PCI received in 1972. A minority DC government could function thereafter only with PCI abstention in Parliament. The Christian Democratic prime minister, Giulio Andreotti, was forced formally to consult the PCI on a new program of government. Meanwhile, PCI Political Bureau member Pietro Ingrao became president of the Chamber of Deputies. By July 1977, the PCI had become one of the six parties of the "constitutional arc" associated through basic agreements reached by the majority parties on the important issues in Italy. In March 1978, a five-party parliamentary majority was formed with the DC and the PCI as the dominating parties. This Italian government could function only with the PCI agreeing not to censure it, based on the bizarre formula of "no-no-confidence," although the PCI stopped short of formal endorsement of governmental policies. Again, the PCI was consulted on all major policies, although it was denied cabinet posts.

That the PCI was so near to sharing political power in Italy bears closer scrutiny. After the exclusion of the Communists in 1947, the Italian state came to be monopolized by the Christian Democratic Party. The Italian Communists were isolated from Italian politics and society in virtually every respect. First, they were ostracized as a threat to Western society in the manner of the other Western nonruling Communist parties. Second, the DC, collaborating with the powerful institution of the Catholic Church, was able to use effectively the "God-versus-Communism" issue to isolate the PCI culturally from important social strata. Finally, with the development of the Christian Democratic state and its system of patronage, the PCI was also excluded from controlling any of the levers for upward social mobility in Italy. A young person entering the PCI could not possibly enjoy the same opportunities for social advancement as someone entering the DC. This peculiar Italian sociological factor was a deterrent to PCI recruitment and added to its social isolation.

The Italian Socialist Party (PSI), as had the old SFIO in France, cooperated with the emerging status quo. However, rather than remaining isolated as the PCF did in France, the PCI managed to absorb Italian Socialism.[4] The PCI built its own counterculture while in isolation; it attached itself to working-class struggles becoming dominant in the trade union movement, and it did so in a penetrating way. Rather than reveling in its own counterculture, PCI culture became integral to *Italian* culture; the PCI absorbed much of Italian society.

By the early 1970s, Italian capitalism had played out its role in the course of the postwar economic boom. Unlike in France, however, where a stronger PCF helped the French Socialists win back lost influence, the Italian Socialists rejected a center-left coalition with the C and found themselves overwhelmed on the left by the strength of the PCI. Even in the 1980s, when the PSI under Bettino Craxi has headed a DC-dominated government with Craxi as prime minister, it has found itself in the PCI's shadow.

The 1976 election to the Chamber of Deputies signaled a watershed in Italian politics, one of parity between the DC and the PCI. The PCI's subsequent association with the DC government was a major achievement for the PCI, a step toward its legitimization in broader circles of Italian politics. Seven years later, in 1983, as the DC and the PCI crossed swords for the municipal elections, the DC president, Ciriaco De Mita, grudgingly admitted in a debate on television with Enrico Berlinguer that the PCI could constitute an alternative to his party.[5] The year of 1947 now appeared a long way off in the realities of Italian politics.

What is striking about the PCI is that Eurocommunist orientation seems to be embraced by the totality of the leadership; it touches on every major faction in the party. An indication of the party's overall economic philosophy was apparent in a report by Berlinguer to the Central Committee in October 1976 in which he discussed the PCI's concept of planning. Berlinguer stated, "The market and private enterprise retain a role, a space—and not just as a tactical concession to the other side, but in order to preserve entrepreneurial and competitive criteria and because only a type of planning that retains a role for market enterprise is consistent with our pluralistic vision of society." He continued, "But we do not believe—and experience has demonstrated it abundantly—that the market and private enterprise are capable of arriving spontaneously at the choices that are necessary to provide points of reference for the whole economy and organize the outlets needed for investment."[6] These choices are to be made, according to Berlinguer, by the public will formed and expressed democratically by both public and private interest groups in Parliament.[7]

While Italian Eurocommunism took up the traditional socialist critique of capitalism that pointed to the lack of economic democracy in capitalist economic organization, it also accepted the liberal concept of the general interest. Pietro Ingrao stated in La Stampa, a conservative Italian newspaper, "But it is contradictory to permit the atomisation and fragmentation of human beings in the process of production and then, outside the production process, to ask them to be 'statesmanlike.' " He added, "How can one create a general will without creating the conditions for it in depth, in the world of labor itself?"[8] What is novel here is that Jean-Jacques Rousseau's concept of the general will is accepted as such, that is, it is not seen as something mythical, as ideology, but as a condition to be fulfilled in the manner of the early Marx. Such a concept implies the possibility for the establishment of a nondominated, nonclass state, which indeed is a part of PCI and Eurocommunist doctrine, clearly distinguishable from Leninist Communism. Luciano Grippi, a member of the Central Committee of the PCI, addressed this theme of Eurocommunism by stating, "We are trying to extend and decentralize the bourgeois democratic state, and in that process we are using bourgeois democracy and Parliament against the bourgeoisie. We are not revisionists of the class struggle. We are revising Lenin's position that the bourgeois state must be 'smashed.' "[9] Thus, the PCI and Eurocommunism do not see the bourgeois state as merely the state form in which the proletariat can best organize itself in the Leninist fashion. Rather, it is seen as the fundamental starting point and appropriate vehicle itself for the transition to socialism. This was precisely the position of Karl Kautsky.[10] The bourgeois state becomes as much a component of socialism as the process of the socialization of the principal means of production.

This is not to say that the Italian Eurocommunist view of democracy goes hand in hand with contemporary liberal notions. Ingrao, for one, views the political party as an integral unit, as a supreme amalgamator, as opposed to the liberal conception of the political party as a simple harborer of disparate interests and interest groups.[11] Such a view of the party is based on what Jean Rony called "organic democracy" as distinct from "associated democracy."[12] The notion of "organic democracy," which may also be applied to the positions of the French Socialists, rests on a critique of contemporary liberal democracy. Liberal democracy is criticized for producing the parcelization and dissipation of political life, which produces alienation among the citizenry.

The PCI seeks to establish Parliament as a mirror image of the larger society.[13] Parliament is to be elected by universal suffrage based on proportional representation with the public financing of parties and their press organs. The state itself is to be decentralized. Democratic rights are to be promoted in the state and in quasi-state institutions (school, army, police, judicial system, mass media). While the PCI acknowledges that in modern societies direct democracy cannot be the principal political form, since in the majority of cases some form of representation is necessary, it seeks nonetheless to reinvigorate direct democracy by promoting it wherever possible as a "corrective principle" to the parliamentary bodies. The forms of direct democracy include workers' councils, local councils, university councils, tenant associations, associations of the unemployed, and so on.[14] However, the workers' councils in particular are not to become organs of a new state. The PCI seeks to combine the socialization of the means of production with the socialization of power itself by diffusing political power throughout the political system. Such a view is analogous to the PS's principle of autogestion. A significant liberal thrust, therefore, exists in the PCI's Eurocommunism. The pluralism of political institutions is stressed, since uninhibited power is viewed as naturally becoming abused. Power can be restricted only by its limitation and its organization into divisions restrained by the counterweight of other, autonomous institutions.[15]

For Bruno Trentin, the workers' councils can become a kind of "second power," a second chamber of democracy, acting as a check on the parliamentary institutions.[16] This is a view strikingly similar to that which was proposed by the Polish workers with reference to the role and function of Solidarity.[17] Nevertheless, for the PCI, representative democracy is still regarded as the primary source of public power. Trentin and the Italian Communists have long since ceased advocating Lenin's (or Gramsci's) conception of the soviets. Ingrao has flatly rejected the notion of substituting a workers' democracy for bourgeois democracy. The planning of the economy, for Ingrao, must be the affair of the entire nation and not just that of the working class. In a manner similar to Karl Kautsky, Ingrao pointed out that giving power strictly to workers' organization means excluding important social strata from political life. Thus the workers' councils are not to mimic those in the U.S.S.R., which came to rest on "the political monopoly of the Bolshevik party" and on a "strong authoritarian centralisation."[18]

Of course, the PCI still had some ideological baggage left over from 1917, and as a result the party's political positions were not entirely consistent. Throughout the 1970s, Berlinguer clung to the notion that the Bolshevik Revolution represented the "first great breakthrough" in the workers' movement; yet he proposed a socialism that would have nothing to do with the form of this "breakthrough," that is, nothing to do with the Soviet model. Instead Berlinguer promoted "a socialism with characteristics that one could not possibly confuse with what has already emerged and exists in countries of Eastern Europe."[19] Yet the Soviet experience was still seen in a socialist context and as a harbinger of a new epoch. Democratic centralism still existed in the party (despite the de facto existence of currents of opinion) although its use had been repudiated for Italian society and institutions.[20]

The PCI, always quick to perceive potential trends in European politics, began to sketch out a new policy in 1978 named "la terza via," or the third way, advocating a type of socialism that would differ from traditional social democracy and from Leninist Communism.[21] The party's thesis on Eurocommunism from its Fifteenth Congress, held in 1979, called for a "recomposition of the working-class movement of Western Europe."[22] This notion of "recomposition" was already implied in Eurocommunism and soon became a basis for the notion of the "Euroleft." The PCI admitted that the historical raisons d'être for the existence of a Communist Party, unconditional support for the U.S.S.R. and the need to override "class collaboration" of social democracy, were no longer relevant. Berlinguer linked the reunification of the European working-class movement to this "third way," which would embody a "third phase" in the history of the working-class movement, the first phase corresponding to the Second International and the second phase to the Third International.[23] "La terza via" comprises the notion that the party is a part of society and of the state but that it is not meant to extend itself into the state.[24]

The PCI's reference to the need to exclude any party from implanting itself within the strictures of the state is one of the pivots of Eurocommunist doctrine and represents a direct criticism of the U.S.S.R. The PCI has firsthand knowledge of the party state. The Christian Democrats have established a hold on Italian political institutions and have developed a system of patronage in carving out positions in government and industry that is rivaled in the industrial societies only by the system of Nomenklatura in the Communist systems. Thus, while the PCI respects the notion of competing political parties as the principal form of political expression in Italian democracy, as it developed concrete programmatic proposals for power in the 1980s, the PCI explicitly stated, "It is indispensable that the parties' functions are clearly distinguished from those of the institutions and the state organs. It is necessary, that is, to put an end to the occupation of the public structures by the parties."[25]

After the Fifteenth Congress in 1979, PCI members no longer had to accept the basic principles of Marxism. Instead, membership depended solely upon acceptance of the PCI's political program. The PCI had begun to develop the twin notions of "la terza via" and a "third phase" before the election of the French Socialists and the events in Poland. These notions were developed by the PCI in part as a response to the defeat of the French left in 1978 as the PCI became disenchanted with the PCF behavior. After the formation of the military regime in Poland in December 1981, the PCI pronounced that the "second phase" of the socialist movement, characterized by the dominance of the U.S.S.R, was "exhausted" and that the evolution of the societies of Eastern European socialism were "blocked."

With these pronouncements Italian Eurocommunism could be clearly distinguished from the Leninist Communism that had spawned the PCI. By taking into account the political and cultural factors relevant to Italian society, along with Italy's weak position in the world economy and the negative burden of the PCI's own "Communist" past, the accomplishments of the PCI have been extraordinary. Still, the PCI was unable to reach power. The abduction and killing of Aldo Moro by the Red Brigades in the spring of 1978 was a setback to the PCI. Moro had been willing to take his Christian Democratic Party into a joint government with the PCI. With Moro dead, PCI-DC relations floundered. By 1979, the PCI had returned entirely to the opposition, responding to growing trade union discontent and remaining frustrated from its inability to initiate public policy changes. Italian society continued to remain stalemated as a result. The PCI, paying a price for its governmental collaboration without tangible results, fell to 30.4 percent in the 1979 elections to the Chamber of Deputies.

THE LIMITS OF SPANISH EUROCOMMUNISM

The Partido Communista Español (PCE) was an instrumental force in the Spanish Civil War. After the defeat of the Republic, however, the party was declared illegal in Spain, and PCE militants were exiled and scattered throughout the world. The PCE was able to use Leninist party organization effectively during its illegal status to become the strongest oppositional force to the Franco regime. In the 1950s, the PCE began to carve out a place in the Spanish trade union movement. Nonetheless, this clandestine activity produced a rigid, embattled attitude within the party.

The PCE was slow in perceiving the relative stability of the Franco power bloc in postwar Spain. Thus, in the 1960s, Fernando Claudin and Jorge Semprun were both eliminated from the Political Bureau and from the party for arguing that, contrary to PCE official policy, the Franco regime was not on the brink of collapse. The two argued that Spanish capitalism possessed a degree of dynamism necessitating a more nuanced formulation by the party concerning its own prospects and the prospects for Spanish democracy.

Still, while a clandestine party, the PCE began to evolve an independent course in international Communism under the leadership of Santiago Carrillo. It strongly condemned the Czech invasion by the Soviet Union in 1968. The CPSU responded to this criticism by threatening to split the party through the loyal faction of Enrique Lister, who was later ousted from the Political Bureau. Despite the exclusion of Claudin and Semprun, the PCE began to develop a strategy of "national reconciliation" based on the notion of the existence of a broad anti-monopolist stratum in Spain, the "forces of labor and culture," which, via a policy of "penetration" of the state, could produce a gradual transition to democracy and then socialism.[26] Small and medium-sized property would be maintained during the PCE's projected phases of first democracy and then socialism, with "surplus value" being paid to sections of big capital during a transitional period.

The political jockeying for power in Spain became intense in the mid–1970s as Franco approached his death. The PCE launched a "Junta Democratica" in July 1974 with a few minor socialist groups and independent Republican leaders intending it to become the basis of a provisional government.[27] The PCE flirted with the idea of "rupture," or a dramatic break in the transition to democracy in Spain, but was careful to avoid using anything that might resemble revolutionary tactics. The Socialist and Christian Democratic groups cautiously kept their distance from PCE-inspired initiatives to avoid being tainted by the negative stigma attached to the "Communist" label in Spain.

A "Plataforma de Convergencia Democratica" that also called for a democratic rupture with the Franco dictatorship was formed by the Socialists and Christian Democrats. The Socialist- and Communist-inspired groups were finally fused into the "Coordinacion Democratica" in 1976 under the first government of King Juan Carlos after Franco's death. Talk of rupture with the Franco dictatorship quickly gave way to the sober realities of power in post-Franco Spain. The PCE was left to count on its legalization and the chance to try its luck in the new Spanish political system. The PCE was legalized in April 1977 but polled only 9 percent of the vote in the elections to the Cortes in June 1977.

Why was the renaissance of Spanish Communism a still birth? The PCE on the eve of the transition to democracy in Spain was the major organized oppositional force, with control of the largest Spanish trade union, and seemed likely to play a dominant role in post-Franco Spain despite the years of anti-Communist rhetoric by the Franco regime. A great gulf existed between 1975 and 1945, however, when the PCI and the PCF reemerged from the war to enter into the political systems in Italy and France, becoming dominant forces on the left. In the years after 1945, the U.S.S.R. was at a peak in terms of its political, moral, and economic image throughout the world, an image which really did not begin to degrade until the late 1960s. In 1975, the U.S.S.R. represented the Gulag and a society of economic stagnation.

The PCE reentered the political stage in the 1970s in a political vacuum; it had no distinct economic project. Both the state and the economy had to be modernized, because Spain would now have to pay for the real cost of the Franco years. But this project could be better implemented by the Socialists, who did not have the negative stigma of Soviet Communism. Ironically, the principal project for the PCE in the 1970s was its strong role in the drive to establish political democracy. Paul Preston noted, "The relative eclipse of the PCE after 1977 should not obscure the fact that prior to mid–1976 the main burden of pressure for democratic change in Spain fell upon the PCE."[28] Carrillo's leadership was scintillating as he became a key figure in the democratization process. Eurocommunism was the key he used to integrate the PCE into Spanish democracy; it was also the only tool the PCE had if it wished to have a chance in carving out a future role in Spanish democracy. But Carrillo and the "Eurocommunists" close to his particular sensitivity could never really let go of the U.S.S.R., which had been the key symbol of their past struggles. Spanish Eurocommunism under Carrillo quickly ran into its narrow limitations, and the PCE paid the electoral price as it has yet to attain more than 10 percent of the vote in a major election.

The PCE militants, hardened in exile for decades, the embodiment of the party apparatus, could not travel the road from Leninism to Eurocommunism fast enough to comply with the swiftly changing political situation in Spain. In Catalonia, where Spanish Communism is a strong force, a sizable contingent of Spanish Communists have scarcely evolved at all in their attitudes to "bourgeois democracy" and the U.S.S.R. For this ideological grouping in the PCE, 1975 and 1945 are coterminous.

If the PCE was unable to attain the status of a major party in post-Franco Spain, it was not due to a lack of effort. The publishing of Carrillo's *Eurocommunism and the State* in 1977 brought considerable attention to the party and launched its Eurocommunist policy in a big way. The dominant position in the PCE represented by Carrillo, however, was still one of a relatively mild version of Eurocommunism. In *Eurocommunism and the State* Carrillo did not see Eurocommunism as denying the historical justifications of the birth of Communist parties. Indeed, socialism was seen to have begun in 1917 and spread throughout the world so that all progressive changes in the world have been a consequence of the Russian Revolution.[29] Carrillo pointed out that Eurocommunism was not an organization, nor did it have a definite body of theoretical knowledge, but he did begin to develop a few building blocks that pointed to a theoretical foundation. He suggested that socialism in the U.S.S.R. was established on an insufficient basis of the development of productive forces and consequently could only have formal socialist aspects.[30] At the same time he argued that the Eurocommunist democratic orientations for power were relevant only to countries with a certain level of industrial development and with established democratic traditions. The "Eurocommunist" Communist parties were seen to be tracing a "line of renewal" in the international working-class and Communist movements in developed countries, a reference that would be merged later into the notion of "the Euroleft."

Carrillo took some distance from Lenin (Lenin's theses were seen as inapplicable today) and was less critical with regard to Kautsky (he was seen to have been right from a "formal" Marxist view), yet his support still went unhesitantly to Lenin over Kautsky.[31] The dictatorship of the proletariat in Russia was an unavoidable necessity. On the other hand, the form of working-class hegemony in a country such as Spain could forgo the dictatorship of the proletariat. As was the case with the PCF's own position, this was a weak denial of the dictatorship of the proletariat.

Carrillo defined democracy as a form of society and not as a particular mode of class-based state. Thus he rejected Lenin's definition of democracy as the domination of the minority by the majority.[32] The democratic road to socialism presupposed the long-term coexistence of public and private forms of property. The Communist Party was not to be the only representative of the working class. The PCE would not establish a one-party system with bureaucratic distortion as was the case in "real, existing socialism." The socialist countries could not be labeled "advanced" socialism or "Communism" because the worker is still aliented there.[33]

For Carrillo, Eurocommunism had to demonstrate that the socialism proposed in the West would not be based on the Soviet model. Instead a more advanced form of socialism would be established in the West.[34] Carrillo went on to delineate the conditions of political democracy under socialism in a manner similar to those posed by the PCF-PCI communiqué in 1975 with the broadest guarantees for individual liberties.

At its Ninth Congress in 1978, the PCE claimed it was not a "Marxist, revolutionary and democratic party inspired by the scientific socialism of Marx and Engels." Leninism would no longer be considered the example of Marxism of the day. The party did, however, see itself as the inheritor of the Bolsheviks of 1917, who were seen to have opened a new epoch. The dropping of the Leninist label produced bitter controversy in the party, particularly in Catalonia, where the semiautonomous Catalan Communist Party rejected the proposal for the removal of Lenin's name from party statutes. However, democratic centralism remained untouched. Manuel Azcarate, who was to call for the radical notion of a federal party with organized currents in the 1980s, in a characteristic justification for democratic centralism at the Ninth Congress argued that without it, democracy within the party would be prohibited, producing a "crystallization of ideas and a battle of personalities."[35]

The Ninth Congress marked the end of the first phase of Eurocommunism within the PCE. The party was not the dominant force it hoped to be. The institutions of a rudimentary political democracy in Spain were still very weak, circumscribing the maneuverability of a Communist Party of any inspiration. The PCE did not get thirty years to travel from Leninist Communism to Eurocommunism, as the PCI had in Italy. By its next Congress in 1981, the Eurocommunists in the party would begin to emerge with a more thorough doctrinal approach, contrasting sharply with Carrillo's "soft" Eurocommunism, a Eurocommunism that had already been challenged in Catalonia from another direction by the party's traditionalists. By 1981, the party had gone too far for the hardliners and not far enough for the Eurocommunist "Renovators." Perhaps more importantly, as Jean Rony suggested, there was no political space in Spain for a distinct Communist project. The whole space of the left would be filled by the Socialist Party.[36] The Spanish elections in 1982 affirmed Rony's position as the PCE fell to just over 3 percent of the vote.

With the PCI's exclusion from power and the failure of the union of the left in France, the first phase of Eurocommunism came to an end in the 1978–79 period. It was a movement that had been unable to attain power in any country, and furthermore, it had been unable to establish a distinct ideology on which to rest in the opposition. With the notion of "La terza via" and a "third phase," the PCI was pointing to a new phase of Eurocommunism destined to merge with the Euroleft. Another push from the outside, however, from the political situation in Europe was needed to set this process in motion. Such a push would come from two directions: the Socialist victory in France in 1981 and the Polish events of 1980–81. As a result of these two events, a second Eurocommunist thrust would eventually emerge, finally establishing the ideology of Eurocommunism.

NOTES

1. Sidney Tarrow, in Howard Machin, ed., *National Communism in Western Europe: A Third Way for Socialism?* (London: Methuen, 1983), p. 125.

2. Massimo de Carolis, in Austin Ranney and Giovanni Sartori, eds., *Eurocommunism: The Italian Case* (Washington, D.C.: American Enterprise Institute for Public Policy Research, 1978), pp. 149–50.

3. Ibid., p. 151.

4. Neil McInnes, in Paolo Filo della Torre, Edward Mortimer, and Jonathan Story, eds., *Eurocommunism: Myth or Reality?* (New York: Penguin Books, 1979), p. 51.

5. *Le Monde*, June 22, 1983.

6. Enrico Berlinguer, in Donald Sassoon, ed., *The Italian Communists Speak for Themselves* (Nottingham: Spokesman, 1978), pp. 125–26.

7. Ibid.

8. Pietro Ingrao, in Sassoon, *The Italian Communists Speak for Themselves*, p. 192.

9. Luciano Grippi, in Carl Marzani, *The Promise of Eurocommunism* (Westport, Conn.: Lawrence Hill & Company, 1980), p. 31.

10. Karl Kautsky, *Terrorism and Communism* (London: National Labour Press, 1920), pp. 229–31.

11. Pietro Ingrao, *La Politique en grand et en petit* (Paris: François Maspero, 1979), p. 123.

12. Ibid.

13. Henri Weber, ed., *Le Parti communiste italien: Aux Sources de l'Eurocommunisme* (Paris: Christian Bourgeois, 1977), p. 41.

14. Ibid., pp. 42–43.

15. Ibid.

16. Bruno Trentin, ibid., p. 134.

17. *Le Monde*, September 6–7, 1981.

18. Pietro Ingrao, in Weber, *Le Parti Communiste Italien: Aux Sources de l'Eurocommunisme*, p. 176–77.

19. Berlinguer, in Sassoon, *The Italian Communists Speak for Themselves*, p. 84.

20. Ibid., p. 73.

21. Sharon L. Wolchik, in Charles F. Elliott and Carl A. Linden, eds., *Marxism in the Contemporary West* (Boulder, Colo.: Westview Press, 1980), p. 71.

22. Pierre Hassner, in Simon Serfaty and Lawrence Gray, eds., *The Italian Communist Party: Yesterday, Today, and Tomorrow* (Westport, Conn.: Greenwood Press, 1980), p. 227.

23. Ibid.

24. Franco Ferrarotti, in George Schwab, ed., *Eurocommunism: The Ideological and Political-Theoretical Foundations* (Westport, Conn.: Greenwood Press, 1981), p. 182.

25. Italian Communist Party, *The Italian Communists: Foreign Bulletin of the PCI* (April–June 1983), p. 48.

26. Eusebio Mujal-León, *Communism and Political Change in Spain* (Bloomington: Indiana University Press, 1983), p. 80.

27. Paul Preston, in Machin, *National Communism in Western Europe*, p. 165.

28. Ibid., p. 157.

29. Santiago Carrillo, *Eurocommunism and the State* (Westport, Conn.: Lawrence Hill & Company, 1978), pp. 9, 83, 137.

30. Ibid., p. 14.

31. Ibid., p. 151.

32. Ibid., p. 88.

33. Ibid., pp. 100 and 161.

34. Ibid., p. 40.

35. *Le Monde*, April 16–17, 1978.

36. Interview with Jean Rony, May 27, 1982.

9

Dark Days of French Communism (1979–1981)

THE PCF'S TWENTY-THIRD CONGRESS

By the time of the Twenty-third Party Congress in 1979, the PCF was firmly on its new autonomous course, even though the policy of the union of the left and Eurocommunism had not yet been openly questioned. The hardliners were now in control of party policy, but what followed—sharp, unequivocal criticism of the PS bordering on hysteria, realignment with the image of the U.S.S.R. (the PCF accepted the Soviet invasion of Afghanistan in January 1980), and the ultraleftist presidential campaign of Marchais, a spectacle of spectacles that was disconcerting to even some of the party's most ardent supporters—could not yet be foreseen. The return of the PCF to the Soviet fold was neither logical nor inevitable. Those who have persisted in viewing the PCF's Eurocommunism as purely tactical have missed the dynamic and volatile confrontations that occurred inside the PCF in the 1970s with each change in policy. The major differences between the period of 1979–81 and that of 1977–78 was that the PCF no longer worked for a left electoral victory. It was concerned exclusively with fortifying itself and weakening the PS, with the latter concern taking precedence. The party would eventually become desperate in attempting to meet these ends. Its goal was to prevent a governmental experience of the left with the PS as the stronger party. In attempting to do so and ultimately failing, it put its long, outstanding presence in French society into jeopardy.

One of the features of the Twenty-third Congress and the period that followed was the PCF's attempt to reaffirm its revolutionary credentials by marking itself off from the PS. The party wished to be viewed as a revolutionary, governmental, and democratic party all in one, but the renewed emphasis went to the revolutionary aspect. According to Georges Lavau, the label of "revolutionary party," reinstalled at the Twenty-third Congress, had been absent from party statutes since 1964.[1] The PCF again became a revolutionary party and a mass party.[2] The PS, in signing the Common Program, had falsely tried to appropriate this revolutionary image.

An important aspect of the Congress, perhaps its defining feature, was the party's attitude toward the U.S.S.R. Marchais came to the happy conclusion that the "balance sheet" of Eastern European socialism was "positive" despite Stalinism and "profound errors" in the past.[3] For Elleinstein, the PCF took a "turn to the East" at the Twenty-third Congress while still affirming its Eurocommunism. While stating that it disagreed with ruling Communist parties over the question of political democracy, the PCF began accentuating Eastern European socialism's supposedly positive aspects.[4]

At the Congress Marchais concluded that if Communist countries have not yet achieved democratic socialism, key institutions had nevertheless been put in place to meet this end, and advancement was being made in the right direction.[5] The balance of world forces was seen to be on the side of social, national, and human liberation: "The great Russian Revolution of October 1917 has been and remains the decisive event of these changes and one should not expect the PCF to minimize or reduce its scope today."[6]

The charge that the PS reneged on the Common Program was a key element in the PCF's attempt to reassert an independent identity vis-à-vis the Socialists. This was closely bound up with the notion that "union is a struggle," which was a key slogan at the Congress. The Socialist view of the union of the left was one constructed at the summit of political power; the PCF view emphasized action at the base, and struggle. The PCF reaffirmed that the PS's strategy was to use left-oriented language to win over PCF adherents, only to then put in place the politics of capitalism. The PS had led the left to its electoral defeat; it carried the full responsibility.[7]

There was no question of the PCF rejecting the Common Program; the Common Program remained the only just and realistic decision that could have been made under the circumstances. The advancement to socialism would be accomplished at each stage not only by universal suffrage but also in struggle. The transition to socialism must represent a veritable rupture with capitalism.[8]

The Twenty-third Congress still cited Lenin in the first rank of those who had sketched the fundamental problems of the socialist revolution. Yet "scientific socialism" was now substituted for "Marxism-Leninism as the PCF's ideology."[9] General laws of socialism existed, although they were somehow nuanced in their application by the par-

ticular conditions in each country. Marchais stated, "We have definitely rejected the idea that there would be a model—or anti-model [a
reference to Elleinstein's term] which would amount to the same
thing—of socialist society."[10] Marchais did affirm that the PCF had
developed a deeper understanding of socialism in contrast to its earlier
visions, which were "a little utopian and abstract."[11]

In a statement that had important policy ramifications for the period
that followed, the party sought to reemphasize its rapport with the
portions of the working class who were the least well off. Marchais
pointed out, "Yes, we are the party of the poor—of the super-exploited.
They can count on us to defend them."[12] The PCF did not renounce
courtship of the better-paid strata of the working class or of the intellectuals officially, but this became attenuated in practice. According
to Fiszbin, the party had also effectively abandoned the intellectuals
after the March 1978 election, assuming that they would naturally lean
toward the PS.[13]

The Twenty-third Congress did have another face to it; it did continue to develop the Eurocommunist policies of the Twenty-second
Congress in certain areas. Marchais admitted to the press in January
1979 that the PCF should have proceeded to elaborate a democratic
socialism, a socialism in liberty since 1956, and not to have done so
was a "retard" or "delay" that worked to the party's detriment.[14] Marc-
chais stated, "Stalinism has existed with its monstrosities. The PCF
does not carry any responsibility in what has happened in the U.S.S.R.
and in the other socialist countries during that period."[15] On Eurocommunism Marchais remarked; "Eurocommunism exists, it is a living
reality. It is an orientation taken by certain Communist parties in
Europe but also by the Japanese party and it is characterized by a
democratic road to socialism and by the construction of Socialism in
democracy."[16]

The Twenty-second Congress was seen to have been "historic" in
defining the socialism the PCF proposed for France. Charles Fiterman
commented, "The Twenty-second Congress has rejected the conception according to which social transformation would be the work of
an acting minority. It has rejected the idea of an authoritarian and
centralized preliminary stage [the dictatorship of the proletariat]."[17]
The party acknowledged "all the implications of pluralism, that is why
we do not identify the party with the socialist society; pluralism means
separation between parties and the state, between parties and
society."[18]

The outstanding feature of the Twenty-third Congress in the Eurocommunist sense was the addition of the notion of autogestion or self-
management to the PCF's repertoire of democratic socialism. A simple
juridical change in property relations creating state ownership was not

enough, the PCF said, to guarantee socialism. The collective appropriation of the principal means of production could not mean simply
their "statization." It was necessary for the workers to have real expression in running the economy, to be able to participate in and to direct
it.[19] The party did not want to replace one bureaucracy for another or
to create a new hierarchy to replace the old (an obvious reference to
Eastern European socialism). The socialist countries maintained a "persistent misunderstanding of the universal demand of democracy of
which Socialism is the bearer."[20]

THE PCF AT THE EDGE OF THE ABYSS

With the death of Jean Kanapa in 1979, a principal advocate for
Eurocommunism in the upper echelon of the PCF was gone. Marchais
was reluctantly left captive of the party hardliners. The party, in effect,
had no political project from 1979 to 1980; it did not act on the political
terrain at all. It treaded exclusively on the syndical plane.[21] François
Hincker has pointed out that the realignment of the party back to the
image of the U.S.S.R. was not the cause but the consequence of the
PCF's isolation on the left and detachment from Eurocommunism.[22]
After 1977, the PCF had stepped up its relations with Communist
parties in power, almost abandoned from 1972 to 1977.[23]

The PCF's sectarian orientation reached the point of the absurd in
January 1980 when Marchais made a television appearance directly
from Moscow supporting the Soviet invasion of Afghanistan. Essentially the PCF recognized the legitimacy of the Soviet explanation for
the intervention in Afghanistan as a response to a call for aid from the
Afghan government. The PCF later also endorsed the justifications of
the martial law government in Poland in December 1981 as a need for
"order." The PCF positions on Afghanistan and Poland were so remarkable for their political ineptness that it is still questionable to
see them as a consequence of even the pro-Soviet Twenty-third Congress in 1979. The PCF's support of the U.S.S.R. on Afghanistan and
Poland ran directly counter to its interests as a French party with the
support of one-fifth of the French electorate. The severity of this error
in political judgment led to the party's own self-destruction evident in
its 1981 election debacle. This PCF self-destructive behavior cannot
be explained by any one factor and certainly could not have been
foreseen.

The recognition of the Soviet invasion of Afghanistan, surprisingly,
did not prevent the party from still addressing the subject of Eurocommunism. Marchais, en route to Moscow, remarked: "Eurocommunism:
it exists, it lives, it persists, it develops."[24] Marchais even mentioned
Eurocommunism in his television appearance from Moscow in which

he supported the Soviet position on Afghanistan! In effect, the party was developing its own restricted (and now meaningless) version of Eurocommunism. For the PCF, the Eurocommunist Communist parties could not deny solidarity with the ensemble of the Communist movement.[25] Eurocommunism could not be a third road between capitalism and Communism, an idea to which the PCF had always been hostile.[26]

The PCF was entering a period that may well turn out to rival the period of the Nazi-Soviet pact as representing some of the darkest days of French Communism. The party was substantially realigning itself with the Communist world, in keeping with its intent to distinguish itself from the PS and hermetically seal off its electorate from the rest of French society. But this occurred at a time when the image of the "socialist" societies in the West was on a steady decline and when their economic performance was stagnating. From January 1980 until the presidential election of May 1981, the PCF reincarnated every negative feature of French Communism in its most blatant form.

In March 1980 *L'Humanité* launched the PCF presidential slogan of the "gang of three," lumping François Mitterrand with Jacques Chirac and Valéry Giscard-d 'Estaing as part of the solid right-wing opposition to Marchais. In April the PCF hosted the conference of European Communist parties held in Paris, a conference not attended by either the PCI or the PCE.[27] Traditional French Communism, thought by many to have been cast off and laid to rest at the Twenty-second Congress, was again alive and well in the party—or so it seemed.

The stamp of the hardliners on party policy in this period was symbolized in the exclusion of Jean Kéhayan in October 1980. Kéhayan, a persistent gadfly to the party, usually one step ahead of even an ardent Eurocommunist such as Jean Elleinstein and a symbol of the new wave of French Communist criticism toward the U.S.S.R., was made into an example by the party leadership to indicate that there were indeed limits as to what could be said against the Soviet Union.[28] After many years of residence in the U.S.S.R. Kéhayan published a book, *Le Tabouret de Piotr*, in which he called the U.S.S.R. a society of failure while insisting that he himself still remained a Communist.[29] The expulsion of Kéhayan meant that Marchais finally had broken the promise he had made in 1978 not to exclude members from the party.

What was more important in the example of Kéhayan was the new emerging critical reality of French Communism. By 1980, French Communism had broken up to the extent that different tendencies, still clinging to the "Communist" label in some manner, had begun to develop sharply different political orientations. In the months that followed many party members left the PCF and attempted to establish alternate poles of French Communism. Kéhayan himself challenged the legitimacy of Marchais's presidential bid for the 1981 elections. The open opposition of French Communists directed at the party leadership in March 1978 was but a mild prelude to the avalanche of opposition in 1981. It is true that dissidents have always existed around the PCF and French Communism. Never before, however, had they attained the slightest measure of legitimacy. The PCF dissidents after the 1978 period were produced by the party itself, as a result of its new style of the 1970s, as a result of Eurocommunism.[30] While it is true that the PCF can still stifle such opposition, this should not obscure the general weakness of the leadership's position vis-à-vis internal opposition. A monolithic French Communism no longer existed, and the legitimacy of the Communist label came up for grabs. But it might have been too late for a Communist Party to be an effective political force—even in France.

The PCF's National Conference in October 1980 finally brought to a logical conclusion what the party had implied since 1977 when it had broken with the PS. The party now questioned the *form* of the union of the left since 1972, and in doing so it proceeded to question all the previous experiences of the united left.[31] If the party did not dare attack the notion of unity itself, which was politically unfeasible, it had at least made an indirect hit. The PCF risked casting a shadow on the supposedly positive experiences of the Popular Front and the Liberation in the process.

The PCF published its 131 points in November 1980 to provide the programmatic basis for the Marchais candidacy. The program was essentially advocative, representing more of a trade union platform than a plausible political program. The PCF would create 500,000 jobs instead of the 250,000 proposed by the PS. It proposed an exorbitant tax on revenues—up to 100 percent on those earning 40,000 francs per month. It would nationalize twenty-three industrial groups, a number well in excess of the earlier Common Program. Nonetheless, the PCF's *categories of demands* were more or less identical to those of the PS (higher minimum wage, shorter work week, taxes on wealth and capital, the nationalizations, lower retirement age, the creation of jobs, etc.), with the PS presenting its demands in a more cautious yet still overly optimistic (in retrospect) form.

THE EUROCOMMUNISTS BREAK RANK

The Polish workers' strike broke out in September 1980. The fate of what came to be a workers' revolution, followed by a counterrevolution by the Polish Communist Party supported by the other party states in the East, finally broke the continued PCI and PCE attachment to what was left of the Communist movement originating from 1917. The

Polish situation was instrumental in presenting the conditions for a second phase of Eurocommunism. By December 1980, Giorgio Napolitano, speaking for the PCI, indicated that a Soviet invasion of Poland would induce the PCI to make a formal rupture with Moscow.[32] In contrast, Marchais considered the warnings of the Italian Communists against an invasion as unfortunate, only complicating the situation. He insisted there would be no invasion of Poland because they (the Soviets) would not want to invade.[33]

In December 1980, the PCF attempted to use a public relations maneuver for the presidential campaign that severely backfired and illustrated the growing desperation of the party. The party supported the bulldozing of a housing project harboring foreign workers at Vitry in the presence of a Communist mayor; this was in keeping with the party's campaign slogan of "produire française," its emphasis on the most downtrodden members of the working class, and its antidrug campaign. These orientations were meant to play on the nationalistic and racist instincts of portions of the French working class who did not want foreign workers living in their neighborhoods. The bulldozing at Vitry was described by Maurice Duverger as the direct application of Stalinism on French soil.[34]

The events at Vitry were soon coupled with the PCF's antidrug campaign at Montigny, in which an immigrant family was implicated by a PCF mayor without trial for drug dealings. This campaign instigated a new wave of PCF defections. Painter Eduard Pignon and author Hélène Parmelin left the PCF in December of 1980, citing the party's comportment as antithetical to its commitment to socialism in liberty. They argued that those who still continued to support the party now had no excuse of ignorance as in the time of Stalin.[35]

Perhaps more telling was the defection of Antoine Spire in January 1981. He was the former commercial director of Editions Sociales, one of the party presses. Spire indicated in leaving that instead of spreading the traditional party message of unity, the PCF had chosen to isolate itself behind a few revolutionary slogans.[36] The party, in renouncing the necessity for alliances, was refusing to take the risk of democracy with all its contradictions and all its richness. If Eurocommunism was a habit "too rigid" for Marchais, for Spire, Soviet socialism was "a costume whose seams were splitting." Spire concluded, "because I am a Eurocommunist, I am leaving the PCF."[37]

Author and journalist Catherine Clement was excluded from her party cell in February after having published an article in *Le Matin* in which she accused the party of "having lost its soul." She indicated that she did not want to quit and said she felt she would be lost without the party. But she could not stand by and see the PCF degraded.[38] This attitude of attachment to the party and high ideals was indicative of much of the intellectual support given to the PCF in the past, a support that threatened to disappear.

The most striking example of discontent centering around the PCF before the presidential elections was the statement of the "Manifesto of Sixty," signed by members still in positions of responsibility in the party and by former members who still considered themselves Communists.[39] The text alleged that the PCF's "ouvrierisme" and "sectarianism" prohibited it from playing its role as an animator of the mass movement, that the PCF had moved away from the principles of the Communist movement. This group made four demands: (1) that the PCF return to the union of the left, (2) that the PCF not be subordinate to an outside entity, in particular, to the Soviet state, (3) that the PCF respect the autonomy of unions and the independent movements stemming from 1968 (ecologist, feminist), and (4) that the PCF contribute to the return of democracy in the working-class movement. Those who signed the statement represented different generations in the party as well as different political lines. The aim of the group was to make the party face another body, with another moral authority, that also had the "Communist" label. It wanted to organize a counterpower to the PCF leadership in establishing "another pole of French Communism" in the hopes of forcing the reconstitution of the party.[40]

In March, as Marchais led his campaign as the anti-Giscard candidate, Jean Elleinstein's book *Ils vous trompent, camarades!*, outlining important doctrinal developments in the Eurocommunist position in France, was published. Elleinstein also revealed important background information on the orientations of the PCF since September 1977. Elleinstein pointed out that the PCF had returned to its simplistic view of the world as one divided into two camps: that of imperialism (the U.S.) and of socialism (the U.S.S.R.). He noted that the difficulties of the party resulted from not taking the consequences of its actions into account, that is, in not taking the Eurocommunist policies to their logical conclusions. The PCF had not accurately gauged the changes that had taken place in the PS in the 1970s. In Elleinstein's view, the PCF aim after 1979 was to prevent the PS from arriving at power by using a strategy of "archeo-communism" harking back to the class-versus-class notions of 1928–34.[41]

With regard to Eurocommunism, Elleinstein no longer hesitated in his criticism of the U.S.S.R., flatly calling it "imperialist."[42] For Elleinstein, apparently borrowing from Michael Voslensky, the U.S.S.R. though not capitalist was characterized by a form of society in which a small minority, the Nomenklatura, constituted a real social class ("une véritable classe sociale").[43] Socialism did not in fact exist in the U.S.S.R., and only a critical analysis of Soviet society could allow socialism and Communism to continue to develop in the West. Elleinstein, citing Milovan Djilas, saw the new social class formed in the Communist systems as directing production because it directed the state.[44] Importantly, Elleinstein brought up the notion of "Nomenklatura" with regard to the PCF itself, outlining different categories of career bureaucrats in the party.

The Soviet Union was seen to have "denatured" the Communist ideal, and the PCF leadership was allegedly now doing the same thing to French Communism with its sectarian orientation. The new basis for an alternate "Communist" orientation, one returning to Eurocommunism, remained to be defined.[45] In 1982 Elleinstein finally gave up even on the hope of transforming the PCF.[46] Meanwhile, Elleinstein in November 1980 was said to have "placed himself outside of the party" by the PCF leadership; he indicated, in turn, that the PCF leadership had "placed themselves outside of communism." He called for a vote for Mitterrand on the first round in March 1981 to punish the party.[47]

Elleinstein saw the need for the left to go beyond the historical split at the Congress of Tours in 1920 between Socialists and Communists by reaffirming the subsequent positive aspects of both traditions. Coming to terms with the past and amalgamating the best of French Communism with the democratic aspects of socialist doctrine would be a way that the PCF could extricate itself from its malaise, Elleinstein concluded.

The PCF was going into the presidential election determined to keep the PS away from governmental power. The PS was a party held together only by the opportunity to govern, the PCF reasoned. Another loss for the left would surely cause the PS to split up, again leaving the PCF as the dominant force on the left. As it was, Mitterrand had barely defeated a bid by Michel Rocard for the leadership of the PS. But the PCF was already paying for its sectarianism, as evident in the wave of Communist dissent preceding the elections. It would pay for its sectarian *derive* in a devastating way in the elections of 1981.

NOTES

1. Georges Lavau, *A Quoi Sert le Parti communiste français?* (Paris: Librairie Arthéme Fayard, 1981), p. 31.

2. *Cahiers du Communisme* (June–July 1979), p. 79.

3. *L'Humanité*, February 3, 1979.

4. Jean Elleinstein, *Ils vous trompent, camarades!* (Paris: Belford), 1981, p. 50.

5. *Cahiers du Communisme* (June–July 1979), p. 45.

6. Ibid., p. 30.

7. *Cahiers du Communisme* (June–July 1979), p. 53.

8. Ibid., pp. 57–58.

9. *Cahiers du Communisme* (June–July 1979), p. 55.

10. Ibid., p. 47.

11. Ibid., p. 48.

12. Ibid., p. 66.

13. Henri Fiszbin, *Les Bouches s'ouvrent* (Paris: Bernard Grasset, 1980), p. 48.

14. *L'Humanité*, January 15, 1979.

15. Ibid.

16. Ibid.

17. *Cahiers du Communisme* (June–July 1979), p. 374.

18. Ibid., p. 77.

19. *L'Humanité*, January 17, 1979.

20. *Cahiers du Communisme* (June–July 1979), pp. 370–72.

21. François Hincker, *Le Parti communiste au carrefour* (Paris: Albin Michel, 1981), p. 211.

22. Ibid., p. 213.

23. Jean Baudouin, "Le P.C.F.: Retour a l'archaisme?", *Revue Politique et Parlementaire* (November–December 1980), p. 38.

24. *L'Humanité*, January 7, 1980.

25. *L'Humanité*, January 24, 1980.

26. *L'Humanité*, February 9–10, 1980.

27. Philippe Robrieux, *L'Histoire intérieur du Parti Communiste, 1972–1982*, vol. 3 (Paris: Fayard, 1982), p. 425.

28. Baudouin, in "Le P.C.F.: Retour a 'Archaisme,' " p. 38.

29. Jean Kéhayan, *Le Tabouret de Piotr* (Paris: Editions de Seuil, 1980), p. 106.

30. Lavau, pp. 255–56.

31. *Le Monde*, November 15, 1980.

32. *Le Monde*, December 9, 1980.

33. *Le Monde*, December 16, 1980.

34. *Le Monde*, March 17, 1981.

35. In "L'Election presidentielle 26 Avril–10 Mai, 1981," *Le Monde*, p. 48.

36. *Le Monde*, January 8, 1981.

37. Ibid.

38. *Le Matin*, February 20, 1981.

39. *Le Monde*, February 27, 1981.

40. Ibid.

41. Elleinstein, p. 97.

42. Ibid., p. 52.

43. Ibid., p. 55.

44. Ibid., p. 153.

45. Ibid., p. 133.

46. Interview with Jean Elleinstein, April 26, 1982.

47. Elleinstein, *Ils vous trompent, camarades!*, p. 133.

10

The French Elections of 1981: The Left Evens the Score

As the presidential campaign came to a close, the PCF threatened a period of strikes in the pattern of the victory of the Popular Front in 1936 should the left win; the possibility of a right-wing Chirac-Giscard runoff appeared real. Contrary to the anticipation before the 1978 election, few now felt the left had a chance of succeeding. On the first round of balloting, Giscard received 28.31 percent of the vote, down from 32.60 percent in 1974, while Mitterrand received 25.64 percent. Marchais obtained only 15.34 percent for the PCF, a stunning defeat. The party had lost a quarter of its electorate. The combined right totaled 49.16 percent of the vote, while the combined left had 46.95 percent with the ecological vote hanging in the balance. These figures themselves may have obscured the relative strength of the two sides, again veiling the real strength of the left, since it was uncertain where the missing 5 percent of the Communist vote went, even on the first round. It can by no means be assumed that all of it went to Mitterrand. Traditional PCF voters, still upset with the party over its flirtation with Eurocommunism, may have decided to sanction the party with a "vote révolutionnaire pour Giscard."

At any rate, the left was indeed on the verge of a long-awaited victory that the PCF helped to bring about but did not benefit from. A leftist France in 1981 was directly a consequence of French Communism, even of French Eurocommunism. Thus, Ronald Tiersky wrote after the failure of the union of the left in 1978, "whether or not the PCF-PS alliance is reconstructed, the fact of having moved the PS so far to the left in recent years must be seen as a striking testimony of French Communism's tenacity in French society, and of the political will of its leadership."[1] The victory of the French left in 1981 was a legacy of French Communism despite the fact that the PCF worked vigorously for the defeat of the left in 1981 and despite the fact that this victory occurred simultaneously with an historic defeat for the PCF. The question that remained regarding French Communism was whether it would self-destruct or whether French Eurocommunism could somehow make a comeback within the party or, alternately, be salvaged by attachment to the PS.

With the results of the second round Mitterrand 51.75 percent, Giscard 48.24 percent—a victory for the left and a thirteen-years-delayed reaction to May 1968—the dam broke. The PS received a whopping 37.60 percent of the vote in the special legislative elections that followed in June. The combined left won an astounding 67.82 percent of the seats in the National Assembly, gaining 333 of the 491 seats. What had happened? Could the left in France suddenly have become so strong? Was the result in June due to the high abstention rate, right-wing voters having chosen to stay home in larger numbers than left-wing voters? The results of the legislative elections were undoubtedly of a conjunctural nature, and yet how could this sudden disparity between the two scores of the presidential and the legislative elections be explained?

As the left had approached the threshold of power in 1974, it became apparent that to "get over the top" was a difficult task. A victory for the left in France represented not just a simple change in government. To a great extent it was perceived by the electorate as a vote to change society itself. The fact that the PS eventually moderated its radical course once in power should not obscure this attitude. This heavy concern over the possibility of radical change produced a latent conservatism in the "swing vote" that delayed an inevitable victory for the left. Once the left had surmounted this threshold and had attained power without a PCF "menace," when it became apparent that French society would not self-destruct as a result of the left in power, the voters who had been "in the wings" sentimentally or potentially for the left expressed themselves as such en bloc.

In 1981, the left and the right in France stood face to face, eye to eye, on equal footing. Neither side blinked. Each could claim a legitimacy to power, and in the decade of the 1980s (and beyond) each side will certainly do so often. But in the case of France, and this is its peculiarity, the choices to be made by the electorate do not represent merely a shift in policy emphasis; the choices involve one's *approach* to society. The two Frances of Jean-Luc Godard's 1965 film *Masculine-Feminine*, of "Marx and of Coca-Cola," still exist side by side in an uneasy relationship based on a changing equilibrium.

FRENCH SOCIALIST IDEOLOGY AND EUROCOMMUNISM

The victory of the French Socialists in May 1981 was significant with regard to Eurocommunism. Soon the PCF was to join the government. Despite the party's previous orientations, this was an important symbolical event for the Euroleft. Meanwhile, Solidarity was chalking up victory after victory in Poland and had begun to sketch a political program similar in many ways to what the Eurocommunist parties in the West were advocating.

Yet what had still been overlooked by most observers, though not all (interestingly enough, not by the PCI), were the political positions of the Socialist Party in France that had swept it into power. What did this party represent? What did its victory mean? Lilly Marcou, discussing the meaning of the Mitterrand election, wrote that it was not a question of "drawing sources of inspiration from the October revolution or the roads already trodden by the old European Social-Democrats. It is a question of something else, and that is what is essential."[2] Maurice Duverger would soon label the French brand of socialism a "socialism of a third kind."[3] The eventual moderation of the French Socialists' policies and ideology, and the question of whether or not the French Socialist experience in government represented a social democratic one, will be discussed in a later chapter.

The Socialist program in 1981 was essentially what the PCF had advocated in the 1970s. The French Socialists called for the nationalization of remaining private banks and credit institutions as well as the dynamic sectors of the economy including the chemical, pharmaceutical, aerospace, telecommunications, and data processing industries. Also nationalized were insurance companies and the problem sector of steel. The impetus for these nationalizations was derived from both practical and ideological considerations. The fortified public sector was to be the pilot for social change. This action was based on a rejection of confidence in the ability of large industrial groups based narrowly and exclusively on the profit motive to solve France's economic problems.[4] A nationalized banking sector would take investment risks that had not been taken under the system of privately owned banks. Concomitantly, state operations were to be decentralized. At the departmental level, the prefect, who represented centralized governmental decision making in Paris, would find his power curtailed. On the economic plane, state firms, while encouraged to act according to the economic signals of the state plan, were to be given a large measure of autonomy on investment decisions. Decentralized decision making was supposedly based on the principle of "autogestion." Nationalized enterprises were expected to show a profit and compete on the competitive market. In other words, the socialism of the French Socialists was to be a socialism of productivity or a "supply-side socialism." Other key elements of the Socialist program included the raising of the minimum wage and family allowances, a fifth week of paid vacation for workers, and a shortened work week. The retirement age was to be lowered to sixty, and public spending would create 210,000 new jobs. A wealth tax on all savings over three million francs was to be imposed.

The quest of the French Socialists since the mid–1960s was previously characterized by CERES' notion of "a search for a lost socialism."[5] Such a search was based on Michel Rocard's view, which was also shared by CERES, that "it is an historical accident which led to the qualification of the economic and social forms born in the poor or very poor countries as 'socialist' whereas, in reality, it is really a question of [putting in place in those countries] authoritarian techniques of development."[6] In *Le Projet socialiste*, "Lenin's revolution against *Capital*" (Gramsci's phrase), in which the Russian Revolution was conceived as a "socialist" revolution despite backward conditions, was criticized as being contrary to Marx's stipulations of the predevelopment of industrialization and the development of the working class for socialism. Marx's analysis was verified as the followers of Lenin were exterminated by Stalinism in the course of the Russian Revolution.[7] For Rocard and the French Socialists in general, socialism can appear only after a certain degree of evolution in production that is in an already industrial society.[8] Jean-Pierre Chevenement criticized the PCF for not mentioning the necessity of a certain level of development of generalized production in its definition of socialism.[9] This is an acute criticism. Such a formulation for a traditional Communist Party is not possible without a thorough criticism of its own foundations and of Bolshevism, since the Communist experience emanating from the Russian Revolution precisely neglected to incorporate the theoretical axis of Marx's analysis regarding the objective possibility of forming a socialist society, which Marx based only on generalized industrial production. Instead Leninist Communism placed the notion of socialism solely in the domain of political voluntarism and the power of the party. The PS's criticism of Communism is fundamental. For CERES, the Leninist conception of the party denatures socialism in principle, and it does so whatever the historical conditions in which it appears.[10]

For the PS, "real, existing socialism" is characterized by inequalities in which one social faction that takes on the character of a ruling class seizes administrative control of the means of production and imposes its domination on the producing classes.[11] The division of labor remains similar to that of capitalism, but there is no political democracy. The U.S.S.R. is seen as a hegemonic and expansionist power based on military and ideological motives. The PS does grant as positive contributions of Communism in Eastern Europe industrialization, aid to the third world, and the fight against fascism.[12] Nonetheless, *Le Projet socialiste* points out that there is a fundamental opposition between the socialism "autogestionnaire" proposed by the PS and the basis of the Soviet regime.[13]

But the French Socialist sword is double-edged: neither Communism nor social democracy (the latter is not seen as a distinct alternative to "capitalist failure") is an "acceptable reference" for socialism.[14] For the CERES group, social democracy has represented something akin to the plague; the critique of social democracy is the springboard of CERES' thought and action. Chevenement wrote, "The problem which was posed to the Socialist Party at Epinay was to understand if it could realize a socialist reformation of Social Democracy, to escape the strong tendencies which have almost always made, in the past, the Socialist Parties as parties of rupture in theory but parties of the system in practice."[15] The goal of CERES has been first to transform the old SFIO and then the new PS into an "authentic" Socialist Party and to develop an original socialism in France going beyond the rupture of the left at Tours by elaborating a Common Program with the Communist Party.[16]

What constitutes the basis of the French Socialist philosophy? Mitterrand acknowledged that a brand of collectivism has been in the thinking of socialists in the past, that is, of those desiring to end the exploitation of man by man. Responding to a period when an entire social class was living without hope, in a state of humiliation, Mitterrand argued, it was natural that the proposed socialist alternative would be the antithesis of what existed, that it would be conceived of in utopian terms.[17] For Mitterrand, what remained true of this original impulse were not the concrete conceptions in which the socialist ideal was once couched but the understanding that it is necessary to change the economic structure of society, to attack a society that is based exclusively on the profit motive to the detriment of all other values.[18] *Le Projet socialiste* placed in a favorable light the century-and-a-half-old notion of a *classless society* that would end the exploitation of man by man. This idea was pronounced still alive.[19] The Socialist Project is none other than to seek the liberation of mankind by gaining access to political power and transforming the structures of society to allow the working class the means for its own emancipation.[20] The Assises du Socialisme, held in 1974, defined the goal of socialism as precisely the end of the exploitation of man by man, the disappearance of wage labor and the state.[21] Chevenement, in referring to the socialist goal, states, "it is a question of constructing apart from the class society stemming from capitalism a *society without classes*."[22] Such a quest is to be based on a strategy in which the means will not pervert the ends, a clear negative reference to Communism. The goal of creating a society "radically different," one in which man would not be "mutilated," cannot be accomplished at the cost of harming existing generations or by the dominance of one group over another. The proposed solution to this antinomy lies in the principle of autogestion.[23]

For the French Socialists, the principle of autogestion means the decentralization of power down to the lowest workable level in every domain of human social activity. Thus, it cannot be confined to a simple notion of workers' control at the economic level; it is much broader in scope, implying citizen's control at the political level as well. In the French Socialist discourse, autogestion is coupled with social ownership of the principal means of production based on a joint management council of state, worker, and consumer representatives, headed by a state-appointed director; democratic planning; and the transformation of the state by the shifting of power from capital to labor. Autogestion in the radical sense is socialism realized: a society characterized by the disappearance of the power of property, the abolition of the "salariat," and the constriction of the market economy. Autogestion is the organization of all social spheres of activity without the distinction between the governed and those who govern. Autogestion for the French Socialists ultimately means the end of any transcending power; it means the decentralization and the end of the state as a state in the authoritarian sense of the word.[24] When people as producers begin to self-manage, just as they begin to self-govern as citizens, then, and only then, will the state begin to wither away.[25]

In the socialist discourse, autogestion is one interpretation of Marx's notion of self-regulated society, that is, communism. For the PS, autogestion is both a guide to concrete proposals and an abstract notion without immediate application; in this latter sense it is also an ideology. As such it can be linked to Eurocommunism at both the practical and the theoretical level.

The aim of a socialist government is to create favorable conditions so that the working class can exercise its influence in the enterprises and challenge the predominance of private decision making under capitalism. The French Socialists do not believe that the government can directly legislate this to happen; it is necessary for the workers and their economic organizations (the unions) to take independent action. Thus Mitterrand has stated, "I wish to permit the worker to be the master of himself."[26]

The basis of the socialist political strategy is the "front de classe." With this concept, the nineteenth-century notion of a homogeneous working class is replaced by the notion of a differentiated working class or more generally a "salariat," which is seen, in the Marxian fashion, to comprise all those who produce surplus value and have only their labor power to sell. The development of this broad sociological category is a consequence of the expansion of the capitalist mode of production to all sectors of the economy, producing a "quasi salariat exploité."[27] The traditional working class still plays a decisive role in the "front de classe," but it is not dominant. Rather, the different categories of labor that become "proletarianized" merge with it. The "front de classe" is then the ensemble of the "exploited" salariat; the "salariat" is never mentioned outside of the "front de classe."[28] The adversary to which the "front de classe" is juxtaposed is monopoly capitalism, the power of the dominant enterprises, the big bourgeoisie and so on. Those who cannot be expected to become socialists are this latter category of "exploiters," and those who culturally, sentimentally, or as a result of tradition identify with the preservation of the dominant structure of capitalism.[29] Despite these precisions, it is not altogether evident how the category of "exploiters" is defined by the French Socialists. For example, it is difficult to ascertain just where the category of small owners of capital would fit into the socialist framework. The "front de classe" is inscribed in the historic movement of the working class and the oppressed and disenchanted who seek to make a rupture with the capitalist system. The union of the left is its political expression.[30]

The other major emblem of the French Socialists is their attachments to liberty and democracy. Here, it is especially evident that the party has evolved out of the social democratic tradition. Yet the definitions given to the terms *liberty* and *democracy* by the French Socialists differ markedly from their definitions in modern liberal discourse. The regimes of modern liberalism and their ideological basis are not held in high esteem by the French Socialists. Pierre Mauroy, in his opening address to the National Assembly as prime minister, called the previous liberal regime of Giscard "arrogant and unjust for embodying a savage Liberalism."[31] Mauroy, in this speech, used the notion of a "new citizenship," an offshoot of the concept of autogestion, to distinguish the Socialist brand of democracy. He stated, "Citizens in their communes, French people should also be citizens at their workplace." Later, in responding to critics who labeled the Socialist program "collectivist," Mauroy asserted, "The power of money, as any other power, should acquiesce before the will of the people: that is the first law of democracy."[32]

The basis of the Socialist criticism of modern liberalism lies with the notion of insecurity. Lionel Jospin, commenting on the liberal ex-president Giscard's juxtaposition of the Socialist notions of liberty and responsibility with collectivism and bureaucracy, retorted that he saw no "liberty" in unemployment, in youth without direction, and in families without lodging. He added that neither did he see "liberty and responsibility" in peasants without control over the price of their products or in a worker unable to prevent his enterprise from closing.[33] For

Jospin, Giscard, in representing modern liberalism, confounds collectivism with collective ambition—the will to form communal ties, an essential human attribute.[34] The Socialist Manifesto of January 1981 stated that insecurity is first of all social: insecurity of employment, purchasing power, income and saving, and so on. When such an insecurity prevails, social disorder is not far away.[35] The Socialists conclude that "the defense of liberty commences with the respect for democracy [of political, social, and economic democracy]."[36] Echoing these themes, and again in the context of a critique of modern liberalism, Mitterrand noted, "My rule is that of liberty. One can be a liberal and not love liberty, a socialist and love it." He continued, "Liberty remains to be known and lived for millions and millions of French people whose conditions of existence do not permit them to experience the liberty which the laws accord them."[37]

The Socialist notion of liberty, when bearing on property, sees the progressive evolution of the enterprise from that of the private domain shielded from societal turbulence (from unions, the state, etc.) to a domain where it (the enterprise) becomes a basic cell of society.[38] The enterprise then does not produce only products; it also produces men. It can deform them, alienate them, or allow them to grow, depending on the social arrangements. This evolution is seen to open up a great gulf between the range of social responsibilities of the enterprise and its strict juridical basis of the right of private ownership.[39]

The elections of May–June 1981 in France brought to power, according to Maurice Duverger, a "third type of Socialism" differing from social democracy and Communism.[40] For Duverger, French socialism has sought a middle ground joining the political pluralism of Western democracies to a certain collective orientation of the economy. The differing views on collectivization of the principal means of production between social democracy and "socialism of the third type" served to justify their differentiation.[41] According to Duverger, social democracy in the past had not sought to end the exploitation of man by man because it had not included nationalization as a key element in its policies, contrary to what Marx had advocated. According to Duverger, social democracy preferred instead to recover surplus value through taxes on revenues and social deductions. It socialized demand but not production.[42]

Many of Duverger's themes were reiterated by Mitterrand himself in his first major television speech in December 1981. Mitterrand claimed "socialisme à la française" was different from social democracy, first, by taking into account the failures of social democracy, and second, on a more fundamental level, in its greater concern for eliminating the exploitation of man by man, in its proposals for nationalization and in its concern for democratic planning.[43] What it still has in common with social democracy is concern for the rights of man and citizen, public and collective liberties, the right to a job, political democracy, and pluralism.[44]

The election of the PS opened up a second phase of Eurocommunism. It is important to note that significant elements of this political party have, as their long-term political project and as their point of ideological reference, a classless society. This element, combined with the PS's differentiation from social democracy and Communism, warrants the utilization of the Eurocommunist label in reference to aspects of PS ideology. The turn of the PS away from notions of "rupture with capitalism" and "class struggle" to the themes of "modernization" after 1982 will be considered in a later chapter. Significantly, in late June 1981, on the heels of the victory of the French left Enrico Berlinguer and Santiago Carrillo met in an effort to relaunch the notion of Eurocommunism.

FRENCH COMMUNISM: AN OVERVIEW

What is it that explains Communism in France? Georges Lavau best sums up the fascination of French Communism to political observers by asking how a party (the PCF) can exist for so long with a significant portion of the vote (20 percent or more) while having so little impact on legislation and on governmental policies.[45] Obviously, such a situation contradicts basic notions in political science about the purpose and effectiveness of a political party. But the PCF has *not* been a "party like the others." Therefore a different gauge must be applied to it. The Communist phenomenon in France cannot be grasped directly at the political level.

The most common notion of the PCF points out that it has been the major representative of the working class. Lavau saw this as its key characteristic in France.[46] François Hincker added that the nucleus of the PCF hard-core vote came from those voters who voted for the party as a result of a "revolutionary choice of class."[47] This latter consideration introduces an ideological element to the picture. For Jean Rony, the PCF represented the most militant, the most concentrated, and the best-organized sections of the working class.[48]

At still another level a reason for the PCF success in the past has been something more intangible, less discernible to political discourse, but no less real. It was the aura about the PCF, its force of attraction, its myth, that has been especially imposing, contributing to its cultural presence in French society. This could be immediately grasped at the street level at the major demonstrations; to march with the PCF was to march as with no other party. Then, too, the PCF, particularly in 1936 and 1941–45, has played a strong Jacobin role, attracting members and voters via French nationalism. The basic camaraderie in French culture found expression in the closed universe of French Communism. Competitive bourgeois values emphasizing the cash nexus between individuals were alien to many aspects of French culture, especially French working-class culture. Until the late 1960s, PCF attachment to the Soviet model brought supporters, not only because of the supposed success of the model but because French working-class culture identified with and idealized the image of Soviet society.

Whatever the reason for the PCF's presence in French society, it is important to note that the PCF has not necessarily been the *party* of the working class. The PCF's tribunitary role as the representative of the working class has not brought to it a corresponding political role. Yves Roucaute has stated matter-of-factly that PCF support comes from its defense of "categorical interests" leaving its position vis-à-vis state power and its seeming inability to attain a share of governmental power as of secondary or no concern to many of its followers.[49] The PCF, in long periods of opposition, played the role of a quasi trade union or of a political party stuck in the revendicative economic-corporatist phase of its development.

The PCF was most comfortable when it played a primarily syndicalist or revendicative role, as it did after 1977. When the PCF was forced to or sought to take on the full-fledged role of a political party, shedding its tribunitary role, when it was forced to change its relation to French society, as it *was doing* intermittently from 1972 to 1977, it found itself in a state of disarray and internal difficulty. This was due not only to the fact that it was forced to take a distance from its secure role as a corporation of civil society, where its main goal was to secure the defense of limited social categories, but also because such a move endangered the status quo of "PCF Incorporated" (Lavau's term) itself. When the PCF moved away from its tribunitary role and became a serious (general) political party in pursuit of a governmental role, it disrupted the delicate internal power structure of the party, that is, it threatened the system of Nomenklatura. Nonruling Communist parties, previously patterned in the Leninist mold, duplicate elements of the system of Nomenklatura. Irwin Wall addressed this phenomenon when he stated, "Stalinism, as adapted to French national traditions, was a mechanism of bureaucratic control by means of which an elite drawn from working-class backgrounds tried to maintain itself in control of the labor movement."[50] The leadership of the PCF has had a measure of relative privilege ensconced in its "safe" role in the countersociety. Unlike the ruling Communist parties, however, it is not locked into this role, nor does the leadership of a nonruling Communist party constitute a dominant class, because vis-à-vis the larger society it is still an outcast, living a subaltern role. It does not have society-wide power. Nonetheless, the phenomenon of privilege does play a role in nonruling Communist parties, and in the PCF in particular, this role has been large. In the past the nonruling Communist parties existed as party classes in embryo. They identified themselves with the party classes in power in the East, because this was their measure of success. For Annie Kriegel, the PCF was a party society representing a "blueprint of the model [of Soviet society]."[51]

But the reality of French Communism has drastically changed. A new element to the equation has been added. The PCF is no longer "safe" in its former role in the countersociety: it can no longer afford to play a principally oppositional role if it wishes to survive as a dominant force in French politics. This has been the lesson of the 1981 French election. Jean Baudouin has pointed out that there has been a progressive transition of French Communism from an "organic epoch" when the PCF held a quasi monopoly as the representative of the most downtrodden social strata, and was able to harvest the advantages that accrued to such a position, to a "critical epoch" marked by the progressive erosion of these very privileges.[52] It was this "critical epoch," beginning after 1968, that saw the emergence of the Common Program and the PCF's Eurocommunism. While the PCF never removed itself from its economic-corporative phase entirely, it had begun to take steps away from a sterile opposition, and in so doing it was becoming a general political party. It could no longer be content to simply play the role of the party that was most outrageous in its demands, not when faced by a Socialist Party that (from 1971) could take the discontent in French society and channel it into positive governmental action.

The PCF, Eurocommunist or not, may be unable to regain its previous stature in French society, lost in the years from 1968 to 1981. Its demise was the result of its own self-destructive behavior stemming from a sectarian tradition after 1978 that was neither logical nor inevitable but that occurred nevertheless. The system of party power, the PCF's version of Nomenklatura, in the end was the principal factor in the PCF's inability to change. The hardliners in the party misread the source of their own power; they disregarded the millions of PCF voters in opting for a fading red star in the East, a political error of great magnitude.

Still, the election victory of the left in 1981 was very much the result of the work of the PCF. It is its legacy and the source of its decline. But will it be its final legacy? After World War II the PCF became the organizer of the working class; it was the dominant force on the left. Its presence was responsible for the weakness and the eventual demise of social democracy in France. The PCF, by organizing and defending the interests of the working class, kept alive the revolutionary tradition that has been so basic to French history. In this sense, it was no coincidence that in 1981, it was France that found itself with a left government and a left Socialist Party bordering on Eurocommunism. The Socialist victory attested to the extraordinary force that has been French Communism.

NOTES

1. Ronald Tiersky, in Rudolf Tokes, ed., *Eurocommunism and Détente* (New York: New York University Press, 1978), p. 195.

2. *Le Monde*, May 22, 1981.

3. *Le Monde*, July 18, 1981.

4. *Le Monde*, May 5, 1981.

5. Michel Charzet and Ghislaine Toutain, *Le CERES: Un Combat pour le socialisme* (Paris: Calmann-Lévy, 1975), p. 244.

6. Michel Rocard, *Parler Vrai* (Paris: Editions du Seuil, 1979), p. 17.

7. Parti Socialiste Français, *Le Projet socialiste pour la France des années 80* (Paris: Club Socialiste du Livre, 1980), p. 66.

8. Rocard, pp. 17–18.

9. Jean-Pierre Chevenement, *Les Socialistes, les communistes et les autres* (Paris: Aubier Montaigne, 1977), p. 32.

10. CERES, *Le CERES par lui-meme* (Paris: Christian Bourgeois, 1978), p. 34.

11. Parti Socialiste Français, p. 68.

12. Ibid., p. 68.

13. Ibid., p. 76.

14. Assises du Socialisme, *Pour le socialisme* (Paris: Stock, 1974), p. 13.

15. Chevenement, p. 265.

16. CERES, p. 34.

17. *Le Nouvel Observateur*, April 28–May 4, 1981.

18. Ibid.

19. Parti Socialiste Français, p. 9.

20. Ibid., p. 33.

21. Assises du Socialisme, p. 24.

22. Chevenement, p. 243.

23. Charzet and Toutain, pp. 141, 177.

24. CERES, p. 135.

25. Nancy Lieber, "Ideology and Tactics of the French Socialist Party," *Government and Opposition* (Autumn 1977), p. 459.

26. *Le Monde*, April 18, 1981.

27. Pierre Bérégovoy, "Le Front de classe: Force et problèmes de la stratégie socialiste," *La Nouvelle Revue Socialiste* 25 (1977):10-11.

28. Paul Bacot, "Le Front de classe," *Revue Française de Science Politique* (April 1978), pp. 280–81.

29. Ibid., p. 284.

30. Bérégovoy, p. 11.

31. *Le Monde*, July 10, 1981.

32. Ibid.

33. *Le Monde*, July 11, 1981.

34. *Le Monde*, May 9, 1981.

35. Ibid.

36. "L'Election presidentielle 26 Avril–10 Mai, 1981," *Le Monde*, p. 67.

37. *Le Monde*, May 16–17, 1981.

38. Jean Boissonnat, *Les Socialistes face aux patrons* (Paris: L'Expansion/Flammarion, 1977), p. 24.

39. Ibid., p. 26.

40. *Le Monde*, July 18, 1981.

41. *Le Monde*, July 19–20, 1981.

42. Ibid.

43. *Le Monde*, December 11, 1981.

44. Ibid.

45. Georges Lavau, *A Quoi Sert le Parti communiste français?*, (Paris: Librairie Arthéme Fayard, 1981), p. 13.

46. Ibid., p. 52.

47. François Hincker, *Le Parti communiste au carrefour* (Paris: Albin Michel, 1981), p. 110.

48. Interview with Jean Rony, May 27, 1982.

49. Yves Roucaute, *Le PCF et les sommets de l'état: De 1945 à nos jours* (Paris: Presses Universitaires de France, 1981), p. 162.

50. Irwin Wall, *French Communism in the Era of Stalin* (Westport, Conn.: Greenwood Press, 1983), p. 5.

51. Annie Kriegel, *The French Communists* (Chicago: University of Chicago Press, 1968), p. 140.

52. Jean Baudouin, "L'Echec communiste de juin 1981: Recul électoral ou crise hégémonique?," *Pouvoirs* 20 (1982): 47.

11

Eurocommunism and the Euroleft

With the invasion of Afghanistan by the U.S.S.R. in 1980, the PCE and the PCI began to accept the full implications of their earlier "Eurocommunist" pronouncements with regard to the Soviet Union and their previous Bolshevik legacy and acted accordingly. An unsigned editorial in *Nuestra Bandera*, an official PCE review, in February 1980 stated that the Soviet intervention in Afghanistan questioned the character of the Soviet state and of the Soviet regime, since the army appeared to be occupying a larger and larger place in Soviet political affairs.[1] The PCI began to view the U.S.S.R. as a full and willing participant in the battle of the superpowers and thus no longer saw the struggle for peace as imposing a choice between two camps in which its support went unequivocally to the Soviet bloc.[2] Instead, the PCI saw the struggle for peace as being based on the concept of Western European unity and the "Euroleft" in conjunction with the movement of the nonaligned nations. The PCI began to participate in international exchanges with the Euroleft, exemplified in the meetings between Enrico Berlinguer and Willy Brandt, the German Social Democratic Party, and Berlinguer and François Mitterrand, as well as an exploratory mission by Giorgio Napolitano with the Labour Party of Britain. These encounters preceded a new phase of Eurocommunism that began to merge with the notion of a radical, non-Leninist and non–social democratic Euroleft.

In late June 1981, on the heels of the Socialist victory in France, Santiago Carrillo met with Enrico Berlinguer in Rome to relaunch the themes of Eurocommunism. At the meeting Berlinguer stated, "The ensemble of ideas and conceptions that Eurocommunism represents are not the sole patrimony of Communist Parties, and its political initiatives may be expected also to extend to Socialist parties as well as to other progressive forces, notably of Christian inspiration."[3] This represented an important statement of Eurocommunist principle and was a significant landmark in the evolution of Eurocommunism even as it began to merge with something much larger, the Euroleft.

SPANISH COMMUNISM AT THE CROSSROADS

In Spain, an electorally weakened and embattled PCE was beginning to show the strains of fierce party factional struggles as the semiautonomous Catalan Communist Party, with underlying support from the Soviet Union, rejected Carrillo's Eurocommunist line.[4] This caused Carrillo to remark that the U.S.S.R. preferred weak Communist parties that were obedient rather than strong ones who thought critically and were independent.[5] This is precisely the case. For the CPSU, Eurocommunism is especially dangerous because of its potential for ideological penetration in Eastern Europe and the Soviet Union. The Leninist Communist regimes in the East can more effectively combat ideologies emanating from a "bourgeois" milieu, since the point of attack of such criticism is external, than an ideology such as Eurocommunism, which claims adherence to socialism, and whose success would tend to undermine the very legitimacy of the existing "socialist" regimes.

Carrillo distinguished three main factions in the Catalan Communist Party: the Eurocommunists, the Afghans or pro-Soviets, and the "true" Leninists.[6] However, a more accurate grouping of ideological tendencies would entail a simple opposition of traditional Communists versus the "Eurocommunist Renovators." The traditional Communists included first the pro-Soviets, who continued to ardently support the Soviet Union as a great socialist society and adhere to the notion of dictatorship of the proletariat or revolutionary rupture with capitalism. They also included the "true" Leninists, who despite reservations about the actual results of Communist principles—democratic centralism, the dictatorship of the proletariat, and so on—still accepted their basis and therefore cannot be grouped with the Eurocommunist Renovators. By the same token the Eurocommunist followers of Carrillo, because they also refused direct condemnation of the U.S.S.R. despite often holding to strident criticisms of certain aspects of Soviet society and Soviet foreign policy, and because they refused to abolish democratic centralism in the party, should also be grouped with the traditional Communists. In contrast, the Eurocommunist Renovators wanted to allow organized currents in the party and to develop a decentralized and federal party with autonomy for the various regional Communist parties as in the Basque region and Catalonia. The Renovators also wanted to move forward with a more rigorous criticism of Eastern European "socialism."[7] In the 1980s, the PCE's strained relations with both Spanish society and the CPSU created contradictory pressures to move the party in either one or the other direction: either the PCE would follow the path of the Eurocommunist Renovators and become a different kind of Communist Party, or it would fall back into a form of orthodoxy.

At the Catalan Communist Party's regional conference in January 1981, the pro-Soviets seized control of the party and suppressed any reference to Eurocommunism. Earlier, in 1978, the Catalan Communist Party had also refused to suppress reference to Lenin in the party statutes. Carrillo intervened by calling an extraordinary Congress in July 1981, regaining control of the Catalan Party. However, there was little chance to restore unity. In April 1982 about 7,000 pro-Soviets, including 29 members of the Central Committee of the Catalan Party who had been expelled for rejecting Carrillo's actions, decided to hold their own Congress. They formed a new Communist Party in Catalonia based on the large working-class base of Barcelona. This group saw itself as guarding the orthodoxy of Spanish Communism based on the principles of Marxism-Leninism and proletarian internationalism. It had had enough of Carrillo's "Eurocommunist reformism" and elitism.[8]

At the PCE's Tenth Congress in July 1981, Carrillo made some additional refinements to Eurocommunism. He stated, "To be a Eurocommunist is to be a Communist at the end of the 20th century in an industrialized Europe where political democracy has attained a great development, and where the workers' movement has social and political weight and where the socialist transformation of society does not pass through the clashing of the two blocs but surpasses them."[9] But Carrillo was now experiencing dissent from another flank of the party. An autonomous Eurocommunist thrust within the PCE, labeled the "Eurocommunist Renovators," captured 25 percent of the vote of the Tenth Congress in 1981. According to Fernando Claudin, the Eurocommunist Renovators sought to deepen the notion of Eurocommunism, moving it from a practical to a theoretical plane.[10] The "Renovators" wished to deny the socialist label to the Communist regimes. They favored political realignment with the Socialist Party in Spain while seeking to form a new type of Communist Party to end what they saw as the contradiction between the Leninist character of the PCE and its Eurocommunist principles. To accomplish this the Eurocommunist Renovators advocated legalizing currents of opinion and instituting proportional representation within the party.[11] The positions of the Eurocommunist Renovators again illustrate the basically conservative character of much of Carrillo's Eurocommunism.

The marked contrast between the Eurocommunist Renovators and the Carrillo "Eurocommunists" was underscored in the events in the

Basque region. In October 1981, the majority of the Central Committee of the Basque Communist Party voted to *merge* with a larger, left nationalist Basque party. When the Basque Communist leaders defied orders from Carrillo and the PCE establishment in Madrid and continued with plans for the merger, they were expelled from the party.[12] The PCF Madrid leadership then intervened to call an extraordinary Congress to regain control of the Basque party.

Meanwhile, Manuel Azcarate and five other members of the Central Committee of the PCE, along with several PCE municipal councilors, organized a public meeting in Madrid with the leaders of the Basque Nationalist Party and the expelled leaders of the Basque Communist Party to explain why they wanted to merge the two parties. This proved to be more than the PCE leadership could countenance as Azcarate and the five other Central Committee members were excluded from the Central Committee by a vote of 67 to 24. A dozen PCE municipal councilors in Madrid were also excluded from the party.[13]

The extent of the political and ideological differences between the Carrillo Eurocommunists and the pro-Soviets, on the one hand, and the Eurocommunist Renovators, on the other hand, is indicative of the breaking up of Spanish Communism. These divergences have emerged in a span of less than ten years, providing stark illustration of the tenuous existence of the Western Communist parties and the reasons for the emergence of Eurocommunism. The Eurocommunist Renovators and the pro-Soviet "Afghans" have no real common basis for existing in the same party. Both groups see themselves as relating to a Communist vision, but they are no longer in the same movement.

The PCE approached the October 1982 general elections in a demoralized condition as the result of these factional struggles. In June 1982, Nicolas Sartorius, once considered a strict ally to Carrillo, argued before the Central Committee that the repeated electoral defeats of the PCE could not be explained away by external factors and that the internal functioning of the party concerning policy formation had to be opened up to all members. Sartorius also called for a rapprochement with those who had recently left or been excluded from the party, but Sartorius really had in mind the Eurocommunist Renovators and not the pro-Soviets. As a result of this intervention Sartorius was forced to abandon his post in the Central Committee although he still remained a member of the Political Bureau.[14]

Despite party dissension, the PCE was stunned by the results of the October 1982 elections to the Cortes, winning only 3.8 percent of the vote and four seats. The Socialist Party swept the elections with 46 percent of the vote under Felipe Gonzalez. In just six years after the formation of Spanish democracy, Spain would be led by the Socialists.

With this major electoral defeat Carrillo's control over the party dissolved. Carrillo still defended his policies, tried to hold the party together at all costs, and criticized the mild reformist policies of the Socialists, but he was forced to resign from the post of party secretary in November. Gerardo Iglesias assumed control of the party leadership.

In the municipal elections of early 1983 the PCE attained a more respectable showing with 8 percent of the vote, but Spanish Communism was still clearly at a crossroads. Was there any political space in Spain alongside of the Socialists for a viable Communist Party, and if so, for what kind of Communist Party? The battle inside the PCE continued for control of the party leadership and the political expression of Spanish Communism.

The Eleventh Congress (December 1983) was approaching, and a "showdown" between Carrillo's supporters and those of Iglesias seemed inevitable. Iglesias's vision of the party was more and more approaching that of the Renovators. Carrillo was outvoted at the Central Committee meeting in late June 1983 in the preparation for the Congress. Iglesias's motion was carried by a vote of 46 to 23 with 12 abstentions. Iglesias wanted to bring back into the party those excluded (the Renovators), significantly reform the party statutes, and offer only mild criticism of the Socialist government while advocating a union of the left.[15] Sartorius argued at the meeting that the only future for Western European Communist parties was through collaboration with Socialist parties.[16]

Carrillo, not content to accept defeat, in the political jockeying leading up to the Congress in October published a series of notes indicating a social democratic orientation of the PCE leadership while strongly criticizing the Socialist government. He was also less critical of Soviet foreign policy and cool toward the notion of Eurocommunism.[17] Carrillo was now trying to line up the pro-Soviets in the party to challenge Iglesias for the party leadership at the Eleventh Congress. Running on the principle of democratic centralism, opposed to allowing official factions in the party, Carrillo and his supporters were outvoted at the Congress and eliminated from the Central Committee.[18] However, Iglesias was reelected only by a 69 to 31 margin, and the course of party policies since he became party secretary was approved only by a vote of 386 to 376 with 25 abstentions. Carrillo called such an unprecedented, tenuous majority a "moral disavowal" of Iglesias's policies.[19]

In this atmosphere Ignacio Gallego resigned in disgust from the Political Bureau and the Central Committee in October, stating in a letter, "Eurocommunist did considerable harm to the party. But your project of 'Eurocommunist Renovation,' if it is pursued, would mean the liquidation of the party."[20] Gallego, after the Eleventh Congress, left the PCE altogether to form a new, pro-Soviet Communist Party in Spain in January 1984. The new party claimed to adhere to Marxism-

Leninism, proletarian internationalism, and the dictatorship of the proletariat. It strongly defended Eastern European socialism and rejected what it called the "political and ideological degeneration of Eurocommunism."[21] The CPSU unabashedly sent an official to attend the Congress that formed the new Communist Party, indicating that it might well have "abandoned" the PCE. In France Georges Marchais, who had felt the Soviet heat when the PCF flirted with Eurocommunism in the 1970s, in a piece of tragicomedy condemned the presence of the Soviet official at the Congress, as did the PCF newspaper, L'Humanité.

The sharp confrontations among ideologically distinct groups in Spanish Communism is indicative of the general dilemma of Western European Communism. Similar confrontations were also taking place inside the PCF from 1976 to 1981 without manifesting themselves in actual splits, and the presence of the Soviet official at the Congress of the new Spanish Communist Party may well have stimulated bad memories for Marchais from this period. What was unusual about Spanish Communism was the openness of the ideological debates.

THE PCI'S REACTION TO THE POLISH COUP

With the martial law regime imposed by the Polish Communist Party's military wing in Poland, the PCI had no choice but to split with the Soviet Union. Giorgio Napolitano had earlier warned the CPSU that the PCI would break relations if military action were to occur in Poland against the Polish workers. The possibility of an eventual split with the Communism that has stemmed from the 1917 Bolshevik Revolution has always existed within any meaningful interpretation of Eurocommunism. Now this came to pass by the force of events. Enrico Berlinguer, on Italian television in December 1981, stated, "A period has ended. The propulsive force which had originated with the October Revolution is now exhausted, as the capacity for renewal in the Eastern European societies is exhausted."[22] Importantly, Berlinguer cited the need for a new socialism founded on the principles of liberty and democracy in the West as necessary to help break the political and social stalemate between the working classes and the Communist parties in the East. Berlinguer concluded, "The road to socialism cannot be founded on Lenin."[23] These conclusions of the PCI, drawn from the events in Poland, followed its earlier negative analysis of "real, existing socialism." In this analysis the PCI saw as necessary a process of evolution in Eastern Europe from a monolithic socialism to a pluralist form, since the previous state socialism had reached its limits. However, as PCI intellectual Lucio Lombardo Radice pointed out, if Poland were to end up like Czechoslovakia, this evolution would be considered blocked, and any future progress would be put in doubt.[24] Such an analysis still sidestepped many key theoretical issues, but it was far from timid.

The PCI published a document December 30, 1981, to illustrate its position on Poland. The document offered a clear condemnation of what was called a "military coup."[25] The measures of martial law were seen as incompatible with the PCI's own democratic and socialist ideals. A regime of a socialist "tendency" could not be saved by military force for such action puts a damaging mark on socialism itself.[26]

The PCI document stated that the Eastern European regimes have been undergoing periodic crises that have challenged their "monolithic conception of power" and a system that does not permit a "real democratic participation" at the point of production or in the political arena. The second phase of the socialist movement that had its origin with the October Revolution was now considered exhausted, just as the Socialist parties and the syndicalist movements around the Second International were previously exhausted. A "third road" as part of a third phase of the workers' movement was on the agenda in Europe. Any separation between socialism and democracy or any divergence from the democratic organization of political and economic power was unacceptable.[27] This "third phase" of the working-class movement was also seen to go beyond the social democratic experiences. In an eye-catching statement, the PCI rejected any notion of a homogeneous Communist movement separated from other socialist, progressive, and liberation movements. In doing so, it was launching its idea of a "new internationalism."[28] Berlinguer had already pointed out the inadequacy of the notion of the "world Communist movement."[29] The PCI, in effect, was authorizing a clean break with Bolshevism and was returning to a Marxian conception of the communist movement, one that existed before 1917. An editorial in the party newspaper, *L'Unità*, in January 1982 stated that the "third phase" entailed a new impulse for socialism in the world meaning "the advance of socialism in the highest points of capitalist development, beginning with Western Europe."[30] The third phase meant "overcoming capitalism at the stage it has reached in the industrialized and developed West."[31]

In response to *Pravda's* critical remarks regarding the PCI theses on Poland, an official PCI statement on the Communist systems asked rhetorically, "in what assembly of the [Soviet] party, in what union meeting can a Communist, a citizen, or anyone who is in fundamental disagreement with state policy express himself and be heard?"[32] The PCI wished to avoid a total break with the Soviet Union. Some constituencies in the party did not agree with the critical assessments of the U.S.S.R. offered by the leadership. However, the PCI's important position in Italian society could be threatened by further association with Eastern European socialism.

Berlinguer felt compelled to step up the pressure in January, presenting a discourse of sixty-eight pages to the Central Committee. He summarized the ills of the socialist countries as bureaucratization, the party state, monolithism, and the loss of specificity of the political party. Berlinguer also criticized the transformation of Marxism in the Soviet Union into an ideology of the state and a dogmatism bordering on fanaticism, obliterating what he saw as Marx's fundamental philosophical innovation of the critique of ideology.[33] Many earlier statements were repeated. Berlinguer revealed the basis of the PCI's political statements on Poland by posing this question to the PCI's Italian audience: "how many workers who really want to go beyond capitalism aspire to a social, political and economic order which exists in the East?" He concluded bluntly, "A strict minority."[34]

The same day, January 11, 1982, on which Berlinguer delivered his long address to the Central Committee of the PCI, the PCE, now minus some of the Eurocommunist Renovators group, also threw its iron into the fire. Carrillo stated that the events in Poland made it necessary "to go well beyond Eurocommunism," and he added, "The organization of the revolutionary workers' movement around the U.S.S.R was definitely dead."[35] Carrillo proposed a new international articulation of Socialist and Communist parties and national liberation movements. He still saw the principles of 1917 as valid but argued that it was necessary to overcome the historic rupture between Socialists and Communists. He stated matter-of-factly, "There does not exist today any Communist country in the world."[36] Carrillo went on to list five principles that would guide subsequent PCE action: (1) pluralism in the organization of state power excluding the notion of a workers' and peasants' state (instead of the dictatorship of the proletariat the party preferred the notion of the democratic hegemony of the "forces of culture"); (2) the long-term coexistence of public and private forms of property in socialism; (3) the establishment of workers' control in the enterprises; (4) recognition that the PCE is not the only representative of the working class; and (5) renunciation by the PCE of any pretense of seeking a monopoly of political power while still aspiring to become a vanguard political force.[37]

The PCE criticisms of the U.S.S.R. over the Polish coup were not as penetrating as those of the PCI. The PCE refused to go so far as to accept the PCI thesis that the October Revolution had lost its propelling force, instead summing up the reasons for the Polish situation as a "bureaucratized state" imposed from without, a reason too timid for the Renovators.[38] Carrillo later stated that he disagreed with the PCI that after the Polish events the Communist movement from 1917 was exhausted, and he could not accept the notion of a "third phase" if it meant a reunification of the working-class movement on the basis of the *failure* of the Communist International and all that has followed from the Russian Revolution.[39] Carrillo would only go as far as to call for "a new pole of attraction" as distinct from a new "center" based on the regional coordination of the Western Communist parties.[40]

In the wake of the Polish coup, Berlinguer did not attend the Congress of the CPSU in February 1981. PCI delegate Gian Carlo Pajetta attended in his place but was not allowed to speak before the delegates, because his speech contained references to and support of independent trade union movements (Solidarity) and because it opposed the Soviet intervention in Afghanistan.[41] The CPSU reemphasized its extreme dislike of the concept of Eurocommunism at the Congress through the condemnation of the Eurocommunism made by staunchly pro-Soviet Alvaro Cunhal, chairman of the Portuguese Communist Party. Cunhal stated that Eurocommunism was "a vehicle which does not have a future and whose influence has already abated."[42]

THE PCI AND THE EUROLEFT

Berlinguer went to Paris in late March 1982 to meet with the head of the PS, Lionel Jospin, to begin to put in place the basis for the "new internationalism" that would permit left Socialists and Eurocommunists to band together for their common interests. The concept of the Euroleft was addressed in this meeting and was defined as the "union of European democratic forces to surmount capitalism."[43] For Berlinguer, the notion of Euroleft was contained in that of Eurocommunism: it meant the search for a new road toward socialism with parties that were not necessarily Communist.[44] The PCI and the PS were seen to have common views in their search for a third road to socialism based on the impracticality of the models of socialism in Eastern Europe but also on the judgment of the inadequacy of social democracy in the West to achieve socialist goals. It was noted that the PCI could be a fundamental element in an alternative force in Italian politics along the lines of the French Socialist government in France.[45]

At its Sixteenth Congress in March 1983, the PCI developed its strategy of the "democratic alternative,"one that it had begun to put in place after leavng its association with the government in 1979. Designed to take the place of the "historic compromise," the democratic alternative projected the PCI, for the first time, as a governmental force in its own right. The PCI saw itself as being able to directly spearhead an alternative to the DC governmental bloc with a projected government based on programmatic accords with potential partners on the left.[46] The PCI had given up on the possibility of working with the DC in government. It now saw the DC as being absorbed by political corruption and entangled in the Italian party state. The PCI felt strong enough to lead a governmental coalition without the DC.

The PCI had developed a series of governmental programs for a future PCI-led government. Party electors had become instrumental in the chairing of several powerful parliamentary committees after 1976 and had fed information back into the PCI regarding policy. In addition, the PCI also commissioned supportive academicians in various fields to develop a series of governmental proposals. The thrust of the PCI's governmental reforms were aimed at administrative reform of the state structures and at the curbing of corruption. The PCI's economic policy, based on austerity, called for the development of the country's backward South and the enhancement of the European Common Market and Italy's role in it.[47]

In relation to the Euroleft Berlinguer, in his address to the Sixteenth Congress, stated, "Not only is a substantial reinvention of Socialism in the East needed, in the West, the fundamental pillars of Social Democracy based on the Welfare State are no longer in place."[48] For Berlinguer, the old ideological disputes on the Western European left between Socialist and Communist parties were no longer tenable. Berlinguer added that the entire European left could agree that the transition to socialism must take place in the framework of democracy and that the model of Eastern European socialism cannot be imitated in the West.[49]

The Socialists, with Bettino Craxi holding the prime ministership in a DC-led government, showed no interest in the PCI's democratic alternative. On economic policy, the Craxi government issued a decree in February 1984 reducing the automatic level of wage indexation that had been established in Italy in 1975. Italian business wanted to move back to a system of contractual negotiations with labor on an individual basis. The PCI and the PCI-led CGIL (Confederazione Generale Italiana del Lavoro), Italy's largest trade union, found themselves isolated in opposition to the decree but nevertheless mobilized a formidable demonstration of one million workers in April 1984 to protest it.

Enrico Berlinguer unexpectedly died in June 1984 prior to the elections to the European Parliament. In this solemn atmosphere, the PCI, aided by a wave of sympathy throughout Italy for their popular leader, finally overtook the DC to become the largest party in Italy. With 33.3 percent of the vote, the PCI edged out the DC (33 percent) and greatly outdistanced the PSI (11.2 percent).[50]

This situation did not endure for long. The PCI, continually a mark for attack by the Socialists at both the local and the national level, lost electoral ground in the municipal elections in May 1985, gaining 30.2 percent of the vote to 35 percent for the DC and 13.3 percent for the PSI.[51] And a PCI-inspired referendum designed to overturn the decree on wage indexation of the preceding year was defeated by a 54 to 45 percent margin in June 1985.[52]

By the mid–1980s, the PCI appeared no closer to government than in 1976. But this was evident only on the surface. Electorally, the PCI stands on equal footing with the DC in Italy and overshadows the PSI. But even this observation does not reveal of the real strength of the PCI in Italian politics and society. The DC has remained as powerful as it is electorally only because the PCI, Eurocommunist or not, is the only real alternative in Italy. The DC maintains its electoral position almost by default; and this position is a tenuous one.

The PCI has shown that it will shed all of its Communist baggage from 1917 in order to accede to political power in Italy. At its sixteenth Congress, the PCI, now under the leadership of Alessandro Natta, renewed its statement that the historic force of the October Revolution was exhausted. It is the CPSU, in fact, that has diminished its attacks on the PCI, because the PCI is too strong a force in Italy and Western Europe for the Soviet Union to easily dismiss. The CPSU has accepted the PCI as a "friendly party," even though it is no longer considered a "fraternal party."[53] But the PCI sees its future in the Euroleft and its relations with the Socialist and Social Democratic parties in Western Europe. And its future in Italy will probably be as the leader of a ruling governmental coalition.

With the positions of the PCI on Poland, the political basis of Eurocommunism had, for the most part, become evident. The victory of the Socialists in France had enlarged its political parameters. Essentially, Eurocommunism is another type of communism that not only is different from but becomes a full-fledged critique of Leninist Communism, producing a new ideology. As such, it harks back to a pre–1917 definition of communism that found its origins in Marx. Eurocommunism merges imperceptibly with the Euroleft on its border. It is the "communist" wing of the Euroleft. But this communist wing comprises many who are in Socialist parties as well, preferring to label themselves "Socialists." Eurocommunism, in making a rupture with Communism, helps to overcome the antinomy between Communists and Socialists stemming from 1917, the potential political implications of which are enormous. Its importance was underscored by Milovan Djilas, who considered Eurocommunism the most significant European event since the cold war.[54]

NOTES

1. In Alexander Adler and Jean Rony, *L'Internationale et le genre humain* (Paris: Mazarine, 1980), p. 238.

2. Lilly Marcou, ed., *L'U.R.S.S.: Vue de gauche* (Paris: Presses Universitaires de France, 1982), p. 224.

3. *Le Monde*, July 2, 1981.

4. *Le Monde*, January 20, 1981.

5. Ibid.

6. Santiago Carrillo, *Le Communisme malgré tout*, interviews with Lilly Marcou (Paris: Presses Universitaires de France, 1984), p. 141.

7. David S. Bell, "Eurocommunism: The Revised Standard Version," *Communist Affairs* (April 1982), p. 569.

8. *Le Monde*, April 14, 1982.

9. *Le Monde*, July 30, 1981.

10. *Le Monde*, July 28, 1981.

11. Ibid.

12. Eusebio Mujal-Léon, *Communism and Political Change in Spain*, (Bloomington: Indiana University Press, 1983), pp. 217–18.

13. *Le Monde*, November 13, 1981.

14. *Le Monde*, November 9, 1982.

15. *Le Monde*, July 2, 1983.

16. Ibid.

17. *Le Monde*, October 20, 1983.

18. *Communist Affairs*, December 1983, p. 362.

19. *Le Monde*, December 20, 1983.

20. *Le Monde*, October 20, 1983.

21. *Communist Affairs*, October, 1984, p. 491.

22. *Le Monde*, December 17, 1981.

23. Ibid.

24. Lucio Lombardo Radice, in Marcou, *L'U.R.S.S.: Vue de gauche*, p. 558.

25. *Revolution*, February 12–18, 1982.

26. Ibid.

27. Ibid.

28. Ibid.

29. Enrico Berlinguer, in Simon Serfaty and Lawrence Gray, eds., *The Italian Communist Party: Yesterday, Today, and Tomorrow* (Westport, Conn.: Greenwood Press, 1980), p. 230.

30. *Communist Affairs*, October 1982, pp. 861–62.

31. Ibid.

32. *Rencontres-Communistes*, February 4, 1982.

33. *Le Monde*, January 13, 1982.

34. *Le Monde*, January 16, 1982.

35. *Le Monde*, January 13, 1982.

36. Ibid.

37. Ibid.

38. Mujal-León, p. 218.

39. Carrillo, pp. 93 and 108.

40. Ibid., pp. 68–69.

41. Richard F. Starr, ed., *1982 Yearbook on International Communist Affairs* (Stanford, Calif.: Hoover Institution Press), p. 309.

42. *Le Monde*, March 1, 1981.

43. *Le Monde*, March 31, 1982.

44. Ibid.

45. Ibid.

46. Stephen Gundle, *Communist Affairs*, October 1983, pp. 508–9.

47. Italian Communist Party, "Berlinguer's Report to the Central Committee, May 11, 1983," *The Italian Communists: Foreign Bulletin of the PCI*, April–June 1983.

48. *Communist Affairs*, October 1983, pp. 510–11.

49. Ibid.

50. Italian Communist Party, reprinted from *L'Unità*, June 12, 1984, *The Italian Communists: Foreign Bulletin of the PCI*, April–June 1984, p. 42.

51. *Le Monde*, May 15, 1985.

52. *Le Monde*, June 12, 1985.

53. *Le Monde*, May 12–13, 1985.

54. Milovan Djilas, quoted in Annie Kriegel, *Eurocommunism: A New Kind of Communism?* (Stanford, Calif.: Hoover Institution Press, 1978), pp. 2–3.

12

The Relations between Socialists and Communists in Power under Mitterrand

Prior to the Mitterrand election, the French left had held power in France for a total of only six years since World War II. While the left stood at parity with the right after 1968 on the social and cultural plane, it had little or no experience with the state apparatus, running the economy, or governing the nation. As the French left swept to power with a rhetoric of "rupture with capitalism," based on a program of democratic rights for workers in the workplace and on extensive nationalization of banking and industry, many feared that a flight of capital would occur, leading to economic dislocation and a quick end to the Mitterrand government. Indeed, the left had never fulfilled the duration of an electoral mandate in France.

The right refused to recognize the legitimacy of the Mitterrand government, hoping that this added pressure would serve to curtail its duration. Although the PCF was severely weakened by the election, Mitterrand invited the participation of Communist ministers both to help consolidate his new majority and to indicate that his government intended to live up to the "Socialist Project" outlined by the PS. The right understood this symbolic message and quickly labeled the government "Socialist-Communist." Amidst this acrimony and institutional uncertainty, the Socialist Congress at Valence in October 1981 projected an image of vengefulness as the Socialists, flushed with their striking electoral success and already impatient with the many obstacles they were confronting in attempting to change the orientations of state structures, called for a systematic cleaning out of adversarial (right-wing) administrators.

It is only with this volatile scenario in mind, at the outset of the Mitterrand presidency, that the subsequent years of Socialist administration may be put in perspective and evaluated. The French Socialists, isolated in the opposition for twenty-five years, came to power on the strength of their ideology and a political program that was devised in the early 1970s, based unrealistically on postwar Keynesian growth models. The French Socialists' ideology was radical left, and their programmatic expectations were high. Mitterrand's conception of the Socialist Project as the "tranquil force" was an attempt to smooth the rough edges of a radical project undertaken by the French left under the institutions of the Fifth Republic, institutions that had been the very symbol of right-wing rule based on the exclusion of the left from political power.

But French Socialists soon discovered that governing a society—and the Mitterrand government was to govern all of France, not just the left constituency—required compromise and a distance from ideological principles. The experience of the French Socialists in power as they turned from ideology to administration, from radicalism to moderation, has renewed the old debate on the European left regarding reformism: Does the delaying of one's ideological goals mean their abandonment? In other words, was the Mitterrand experiment merely another turn after all in the history of social democracy?

The Mitterrand presidency may be divided into three stages: (1) July 1981 to June 1982, during which the government implemented its "Socialist," program highlighted by extensive nationalizations of industry and banking; (2) June 1982 to July 1984, when the government began to administer the economy while implementing austerity measures; and (3) July 1984 to the March 1986 legislative elections, when government policy recognized the economic constraints of the capitalist world economy, giving the modernization of French industry top priority. In this latter phase the French Socialists began to modernize their conception of socialism as well. In the course of the Socialist governmental experience the PS was transformed from an ideological club that aspired to political power into a governmental party. The period of ideological gestation for power in the 1970s gave way to a period of practical administration, as the French Socialists began to realize the natural distance between ideology and policy. By its October 1985 Congress at Toulouse the PS had concluded that if the Socialist government had yet to establish socialism in France, it had at least proved it could run the economy and govern society. Thus the Mitterrand experiment legitimized the left, that is, the PS, as a governing force in France.

As for the PCF, at each turn of the Mitterrand government toward realism, it hid behind the purity of ideology; once again the PCF balked at becoming a governing party, drifting instead into its corporatist role of defending categorical interests of sections of the working class. After leaving the Mitterrand government in July 1984, the PCF adopted a posture of outright opposition to government policy, abandoning all political perspective and becoming, in effect, a quasi trade union. The experience of the Communist ministers were not allowed to become the experiences for the PCF as a political party and were circumscribed from having any effect on party policy. Consequently the PCF did not receive the benefit of legitimization from its governmental stint. Electorally, the PCF continued to decline after 1981, a decline that Jean Elleinstein saw as destabilizing the previous political balance in France.[1] The decline of the PCF has had at least short-term negative consequences for the left and for the Socialists' ability to reconstitute a governmental majority. The decline of the PCF as a key political force is the major new given in French politics.

THE PCF IN THE AFTERMATH OF THE MITTERRAND ELECTION

After the election of François Mitterrand, dissension in the PCF resurfaced quickly. An independent pressure group, Rencontres Communistes, was created, designed to be a "center for initiative, reflexion, research and debate" within the PCF. It was headed by Henri Fiszbin. Rencontres Communistes maintained that the PCF leadership had not followed official party strategy since 1977 and that the party was not playing its vanguard role.[2] They began publishing a weekly entitled *Rencontres Communistes* with the participation of such noted PCF figures as François Hincker, Eddy Koenig, Pierre Li, Maurice Goldring, and Yvon Quiniou. The pro–martial law orientations of the PCF on Poland, the rejection of the union of the left, and the lack of even a semblance of internal party democracy were of such consequence in their estimation that they felt compelled to take the leap into the unknown by openly criticizing the party. They were not people to take such an action easily. For the Rencontres Communistes group, the PCF in a government of the left was an important event, vindicating the long unitary policy of the PCF from the 1960s. However, PCF governmental participation occurred at a time when the party had lost its credibility due to its recent sectarian orientations. It was in the discussion in *Rencontres Communistes* that the incredible phenomenon of a possible Communist vote for Valéry Giscard d'Estaing in the 1981 elections, alluded to earlier, emerged. *L'Humanité* journalist Alain Leygnier stated that certain high- and middle-level bureaucrats and certain journalists of *L'Humanité* advocated abstention or a "revolutionary vote" for Giscard on the second round of the presidential elections.[3] This phenonmenon was corroborated by Hincker.[4] Apparently, the appeal to vote for Giscard or to abstain had roots even in the Political Bureau![5] Pressure was brought to bear on party members through person-to-person contact and by telephone. The Central Committee was reported as divided between those who favored Mitterrand and those who favored Giscard, the latter refusing to drink champagne after the Mitterrand victory.[6]

The first meeting between the leadership of the PCF and that of the PS since March 1978 occurred in June 1981. The purpose of this meeting was to draft a political accord that would provide a basis for Communist ministers in the Socialist government. The PCF agreed to put aside the 131 propositions it had advocated during the presidential campaign, although it would never admit they were inappropriate. Disagreements still existed between the two parties over Poland, Afghanistan, the SS–20 missiles, the Camp David accords, and the extent of the nationalization policy. Yet there was substantial agreement over social policies, including a host of transfer payments and, importantly, over the extent of the new rights of workers in public enterprises. Directors of nationalized industry would be appointed by the government according to the Socialists' model of industrial relations. The PCF was promised four ministers: of public administration, transportation, professional training, and health. Georges Marchais called the accord a serious and constructive one, an accord of government.[7] Roland Leroy denied that it was an accord of government, but he affirmed that it did have some political content.[8]

However, Charles Fiterman, the future minister of transportation, after the first round of presidential balloting, had stated that the PCF refused to denounce its policies leading up to the elections. To have taken another course (since 1977) would have been to support a policy of social democratization (referring to the PS). It would have meant that the party had lost its revolutionary soul.[9] Fiterman and Marchais both blamed the French presidential system itself, which tends toward bipolarity, as the reason for the PCF's poor results.

Nonetheless, after the election of Mitterrand, while still holding to a stonefaced front the PCF capitulated to the PS. It had no other choice since the leadership's policies after 1977 had put the PCF at the Socialists' mercy. And the Socialists needed the Communists if their efforts at a national reconciliation ("rassemblement") were to be successful. Marchais, in a distinct change in tone, cited the autonomy of the two parties while recognizing the importance of the defeat of the right. He mentioned that there was a possibility of governing together founded on cooperation, loyalty, mutual respect, and democratic discussion.[10] On the other hand, the PCF did not give an inch to the Eurocommunist "contestataires," who would eventually be excluded from the debates prior to the Twenty-fourth Congress held in February 1982.

Marchais summed up the positions of the PCF leadership with regard to the party's "serious reverse" in the 1981 elections at a Central Committee meeting in late June. The PCF criticized itself for not presenting a presidential candidate in each election since 1965. By not always presenting its own candidate in the past, the PCF felt it had encouraged PCF electors to vote Socialist from the first round of balloting ("vote utile"). Marchais questioned the form of the union of the left from 1972–1977, which, he said, saw the PCF and the PS imperceptibly merge in the eyes of the electorate. He refused to admit that a better score for the PCF in the 1981 election was possible had it assumed a different course after 1977, that is, if the PCF had continued with its unitary, Eurocommunist policy. This assertion was buttressed by pointing out that the electoral decline of the party had begun well before 1977.[11] Marchais admitted that the party had shown bad judgment in its electoral campaign, specifically in its vituperations against immigrants at Vitry and Montigny, and he saw as unfortunate the timing of his meeting with the CPSU in January 1980 during the invasion of Afghanistan. Marchais acknowledged that too much attention had been paid to the most deprived workers in his electoral campaign.

Fiterman, in a July issue of the PCF journal, *Revolution*, noted that the Communists would not have entered the government if there had been a question of putting into place a classical experiment of social democracy.[12] But this was not the position of many in the party. Apparently dissent was expressed in assembly sections before the second round of the presidential elections against the party's official support of Mitterrand, and this was followed by similar dissent for its running on the majority ticket for the legislative elections.[13]

Also, in early July, eleven members of Rencontres Communistes were excluded from the Federal Committee of Paris by a vote of seventy-one to twelve for having formed a parallel party and press, which was seen as contrary to the party statutes.[14] In October the Rencontres Communistes group was said to have "put itself out of the party." The PCF was now cleaning house to prepare for the Twenty-fourth Congress, a Congress that would be a sterile operation having little impact on the party's subsequent policies.

The discussion for the Twenty-fourth Congress began in October 1982 and carried through the remainder of the year. One of the reasons promulgated by the PCF to justify its position in the Socialist government during this period was the staunch opposition of French business to the government. It was natural for the PCF, which always opposed the business sector, to then support the government. The favorable conditions created by the elections made possible the implementation of measures the party judged important. Marchais, in an address to the Central Committee in December, stated that the government was going in the right direction and that there had been an "undeniable amelioration" in the living conditions of the French workers.[15]

Yet, in September, at the Fête de L'Humanité, Leroy had announced that the PCF was a "party associated with the government" and not a "government party" ("parti au gouvernement," not "parti de gouvernement").[16] And in October, Marchais called Eurocommunism a formula that was out of date.[17] François Hincker, in *Rencontres Communistes*, replied that Marchais's statement on Eurocommunism was contrary to the PCF Congresses, even to the document for the pending Twenty-fourth Congress.[18] Finally, in December 1981 when the Polish workers' revolution was crushed by the military wing of the Polish Communist Party, causing an open split of the PCE and the PCI with the Soviet Union, the PCF tacitly supported the actions of the new Polish military government. The Polish situation was one of several foreign policy issues that would see the Communist ministers supporting the Socialist government (which, in this case, severely condemned the Polish military action), while the PCF took a contrary position.

Marchais opened the PCF's Twenty-fourth Congress stating that a new period of French history had been opened up by the election victory of the left in 1981. The PCF, following its Twenty-second and Twenty-third Congresses, was taking its place in the new majority. Socialism was now the order of the day, a situation that was without precedent.[19] The party had been too late in specifying a French road to socialism, beginning only in 1976 with the Twenty-second Congress and not in 1956 after the Khrushchev revelations about Stalinism. This time lag was responsible for some of the PCF's poor electoral results. The union of the left had been necessary in the 1970s, but its content and form were inappropriate, because it authorized a fundamental and global accord with the Socialists. This form of union effaced the differences between the PCF and the PS. Future unitary actions and political accords with the Socialists must be conducted according to the criteria of the moment and not in advance.

The bourgeoisie, the PCF said, had tried to use the PS to effect a continual erosion of the PCF vote after 1973. The PCF was therefore correct not to have capitulated in 1977 to the Socialists, who were playing the game of the bourgeoisie. Without PCF perseverance the political situation in France would not have been as favorable as it was at the present.

It was impossible to fathom just how the PCF was able to prevent the PS from collaborating with the right, given the manifest weakness of the party in 1981, when previously, in 1977, it had been unable to do so. But the PCF was in the government, and the first measures of the government were seen by the leadership to have gone in the right direction. A social democratic experience was not seen as fatal.[20] The

Rencontres Communistes group called such a presentation a "insurmountable contradiction."[21] The party was in the Socialist government, yet it had not changed its point of view on the Socialists or its sectarian strategy since 1977. Indeed, this strategy was still intended to be the basis of the party revival.

In fact, the PCF was in a government the policies of which it not only supported but recognized as "left" in orientation, at least in the 1981–82 period. But it would not return to a form of unity with the Socialists that might sacrifice its Communist identity. Thus, in foreign affairs the PCF continued to cultivate its link to international communism; the text of the Twenty-fourth Congress cited the influence of the socialist countries as growing and decisive in the evolution of the world.[22] At the same time, reference was made to Eurocommunism. Eurocommunism was seen to embody the relations of various Communist parties of the capitalist countries that placed democracy at the center of the road to socialism. Eurocommunism was an element of the diversity in world Communism but not, in itself, a general model of socialism.[23]

Meanwhile, the PCF leadership was having renewed difficulty keeping a lid on internal party dissent, despite the renewed threat of exclusion. In December the PCF position on Poland began to have its fall out. Twenty-five Communist journalists who worked for *L'Humanité* and other party organs strongly condemned the "state of siege" in Poland and demanded that the PCF follow suit.[24] Even more startling was an intervention during the discussion for the Twenty-fourth Congress in a January issue of *L'Humanité* by Jacques Arnault, the former editor of the PCF journal, *La Nouvelle Critique*, in which he asked the Central Committee not to retain Marchais as party chairman.[25] This view was quickly followed by a stream of rebuttals in *L'Humanité*, refuting Arnault's lone dissenting voice. What was significant was that the party felt compelled to air Arnault's opinion, if only to refute it.

The trouble inside *L'Humanité* continued in January, when fifteen journalists of the newspaper who had been laid off cited political reasons as the cause, contending that they were seen as too independent by its director, Roland Leroy. They complained that during the presidential campaign every reference to the PS had to indicate its turn to the right.[26]

In February the Rencontres Communistes group, excluded from participating in the Twenty-fourth Congress, claimed that "another Communist policy" was necessary, one based on a creative and critical heritage of the PCF, inscribed in the renovating international working-class movement (the Euroleft).[27] They refused to recognize that they were no longer in the party. For this group, the PCF, in approving the "coup de force" in Poland, was contradicting its attachment to democratic rights and liberties. They lamented the PCF's persistent lack of analysis of the regimes of the East and of the Soviet model, which, in their view, could not in any way provide a reference for French socialism.

THE PCF COURTS THE MITTERRAND GOVERNMENT

With the Twenty-fourth Congress out of the way, the PCF began seeking to improve its relationship with the government. The party began to earnestly work for the success of the government while maintaining some distance on specific issues and while guarding its Communist identity. The PCF was still in a weakened condition, but it was attempting to place itself strategically so that it could reap any successes of a government of the left. And as for the failures, the Mitterrand government was, after all, a predominantly Socialist government, so the PCF could not be held at fault. PCF solidarity with the government was stepped up after the cantonal elections in March 1982. The PCF's electoral decline was reconfirmed in these elections, but this time in the context of a general decline of the left. The PCF concluded that its own lot rested with the success or failure of the government.[28] The Paris Federation began organizing meetings and public debates on key political questions in an effort to help the government succeed. Marchais made a remarkable speech citing an "uncontestable amelioration" of conditions due to the actions of the government. He argued that if the party only accentuated the negative, acting as if nothing had changed since the Mitterrand election, then it would be "putting itself outside of reality."[29] Marchais's statements were a long way from notions of a "gang of three" lumping Mitterrand with Valéry Giscard d'Estaing and Jacques Chirac as part of the PCF's campaign buildup in September 1980. In May 1982, Marchais continued in this positive vein vis-à-vis the government, arguing that if the party left the government, it would be disastrous. To counteract the political offensive of the right the union of the left had to be refortified. Charles Fiterman went so far as to criticize certain *L'Humanité* journalists for "excessive attitudes" in their one-sided support for Argentina in the Falklands affair. Apparently, this was the first time a PCF leader publicly criticized the newspaper of the Central Committee.[30] Roland Leroy then acknowledged Fiterman's criticism, stating that he had been in the countryside and had not directly supervised the matter!

At this time the government was feverishly putting in place many of Mitterrand's presidential propositions including the decentralization of governmental administration, the nationalization program, and the new charter for the rights of workers in public enterprises (Auroux Laws). Workers had been given a fifth week of paid vacation, the work week had been reduced one hour, and the minimum wage had been raised.

The PCF's positions vis-à-vis the government of the left flipflopped for the remainder of 1982 while in a basic framework of solidarity. At times, the PCF gave the government unquestionable support. At other times it gave the government support with mild reservations or warnings with regard to particular aspects of governmental policy. Importantly, the PCF continued its strong support of the government even after the initial turn to austerity measures of wage and price controls in June 1982.

In September 1982, Leroy was made to atone for his remarks of the previous year when he had noted that the PCF was a party "associated with" the government and not a party "of" government. Leroy now declared that the PCF could not have one foot in the government and one foot out ("un pied dedans et un pied dehors"), that it could not be 50 percent for and 50 percent against it, but that the PCF could only be totally "in the government" (dans le gouvernement").[31]

In terms of foreign policy, after the Mitterrand election, the PCF continued its strict alignment with the international Communist movement while the PCE and the PCI, in the meantime, flirted with the Euroleft. To illustrate the PCF approach, in 1982 Marchais went to China, met with Enrico Berlinguer, and attended the Congress of Yugoslav Communists. Yet Maxine Gremetz, responsible for PCF foreign affairs and a member of the Central Committee, went to Czechoslovakia to renew ties with the Czech party, which just two years earlier the PCF had accused of putting in place a caricature of socialism.[32] In November, before students at a school for party cadres, Marchais illustrated the PCF's continued and reinvigorated attachment to East European socialism, noting that one could not speak of a crisis in the socialist countries in the same sense as of a crisis in the West.[33] Still, the PCF did show signs that the germ of Eurocommunism had not been completely exterminated in the party. An editorial in *Revolution* mentioned that the "coup de force" in Poland did not resolve anything. This editorial stood up thereafter in the face of attempts by Leroy to get the Political Bureau to issue a disavowal.[34] *Revolution* printed the text of the PCI's critical statement on Poland, although only after *Rencontres Communistes* had already done so. The Communist minister of professional training, Marcel Rigout, supported the critical comments of the French government that challenged the nature of the Polish system.[35]

In February 1983 the Political Bureau, in preparation for the March municipal elections, stated that the social and economic reforms achieved by the government were some of the greatest reforms in French history.[36] But the government's popularity had nevertheless declined in public opinion polls, and the left lost thirty mayorships in the election; the PCF score remained near its 1981 showing (15.9 percent), and the Socialists lost electoral ground.

The Mitterrand government, under the initiative of Finance Minister Jacques Delors, began to put in place a concentrated austerity program after the March elections. The "Socialist," or modification-of-structures, phase of the governmental action would now be consolidated. With the public sector enlarged and a temporary reflation of the economy concluded, the Socialists now turned to matters of "gestion," that is, to managing the state and the economy; the reforming impulse was momentarily spent. Delors and the majority of Socialists were concerned about France's growing trade deficit and a persistently higher inflation rate than those of its Western economic partners. The state budget was being strained by the new demands of both the purchasing and the financing of capital investment for the nationalized firms and also the increase in social welfare costs derived from a series of transfer payments to the least well off. While a tax on wealth had gone into effect, the economy was not growing at a rate at which these combined costs could be absorbed. Several devaluations of the franc had occurred, which added to business uncertainty.

The Socialists had begun to realize that the private sector needed relief from taxation. Even the CERES group, which criticized the Delors plan for paying too strict attention to France's international financial standing, stated in its polemical treatise *Le Socialisme et la France* that in France's economy, "The power of decision over investment and production is largely held by the private sector." The Socialists, managing the enlarged state sector alone, could not stimulate the economy without complementary private investment in the private sector. In other words, industrial socialism was still forced to rely on capitalist investment.

The Socialists were also having second thoughts about pumping state funds into declining industries like the iron and steel industry, reasoning that these funds could be better utilized in other sectors of the economy. These changes in Socialist attitudes presented a real dilemma for the PCF. Could the PCF remain aligned to a government whose policies would begin negatively to affect the traditional PCF working-class base? Could the PCF, which has never acknowledged the legitimacy of any claims coming from business, countenance a government that was now working comfortably with the business sector in devising economic policy?

THE PCF'S STRATEGY OF CRITICAL SUPPORT

The PCF began a period of critical support for the new government of Pierre Mauroy after the announcement of the Delors austerity plan in March 1983. The party insisted that its own amendments to the plan be "taken into consideration" and waffled between the position either that the plan was contrary to the objectives of the Mitterrand electoral program or, alternately, that the objectives of the plan were correct but that the means used were erroneous. At one point, Leroy wrote in *L'Humanité* that the Delors plan did not have the PCF's approbation.[37] The PCF was not against the notion of austerity as such, but its own notion of austerity related only to capitalist waste ("gachis") and speculation. Of course, the PCF could not be outflanked on the left by the CERES group inside the PS, which had quickly declared the Delors plan to be contrary to the "Socialist Project" for the 1980s.[38]

The establishment of austerity measures revived existing tensions inside the PCF. Reportedly, Fiterman did not want to participate in the new Mauroy government in March, preferring to return to the party to better defend the governmental orientation policy within the party.[39] Antoine Spire outlined the split inside the PCF; he lumped together Fiterman, PCF spokesman Pierre Juquin, and Ministers Marcel Rigout and Anicet Le Pors on the one hand as favorable to the PCF's governmental orientation and the need for the PCF to take distance from the U.S.S.R. and cited hardliners Gaston Plissonier, Roland Leroy, and Andre Lajoinie on the other hand, who were opposed to social democracy and who embraced Eastern European socialism.[40] Presumably, Marchais played his usual role of "sitting on the fence." These differences in party attitudes were reflected in the CGT in contrasting statements made by Henri Krasucki, the secretary general of CGT, who called for a "reasonable autonomy" from the government in April, and former Secretary General of the CGT Georges Seguy, who called for a much stronger "critical participation" by the PCF in June.[41]

PCF ministerial participation did present a potential new outlook for the party, but this was largely circumscribed.[42] Anicet Le Pors, who was minister of public administration, wrote in the June 1983 issue of *Cahiers du Communisme* that the PCF needed to reevaluate the role of the state in social change by seeing it in more nuanced terms. The state represented more than merely a locus of class struggle and or bourgeois domination[43] However, Georges Lavau noted that aside from the ministers and their immediate collaborators PCF governmental participation did not filter back into the party.[44] Nor has any evidence emerged that the PCF has been able to secure many posts in the public administration or in nationalized industry. The PCF had hoped that the new laws on workers' rights in nationalized industry would allow the CGT greater leverage. However, the number of official CGT adherents dropped 15 percent from 1981 to 1983.[45]

The Mitterrand government was hit by a series of corporatist demands in the 1983–84 period, the most notable being opposition to the plan for unifying all education under the public aegis. This temporarily served to reinforce the PCF's participation. The Central Committee meeting in September 1983 saw the right as menacing the government; the PCF reasoned that the right did not wish to govern through intermediaries (the PS).[46] Incredibly, the PCF began to loosen its conception of the economic crisis, allowing for problems in the international economy and the problem of technological change, although it would not agree to the possibility of technological change producing unavoidable unemployment. The party leadership announced it would now judge the government from a global perspective.

Mitterrand and the Socialists, under the institutions of the Fifth Republic, were willing to grant more autonomy to the PCF on matters of foreign policy than in internal policy. In May 1983, for example, Marchais created a furor by reversing PCF policy on the Euromissile issue to fall directly in line with that of the CPSU when he called for the "taking into consideration" of France's nuclear forces in the Geneva negotiations among the superpowers.[47] He followed this statement by conferring with the Soviets in July in Moscow. Mitterrand then personally reiterated government policy concerning the autonomy of France's nuclear forces in a rebuff to Marchais's statements. However, the matter abruptly ended without the Socialists calling for a vote of confidence from the PCF in the National Assembly despite demands from the right that the Communist ministers be removed from the government.

By the end of 1983, the PCF still saw possibilities for stimulating working-class action in the enterprises through the implementation of the Auroux Laws on workers' rights. On this score, it sided with governmental policy. At the same time the PCF began to support working-class demonstrations and defend workers' rights *against* the effects of government austerity measures such as the closing of plants. However, without a realistic program of economic modernization, the PCF was doing little more than playing its usual role as a quasi trade union, leaning heavily on the CGT. As a result, the PCF's public image was not enhanced by its participation in government, since it was seen to be playing a double game of support and opposition vis-à-vis the government.

Delegations from the PS and the PCF met in December 1983 to verify the June 1983 accord for government; the agreement pointed out in a positive tone the government's considerable accomplishments. Although the PCF had voted to accept the government's budget for 1984, its relation with the government was clearly beginning to show strain, and hardliners in the party were already crying the alarm of "social democracy" in reference to the governmental orientation. Marchais made a speech in October 1983 supportive of the government that was given a large dissemination by the party. However, the speech was not given choice space in *L'Humanité-Dimanche*.[48]

While the PCF gave no hint that it might actually leave the government, it was beginning to strongly imply that the government was "Socialist" despite the presence of Communist ministers. Alternately, the PCF implied that the government was not holding to the Mitterrand program agreed to by the PS and the PCF in 1981, despite the new agreement of December 1983. In April 1984, Marchais called the government's decision to close several steel plants a "tragic error," and along with several members of the Political Bureau, he marched with unemployed steel workers from the Lorraine region in a protest on the streets of Paris.[49] The PS, sensitive on issues of national politics, felt that this symbolic action was going too far and forced the PCF to deliver a vote of confidence for the government in the National Assembly. The PCF made it clear, however, that being a part of the governmental majority did not imply unconditional support on each and every policy.

With Laurent Fabius replacing Pierre Mauroy as prime minister in July 1984, the PCF chose to leave the government. The Socialists now embarked on a modernization of France's economy within the context of austerity. But it was the PCF's continual electoral decline that made continued participation in the government problematic. In the June 1984 elections for the European Parliament, the PCF fell to 11 percent of the vote. Its participation in the government had not helped it retrieve lost electoral ground, and now the PCF was asked to support policies that directly injured its traditional working-class base. The Central Committee meeting in late June stated that the high rate of abstention on the left in the European elections was due to deception and discontent provoked by government policy. It stated, "The traditional Communist electorate ... is today hurt the most by the policy of rigor [austerity]."[50]

Most observers were nonetheless surprised when the PCF decided not to accept ministerial participation in the Fabius government and abstained on the vote of confidence called for by the government in the National Assembly. The Central Committee stated that after initiating a number of important measures, the government had reoriented its policies producing the aggravation of unemployment, economic stagnation, and the reduction of purchasing power, which, if continued, would result in the failure of the left in the legislative elections in March 1986.[51]

While the PCF was leaving the government in July, it still considered itself a part of the governmental majority. However, in September, Leroy set the tone for the PCF's new orientation by stating point blank, "We are no longer a part of the majority."[52] In December 1984, the PCF joined the parties of the right in voting against the government's budget for 1985, stating that it favored capital over labor.[53] The PCF was moving to a position that would culminate in a virtually total opposition to the Socialist government. The PCF openly classified the government as on the right and saw its policies as indistinguishable from the right-wing policies of previous non-Socialist governments. A year later, in December 1985, Lajoinie discounted any positive characterization for the Socialist-dominated legislature under Mitterrand, stating that history would pass a severe judgment on a Socialist majority that had inclined before the power of capital.[54] Forgotten was the time of the PCF participation in the government; the 1982–83 period of high solidarity with the Mitterrand government now seemed a long way off.

The "trade union" strategy of total opposition to the government was put in place at the Twenty-fifth Congress in February 1985, and it did not go unchallenged in the PCF. However, most of the life had already been taken out of the party in the 1978–81 period; the Eurocommunists had been largely excluded. The project of resolution for the Congress in October 1984 witnessed six abstentions at the Central Committee meeting, including those of Juquin and Rigout. In *L'Humanité*, Juquin criticized the project for not allowing any criticism of the comportment of the leadership from 1977 to 1984 and for not developing a more "profound" analysis of the PCF's inability to propose a French road to socialism. Juquin called for a total independence of the PCF, both "intellectual and practical," from the socialist countries.[55]

At the Congress, for the first time in PCF history, three Federations rejected the project proposed by the leadership. Juquin defended his positions at the Congress, but unlike Roger Garaudy at the Nineteenth Congress in 1969, instead of dead silence, Juquin received scattered applause. The PCF leadership, despite stamping out most of the dynamic element in the party with the exclusion of the Eurocommunist tendency, has not been able to prevent noticeable changes in party psychology relating to party discipline. While Juqin was removed from the Political Bureau, both he and Rigout were retained by the Central Committee, thus maintaining official dissenters at this high level for the first time in PCF history.

The PCF had in effect given up on any political project after its Twenty-fifth Congress in February 1985. Those who defended the governmental orientation were rebuffed as the PCF chose to use the arm of the CGT to menace the government and arouse working-class dissent, but without any political perspective. If successful this negative force would allow the PCF to recoup its electoral loses and, in the face of an electoral decline of the PS, emerge in a stronger position on the left. With Mitterrand being forced to compromise with the right in the

National Assembly, the PCF could again play its freewheeling role in the opposition concerned with defending categorical interests and the interests of "PCF Incorporated." However, the PCF policy of absolute opposition is a sterile one, and whether or not the PCF gained a few points in the March legislative elections mattered little as the PCF sacrificed and lost its prominent role in French politics.

THE OLD RUT OF SOCIAL DEMOCRACY OR A THIRD WAY OF SOCIALISM?

The Socialist legislature stayed the entire duration of its electoral mandate and established the left, that is, the PS, as an instrumental force in French politics for some time to come. But what other conclusions can be drawn from the Mitterrand experiment?

The Socialists entered the government determined not to duplicate the experience of social democracy in the West; there was a keen desire to transform the structure of French capitalism and of the French state. While a left PS was a product of the tenacity of French Communism, to cast the PS in the light of the PCF would be a mistake.[56] The bickering over economic policy between the "right" and "left" in the PS in the 1970s was largely rhetorical.[57] All the Socialists, including Michel Rocard and Jacques Delors, saw the nationalizations as a privileged tool of governmental policy.[58] Industrial socialism was necessary for France because a capitalism dominated by finance capital had failed to invest in the economic future of the country. The French Socialists did not reject the market as an important allocator of capital and labor, but they clearly preferred an indicative plan, developed by the state, to assure that key economic projects be carried out. The French Socialists never envisioned the breaking of economic relations with the capitalist world market as a viable policy. The Socialists, on the contrary, via industrial socialism sought to elevate France's position on the world market and in the international division of labor. Following the theses of Alain Boublil, only the technological leaders at the "core" of the world economy have the freedom to decide on their pattern of economic development. For countries in the "periphery," the "type of society" is handed down to them.[59] In a nutshell, freedom of maneuver for Socialist goals in France depended on how effective a force Socialist policy would be in conquering capitalism on its own terrain.

In the area of the functioning of nationalized industry, the problems of central planning were to be avoided by decentralizing decision making, following the model already used by Renault. Managers of the nationalized firms were to make a contract with the state concerning investment and production goals ("plans d'entreprise"). It is difficult to tell how successful this form of indicative planning has been. In the area of administration, the nationalized firms have been inhibited by not having enough leeway to form mergers or to sell off units to enhance their efficiency.[60]

In terms of workers' rights, the Auroux Laws proposed that workers in firms with more than fifty workers form work groups ("comités d'entreprise") where they would have a right of self-expression on working conditions and a right to be informed by management about new technology, layoffs, and other issues affecting their jobs. While the Auroux Laws still recognize the right of management to manage, they have uplifted the status of the working class in the workplace considerably. In other areas of governmental policy—culture, education, the media, governmental administration, and so on—the Socialists embarked upon ambitious projects with varying results.

The Mitterrand experiment represented a radical departure from previous, rightist governments in France, and it tried to find new directions for Socialist policy. On the other hand, self-identified limits to the French Socialist Project existed at the outset of the Mitterrand presidency, limits relating primarily to France's freedom to maneuver vis-à-vis the world economy. The French Socialists came to power with an idyllic view of what they could accomplish in power as a result of having rested so many years in the opposition; a turn away from ideology toward administration was inevitable. However, the thread of continuity that unites the dual moments of the Socialist experience while in and out of power is often lost by observers, who tend to view either Socialist ideology before 1982 or Socialist policy after 1983 in absolute terms.

THE MODERNIZATION OF FRENCH SOCIALISM

By 1983, scarcely two years into the Socialist-dominated legislature, it became apparent to the French Socialists that the early spate of reforms had to give way to the administration of the economy; it was really then that the Socialists understood concretely, in power, what they had only theorized about when out of power, namely, that their ability to implement policy was subject to the economic constraints of the world economy and to the laws of productivity in general. CERES, at that time, argued that the government had to act both on demand and on *production*, to reorient savings toward productive investment.[61] Distribution could only follow from production; state spending could not be maintained beyond certain limits. This was certainly not a position of postwar social democracy; it would be more accurately labeled one of "supply-side" or "industrial" socialism.

The "left-wing" CERES concluded that socialism was not on the immediate agenda for France: "We cannot remove ourselves too far away from the margin of maneuver that will be tolerated [by the other capitalist powers and principally the U.S.]"[62] This view of CERES occurred in the context of a lively economic debate among the Socialists concerning the Delors austerity plan, with CERES purportedly proposing an alternate economic strategy. But once again disagreements among the Socialists were overplayed by the French press. CERES' criticism was merely that greater attention be paid to the economic restructuring of French industry, that is, to industrial capital, than to the monetary concerns of the balance of payments and the exchange rate of the franc, highlighted in the Delors plan.[63]

By the fall of 1983 Prime Minister Mauroy summed up the Socialist predicament by pointing out that the left had to manage an economy and a society that it challenged in both structure and organization. The government was subject to the constraints of "a system that is not our system."[64] At this time Mitterrand acknowledged that the Socialists' goal was that of a "mixed economy"and made explicit that while the PS was a party that acknowledged the existence of social classes and class struggle, the aim of the government was to establish peace among the classes.[65]

The PS approached the March 1986 legislative elections in a political situation radically different from that of the 1970s. The PS was now a governmental party and the sole major party defending the policies of the Mitterrand government. The Socialists felt that the decline of the PCF was permanent, meaning that the PS now had to fill the entire space of the left in France; the union of the left with the PCF was outdated. In the meantime, the PS had to try to bring into line the existing disjunction between the ideology and expectations it developed and was associated with in the 1970s and the sober reality of the actual governmental experience in the 1980s. The Socialists' conception of socialism and what was implied by "Socialist" policy had to be rethought if they were to reinvigorate the PS as a force of attraction.

The PS held an important Congress at Toulouse in October 1985 that produced considerable unity in the party and positioned the party so that it could compete for the centrist "swing" vote with the right while also fulfilling the void left by the PCF on the left. While the Socialists rested on their "choice of society," they acknowledged that it was necessary to produce in order to be able to distribute and be able to fulfill Socialist ideals. In an attempt to rekindle interest on the left the PS called for a minimum social income in France for workers who had exhausted their unemployment benefits.[66]

Prime Minister Fabius called for the modernization of socialism or the "socialism of the possible" while stating that the Socialist Project rested on more justice combined with more efficiency.[67] Rocard no longer saw two socialisms in France, one centralist and the other "autogestionnaire," as he had in the 1970s, but rather he saw a single socialism operating within economic constraints and in the interests of society as a whole. Instead of conceiving PS strategy in terms of the "front de classe," he saw the PS as a catchall "parti de salariat."[68] PS party chairman Lionel Jospin responded to the question of whether or not the PS was social democratic by stating, "If it [social democracy] means to distinguish us from the Communist movement, then yes. If it means that we believe in socialism and in democracy, then, of course. If it means that we renounce structural reform and the public sector, then, that is out of the question. . . . Are we a class party? I don't know. But we are a party tied to the salariat."[69]

The major campaign debate for the legislative elections between the PS and the right hinged on the nationalization issue, with the right calling for a major denationalization of banking and industry should it gain control of the legislature. It was important for the right not to let the principle of nationalization or the enlarged state sector stand. Otherwise the structural changes brought about by Socialist policy would be conceived of as "givens" in future elections and the right would find itself doing battle on "Socialist" terrain.

The PS, whether victorious or not in the legislative elections, will probably remain the largest party and the pivotal force in French politics in the future. But the Socialists, as they realign and come to reflect the image of French society as a whole, must respond to this fundamental antinomy posed by CERES, which is relevant to the entire Euroleft: "How can we realize Socialism in France, when it is not on the agenda in Germany, Italy, Spain, Britain or the US. . . . What would it mean to do so?"[70] The French Socialists, as key actors among the Euroleft, have gained considerable insight into this question in the course of the Mitterrand experiment. But that is only a beginning.

NOTES

1. Jean Elleinstein, speech at the Western Society for French History, University of Southern California, March 22, 1985.
2. *Rencontres-Communistes*, June 26, 1981.
3. *Rencontres-Communistes*, July 3, 1981.
4. Interview with François Hincker, April 19, 1982.
5. *Rencontres-Communistes*, January 16, 1982.
6. Ibid.
7. *Le Monde*, June 12, 1981.
8. Ibid.
9. *Le Monde*, April 30, 1981.
10. *Le Monde*, May 17–18, 1981.
11. *Le Monde*, June 28–29, 1981. This view was expressed to me by Danielle

Tartakowsky and by Roger Martelli. Interview with Danielle Tartakowsky, April 28, 1982; interview with Roger Martelli, May 13, 1982.

12. *Le Monde*, July 3, 1981.
13. *Le Monde*, July 17, 1981.
14. *Le Monde*, July 2, 1981.
15. *Le Monde*, December 6–7, 1981.
16. *Le Monde*, May 7, 1982.
17. *L'Humanité*, October 30, 1981.
18. *Rencontres-Communistes*, November 6, 1981.
19. *L'Humanité*, October 13, 1981.
20. Ibid.
21. *Le Monde*, December 3, 1981.
22. *L'Humanité*, October 13, 1981.
23. Ibid.
24. *Le Monde*, December 24, 1981.
25. *Le Monde*, January 6, 1982.
26. *Le Monde*, January 21, 1982.
27. *Rencontres-Communistes*, February 20, 1982.
28. *Le Monde*, May 7, 1982.
29. *L'Humanité*, April 21, 1982.
30. *Le Nouvel Observateur*, May 22, 1982.
31. *Le Monde*, September 10, 1982.
32. *Le Monde*, October 15, 1982.
33. *Le Monde*, December 22, 1982.
34. *Le Monde*, October 15, 1982.
35. Ibid.
36. *Cahiers du Communisme*, (March 1983).
37. *L'Humanité*, April 26, 1983.
38. *Le Monde*, April 5, 1983.
39. *Le Monde*, October 29, 1983.
40. *Le Monde*, August 1, 1984.
41. *Le Monde*, April 12 and June 11, 1983.
42. For a detailed discussion on the Communist ministers and the Mitterrand government see Armen Antonian and Irwin Wall, "The French Communists under François Mitterrand," *Political Studies* 2 (June 1985).
43. *Cahiers du Communisme* (June 1983).
44. Georges Lavau, "Le Parti communiste: Un Congrès de survie," *Revue Politique et Parlementaire* 914 (January–February 1985): 14.
45. *Le Monde*, November 19, 1985. For recent analysis of the CGT see Mark Kesselman, ed., *The French Workers' Movement* (London: Goerge Allen & Unwin, 1984); Peter Lange, George Ross, and Maurizio Vannicelli, *Unions, Change and Crisis: French and Italian Union Strategy and the Political Economy, 1945–1980* (London: George Allen & Unwin, 1984).
46. *Le Monde*, September 21, 1983.
47. *L'Humanité*, June 1, 1983.
48. *Le Monde*, October 29, 1983.
49. *Le Monde*, April 13 and 15–16, 1984.
50. *Le Monde*, July 27 and 29, 1984.

51. *Le Monde,* July 20, 1984.

52. François Platon, "Les Communistes au gouvernement: Une Experience complexe et contradictoire," *Revue Politique et Parlementaire 914* (January–February 1985): 38.

53. *Le Monde,* December 20, 1984.

54. *Le Monde,* December 20, 1985.

55. *Le Monde,* January 12, 1985.

56. For an opposite view see D. S. Bell and Byron Criddle, *The French Socialist Party* (Oxford: Clarendon Press), 1984.

57. See David Hanley, "Les Variable de Solferino or Thoughts on Steering the Socialist Economy: An analysis of the economic discourse of the French Parti Socialiste," in Stuart Williams, ed., *Socialism in France: From Jaurès to Mitterrand* (London: Frances Pinter, 1983).

58. Volkmar Lauber, "The Economic Policy of the French Socialists," paper delivered at the American Political Science Association, Denver, Colorado, September 2–8, 1982, pp. 313 and 245. See also Volkmar Lauber, *The Political Economy of France: From Pompidou to Mitterrand* (New York: Praeger Publishers, 1983).

59. Ibid., p. 307.

60. This was pointed out by Alain Minc, director of CIE de Saint-Gobin, in a paper delivered on the theme "Continuity and Change in Mitterrand's France," December 5–8, 1985 at Cambridge, Massachusetts.

61. Jacques Mandrin, [Didier Motchane and Pierre Guidoni], *Le Socialism et La France* (Paris: Le Sycamore, 1983), p. 110.

62. Ibid., p. 120.

63. Ibid., p. 107.

64. *Le Monde,* September 2, 1983.

65. *Le Monde,* September 17, 1983.

66. *Le Monde,* October 15, 1985.

67. Ibid.

68. Ibid.

69. *Le Monde,* October 13–14, 1985.

70. Mandrin, p. 118.

13

Eurocommunism in Perspective

What is Eurocommunism? In the 1970s, journalists, politicians, academicians, and political observers were all buzzing about the term. Then, for a time, Eurocommunism as a concept seemed to disappear altogether. After 1979, when the Italian Communists ended their flirtation with governmental power, an event that followed in the wake of the defeat of the union of the left in France and a return of the PCF to Communist orthodoxy, Eurocommunism as a political movement certainly seemed to have lost its momentum. Yet the term *Eurocommunism* has found its way back into political discourse in the 1980s; it has become almost passé. But other than the nebulous criticism and disassociation from the image of Soviet society and from certain aspects of Soviet foreign policy by some of the nonruling Communist parties, does Eurocommunism have any meaning? If not, then how does Eurocommunism differ from other previous deviations in international Communism? In other words, why use the word at all?

In order to determine Eurocommunism's political specificity, it was necessary to approach the subject from a historical perspective. Eurocommunism emerged from the remnants of International Communism centering around the Bolshevik Revolution of 1917. Yet Eurocommunism is a contemporary concept even though many of its elements were traced to earlier political formulations among the European left from both Communist and Socialist inspiration. The positions of the Eurocommunist parties were scrutinized for content and for direction as Eurocommunism came to represent an unfolding ideology with its own rhythm of development apart from the fortunes of Eurocommunism as a political movement. But how were "Eurocommunist" positions really different from orthodox Communist positions? At what point did a mere political tactic become transformed into a veritable ideology? A balance sheet on Orthodox or Leninist Communism was developed to provide a basis to compare and contrast "Eurocommunist" formulations, to assess their authenticity.

Key reference points for Eurocommunist ideology began to emerge: the criticism of the party state and Soviet "socialism," the criticism of democratic centralism and Leninist ideology, the embracing of political democracy combined with the maintenance of a criticism of capitalist society, and the continued adherence to a vision of a classless society, that is, a communist vision. Eurocommunists or Eurocommunist Renovators were distinguished from orthodox Communists, and it was found that many left Socialists, with certain groupings in the French Socialist Party as the best example, could also be categorized in some sense as "Eurocommunist." Paradoxically, the parameters of Eurocommunism were both broader in scope than imagined, with the inclusion of certain elements of Western socialism, and also narrower, since it became apparent that the term *Eurocommunism* was specific to nonruling Communist parties in industrial democracies and that it was not relevant to the disagreements among ruling Communist parties. Eurocommunism not only became distinguishable from other schisms within the international Communist movement, such as Maoism or Titoism, but was projected outside this movement, becoming a distinct political ideology, whose fundamental ideological pillars rested on a criticism of the historical experiences and the political parties and models of society that currently embody international Communism. In other words, Eurocommunism ultimately challenged the very legitimacy of Leninist Communism as embodying the ideals of socialism and of carrying the aspirations of the majority of citizens where it had emerged in Eastern Europe.

By the 1980s the remnants of what was left of Eurocommunism as a political movement stemming from the Western Communist parties, with the PCI as the principal force, began to be compared to and aligned with an anticapitalist militancy within some of the Socialist parties in Western Europe, with the PS as the principal reference point. The concept of the Euroleft has come to the forefront with Eurocommunism as one of its components. Does this mean that a recomposition of the working-class movement in Europe is at hand, as the PCI suggests?

Certainly, many old conceptions and phrases relating to the European left have to be reworked. Communism and Eurocommunism, socialism and social democracy were clearly differentiated in order to describe the emerging reality on the European left, a reality that can no longer be explained by the dichotomy of Communism versus social democracy. Instead, the concepts of Eurocommunism and the Euroleft must be brought to the forefront.

A major analytical problem in dealing with a phenomenon such as

Eurocommunism is to decide whether it should be approached as a political movement based on popular orientation, as a temporary political strategy correspondng to the orientations of certain Communist parties, or as a full-fledged ideology. The difference therein determines whether or not Eurocommunism should be viewed as a conjunctural phenomenon or whether it should be viewed in the longer term as a basic set of ideas that go beyond the positions of a certain group of political parties at a given moment in time. Without question, the majority of earlier interpretations of Eurocommunism viewed it as a conjunctural phenomenon. Georges Lavau noted that the word was dropped by most political observers after the autumn of 1978 because the "certain reality" that Eurocommunism then represented, the convergence of the Italian, French, and Spanish Communist parties with common strategies and a similar ideological approach, on the threshold of government, seemed to be at an end.[1]

By 1979, these three parties had all been thwarted in their attempts to attain a share of governmental power, and one of them, the PCF, had changed its orientation, returning to an image more in line with orthodox Communism. The defection of the PCF supported those who doubted the authenticity of Eurocommunism's liberal thrust, preferring to see it in terms of a "Trojan horse" tactic. In addition, scholars who began to address the Eurocommunist phenomenon found "Eurocommunist" positions to be not unlike many earlier formulations of the three major Western Communist parties scattered here and there in the past, which detracted from the supposed novelty of the phenomenon.[2] Many argued that what was referred to as Eurocommunism actually had emerged separately in the Western Communist parties at earlier points in time.[3]

It is always incumbent upon a new phenomenon to prove its worth. With a phenomenon such as Eurocommunism, it was much easier, and indeed it was possible to view it initially as a national Communism and not as another communism. Such a view was made more plausible because the Eurocommunist parties persistently refused to claim universality for the democratic socialist model they propounded. In his famous *Eurocommunism and the State*, Santiago Carrillo noted explicitly that Eurocommunism was not a third road to socialism, nor would it deny the justification of the birth of the Communist parties.[4] The Eurocommunist parties wanted to remain attached to Eastern European socialism internationally while still being perceived as offering something different from Eastern European socialism nationally. Clearly, this state of affairs could not have endured for long without an "epreuve de verité." There was a period of "safe" Eurocommunism, during which the Western Communist parties had everything to gain by accentuating their differences with Eastern European socialism; by not, at the same time, having to make significant doctrinal concessions, they had nothing to lose. Thus, the following typical remark by Bogdan Szajkowsky was quite accurate during the early stages of Eurocommunism in the mid–1970s: "It is highly questionable whether Eurocommunism exists as a definable ideology as against Eurocommunist strategy."[5] But this period of "safe" Eurocommunism passed after 1978, and it was then that the PCF balked. Yet this turn of events, in which Eurocommunism seemed to evaporate as quickly as it had emerged, proved also to be temporary. What was planted in the first phase of Eurocommunism came to take root, if for no other reason than by the force of events.

The problem with viewing Eurocommunism in conjunctural terms is that it is then difficult to explain the series of events that I associate with a "second phase" of Eurocommunism hinging on the victory of a left Socialist Party in the key country of France whose positions bordered on the positions associated with Eurocommunism. The Socialist victory in France brought the PCF, Eurocommunist or not, directly into government. This occurred after a Eurocommunist "contestation" in France that first surfaced in 1978 and that continued thereafter unabated, with individual Communists taking positions that went well beyond earlier, more timid Eurocommunist notions. In fact, Jean Elleinstein has pointed out that the abandonment of Eurocommunism by the PCF radicalized those who were really attached to it by forcing them to take clearer positions.[6]

Then, with the events in Poland and the imposition of martial law in December 1981, the other major factor I associate with a "second phase" of Eurocommunism emerged as the PCI effectively split with Moscow, claiming that the evolution of the Eastern European societies toward democracy and socialism was blocked. In the process, the PCI and the PCE both called for a new internationalism, which would make the historical differentiations between Socialists and Communists obsolete. To comprehend these new events, a new term has been employed: *Euroleft*. However, as Enrico Berlinguer noted, the concept of Eurocommunism always contained within it the concept of the Euroleft.[7] So, again, things come full circle. What is Eurocommunism and what does it represent?

The political reality underlyiing the appearance of Eurocommunism in the West goes much deeper than the short-term policies of any one party or political formation. In this sense, Eurocommunism is but one form of a multivaried response of the European left to the crisis of the Western social system; socialism in France is another form that aims at the same reality. It then makes little sense to gauge the existence of Eurocommunism *solely* on the policy positions of a few political parties. A political party has its own specificity in the field of politics with its corresponding limitations. A political party rarely contains within it all the basic principles of any given ideology. Eurocommunism must be approached at both the political level (of parties, social movements, elections), and the ideological level—at the level of political discourse.

It is evident that the PCF did not make it to Eurocommunism in the 1970s. But it almost made it, and this is important. And the steps it did not take were taken for it by the PS. The PCF's positions in the 1960s, however similar in appearance, were not those of even the "safe" Eurocommunism the party flirted with in the 1970s. In the 1960s, the image of the Soviet Union was still solid in the eyes of substantial sections of the PCF electorate and beyond, into French society itself. Therefore, the PCF raison d'être was not challenged in its political overture with French society as it was in the 1970s, when it reiterated, albeit more forcefully and more coherently than before, the same democratic-oriented positions.

The example of the PCF demonstrated, above all, the immense difficulty in transforming a nonruling Communist party based on the principles of Leninism into a "Eurocommunist" party. As the PCF began to adopt Eurocommunist principles in the 1970s, it became evident to the party leadership that the system of party power, or Nomenklatura, would be undermined. It was then that the PCF hesitated and eventually turned away from Eurocommunism. The subsequent political decline of the PCF in France, after the abandonment of Eurocommunism, highlighted with éclat the problem of the continual existence of the Western Communist parties.

But that which came to pass with the PCF did not happen in the example of the PCI. The PCI, despite the system of Nomenklatura, has broken with its historical foundations; it has become a full-fledged Eurocommunist Party and is no longer a part of international Communism as it has been traditionally understood. A nonruling Communist Party, since it is not ensconced in a position of society-wide power in the manner of a ruling Communist Party, *can change* its orientation to power and society; in the cases of the PCI and the PCE, they have changed.

The PCE, since its legalization in 1975, has lived out the forty years of the postwar history of the Western Communist parties concomitantly, in a very short period. That there are now two Communist parties in Spain, one Eurocommunist and one pro-Soviet, with the CPSU supporting the latter, should come as no surprise. Eurocommunism, because of its merging of socialism and democracy, was always on a collision course with Soviet Communism. Those in the Western Communist parties who were unwilling or unable to maintain this course, with the figures of Santiago Carrillo and Georges Marchais as symbols, were soon eclipsed. Carrillo was eliminated from the PCE leadership, and his positions pale next to those of the Eurocommunist Renovators in Spain. As for Marchais, his party was displaced by the French Socialists and eclipsed by the evolution of French society. The PCF sacrificed its prominent role in French politics, that is, it sacrificed its *real* interests in France, for a fading Soviet star. The PCI, on the other hand, has labeled the further development of Soviet society as blocked and has faced up to its challenging role as a party with a third of the Italian electorate that seeks to transform the basis of Italian capitalist society. It is likely that the PCI will find itself in this role as the head of the Italian nation.

In the broadest sense, Eurocommunism is an emerging response to the splitting of the European left into Socialist and Communist factions predicated on differing views of the meaning of the Bolshevik Revolution. It is another attempt to overcome the historical breach between Communists and Socialists. As nonruling Communist parties shed the umbilical cord of Soviet Communism, so too have Social Democrats come to reevaluate their relation to capitalism in the West, readopting a critical attitude toward bourgeois society. Thus, the basis for the mutual antagonisms between Communists and Social Democrats has all but evaporated, and it makes more sense in contemporary European politics to refer to the two groups as "Socialists" and "Eurocommunists."

Because Eurocommunism emanated from Leninist Communism, its critical direction has been most often aimed at the U.S.S.R. Not surprisingly, then, the Eurocommunist target sooner or later had to be Lenin. The PCE dropped specific reference to Lenin as one of its founding fathers in its party statutes at the Nineteenth Congress in 1978. But only with the events in Poland did the PCI and the PCE remove most of the residue of their Leninist pasts. The PCI declared that the phase of the international working-class movement springing from 1917 had been exhausted, and that the evolution of the Eastern European countries toward socialism was blocked. Enrico Berlinguer indicated that the road to socialism in the West could not be founded on Lenin.[8] Maurice Duverger remarked that such a statement really went to the heart of the problem regarding the Soviet regime instead of meekly attributing the negative effects of Stalinism to historical conditions, as had traditionally been the explanation used by Western Communist parties to justify their continual alignment with the CPSU.[9] The PCE explicitly acknowledged the need to go beyond the scission of 1917, and it no longer considered itself the only legitimate representative of the working class in Spain.[10] The PCI rejected the notion of a homogeneous Communist movement separated from other socialist or "progressive" movements.[11] In doing so, the PCI rejected Lenin's major break with Marx centering on the political specifity of communists in the labor movement. This position of the PCI is congruent with the position of the French Socialist Léon Blum at the Congress of Tours in 1920. Blum had insisted at Tours that the Communist movement, as indicated by Marx and Engels in the *Communist Manifesto*, was to be based on recruitment from the widest possible range of social categories and that a Communist Party was not to be constituted by itself, as a party set against the other Socialist parties.[12] Pierre Hassner pointed out that the ideological meshing (with the Euroleft) implied by the PCI's conception of the European working-class movement breaks an essential dogma which Communist Parties have been based upon: "Their essentially different nature from the Socialist parties."[13]

Eurocommunist ideology never really conceded anything to social democracy in its opposition to capitalism. Thus, in an important sense, there was never really a social democratization of the Eurocommunist parties, as many had thought, and Eurocommunism as an ideology is not a brand of social democracy even though it has adopted the attitude of social democracy toward political democracy and pluralism. If the analogy must be made, Eurocommunism is more a throwback to the social democracy before 1917 in which communists existed alongside of socialists in the same movement. Thus, Eurocommunism has always remained "communist" in an important sense, even though, paradoxically, it rests above all on a criticism of *the Communism stemming from 1917*.

But Eurocommunism can also be approached from another angle, from elements of the Socialist International that have reradicalized social democracy's criticism of the capitalist economy and bourgeois society. The French Socialist Party is the best example of such an approach in spite of its seeming moderation in power. The PS, coming from social democracy, and the PCI, coming from Communism, have become the pivots of the Euroleft and the emerging "third road" to socialism.[14] While the PCI today represents the principal lever of the communist wing of the Euroleft, not to categorize the PS as also in some sense Eurocommunist would be shortsighted. It matters little whether or not the members of the PS, who uphold many of the Eurocommunist positions, actually consider themselves "communists." In point of fact, the antinomy between Socialists and Eurocommunists in France is still very strong. Most Socialists will not employ the "communist" label in any form. But matters viewed at this level remain superficial. Henri Fiszbin, head of the PCF's Paris Federation in the 1970s, who now considers himself a "Democratic and Unitary Communist," ran on the Socialist Party's list of candidates for the 1986 legislative elections. In relation to the recomposition of the working-class movement in France, Fiszbin has called for "a grouping of all social forces attached to Democratic Socialism in one great Socialist organization [the PS], capable of federating, within itself, the pluralist character of the left. Of course, within this formation, the Eurocommunist inspiration would take its full place."[15]

The political space the PS occupies in France has been previously held, at least partially, by the PCF. More importantly, the political ideology of the PS has many elements: the quest for a classless society, the elimination of the state as a state in the strict authoritarian sense of the term, the drive for the self-emancipation of the proletariat, itself broadly defined, that have a decidedly communist ring to them and hark back to Marx. For all intents and purposes, the PCI and the PS are occupying the same political space in their respective societies.

Jean Elleinstein has zeroed in on this phenomenon, noting that the words *Socialist* and *Communist* no longer have the same meaning *since the basis for their distinction, the historic split of 1919 to 1921, is no longer relevant.* The words *Socialist* and *Eurocommunist* have begun to convey the same political orientation as Eurocommunism becomes an integral part of the Euroleft.[16]

Jean Rony believes that the PCI will be the only Communist Party in Western Europe to maintain a major influence precisely because it changed in time, that is, ceased to be a traditional Communist Party and began to resemble more a Socialist Party.[17] The head of the Left Independents in Italy, Luigi Anderlini, whose group often runs on the PCI slate of candidates, calls the PCI a different Communist Party, a party that fills much of the political space of socialism and social democracy in Italy.[18]

The main difference between a Eurocommunist and a Democratic Socialist is that the former is more adamant, more ideological in his vision of a future classless society. A Eurocommunist is a Democratic Socialist who holds to a communist vision. Eurocommunism is the communist wing of the Euroleft, just as communism before 1917 was an element of the larger Socialist movement.

Eurocommunism then, is a throwback to the pre–World War I Socialist movement in an effort to retrieve a lost socialist heritage that originated in Marx. The distinction between Marx and Lenin and the emergence of a more solid critique of Soviet society in Eurocommunist thinking were brought out forcefully by Yvon Quiniou in France writing in the Eurocommunist-oriented *Rencontres Communistes*. Quiniou found Lenin's conception of vanguardism surprising in a theory (Marx's) that, in the beginning, had as its basis the recognition of the decisive force of the popular masses. The Leninist conceptions have instead dispossessed the masses of their sovereignty since the right to make history became concentrated in the apparatus of a minority. Quiniou believed that this was so because of a double substitution:

first, the substitution of the party for the class (since the working classes can exist only through the party), and the second, the substitution of the leadership of the party for the entire party (inference to democratic centralism). Quiniou called this a "totalitarian deviation of Communist political practice contradicting the letter and the spirit of the Marxism of Marx."[19]

As I have pointed out, the critique of this "totalitarian deviation" was already developed by Rosa Luxemburg, who, despite her support for a minority seizure of power in a backward Russia, criticized Lenin and the Bolsheviks regarding the formation of the Communist Party, characterizing Lenin's party policies as outlining a "most pitiful centralism." For Karl Kautsky, the Bolshevik Revolution as a *socialist* revolution under backward conditions was "a wild experiment," and the key relationship between the working-class party (the Communist Party) and the working class was distorted, since a small fraction of the working class (the Bolsheviks) claimed to rule all of society. In other words, dictatorship was instilled in the Bolshevik logic of power from the outset, irrespective of historical conditions, and apart from the state ownership of the means of production, which came later.

Fernando Claudin has outlined three points of reference by which to judge the credibility of Eurocommunist parties. Claudin noted that Eurocommunist parties must (1) deny the Socialist label to the U.S.S.R., (2) reject any hegemonism in the labor movement, and (3) reject democratic centralism in the party.[20]

Jean Elleinstein has summarized the Eurocommunist intervention as the critique of "real, existing socialism"; a radical response to the advanced capitalist societies of the West, which are experiencing a crisis; and the definition of a new politics beyond the established traditions of Communism, socialism, social democracy, and extreme-left politics, which, nonetheless, integrates aspects of these earlier formations.[21] For Elleinstein, Eurocommunism assimilates from the Communist parties the Communist role in the resistance, the obdurate defense and organization of workers, and support for previous anticolonial struggles. From the Socialists and Social Democratic parties, it conserves the idea of political democracy as a universal idea and many important social reforms initiated by social democracy. The new element to the question of the European left, according to Elleinstein, is the renewed willingness of Socialist and Social Democratic parties to make a rupture with capitalism and the intention of some Communist parties to find a new way between reform and revolution based on a democratic, pacific, legal, and gradual road to socialism.[22]

For Georges Lavau, the prefix *Euro* that precedes *communism* connotes "liberal."[23] Indeed, Eurocommunism is a liberal communism that contains and that emanates from many elements of the radical liberal tradition. The Eurocommunist position goes back to the Socialist Jean Jaurès, who, interpreting the liberal political philosopher John Locke, wrote, "Social property has to be created to guarantee private property in its real sense, that is, the property that the human individual has and ought to have in his own person."[24] Eurocommunist theory rests on one interpretation of the liberal definition of property that Guido de Ruggiero noted led to Communism.[25] Eurocommunism recognizes major elements of the liberal tradition: the separation of powers, universal suffrage, free elections, and the basic freedoms of speech, association, and so on. It supports the concept of the democratic state. It differs politically from the modern variations of liberalism in its critique of capitalism and in its decidedly socialist philosophy. It still must be considered a type of communism since it maintains a vision of a classless society as a central ideological principle.

NOTES

1. Georges Lavau, "Eurocommunism: Four Years On," *European Journal of Political Research* 7 (December 1979): 359.

2. Ibid., p. 360.

3. Bogdan Szajkowski, "Roots of Eurocommunism," *Contemporary Crisis* 3 (July 1979): 256.

4. Santiago Carrillo, *Eurocommunism and the State* (Westport, Conn.: Lawrence Hill & Company, 1978), p. 9.

5. Szajkowski, p. 255.

6. Interview with Jean Elleinstein, April 26, 1982.

7. *Le Monde*, March 31, 1982.

8. *Le Monde*, December 17, 1981.

9. *Le Monde*, December 24, 1981.

10. *Le Monde*, January 13, 1982.

11. *Révolution*, February 12–18, 1982.

12. Léon Blum, in Annie Kriegel, ed., *Le Congrès de Tours* (Paris: René Julliard, 1964), p. 107.

13. Pierre Hassner, in Simon Serfaty and Lawrence Gray, eds., *The Italian Communist Party* (Westport, Conn.: Greenwood Press), 1980.

14. Interview with Jean Elleinstein, April 26, 1982.

15. Henri Fiszbin, "Il y a encore des communistes à gauche," *Revue Politique et Parlementaire* 914 (January–February 1985): 55.

16. Interview with Jean Elleinstein, April 26, 1982.

17. Interview with Jean Rony, May 27, 1982.

18. Interview with Luigi Anderlini, May 24, 1982.

19. *Rencontres-Communistes*, November 28, 1981.

20. Fernando Claudin, in Carl Marzani, *The Promise of Eurocommunism* (Westport, Conn.: Lawrence Hill & Company, 1980). p. 45.

21. *Le Monde*, February 3, 1982.

22. Ibid.

23. Georges Lavau, "Eurocommunism: Four Years On," *European Journal of Political Research* 7 (December 1979): 361.

24. Jean Jaurès, *Studies in Socialism* (London: Independent Labour Party, 1906), p. 29.

25. Guido de Ruggiero, *The History of European Liberalism* (Boston: Beacon Press, 1959), p. 27.

Bibliography

BOOKS AND ARTICLES

Adler, Alexandre, Francis Cohen, and Maurice Décaillot. *L'URSS et nous.* Paris: Editions Sociales, 1978.

Adler, Alexandre, and Jean Rony. *L'Internationale et le genre humain.* Paris: Mazarine, 1980.

Albright, David E., ed. *Communism and Political Systems in Western Europe.* Boulder, Colo.: Westview Press, 1979.

Amyot, Grant. *The Italian Communist Party.* New York: St. Martin's Press, 1981.

Antonian, Armen, and Irwin Wall. "The French Communists under François Mitterrand." *Political Studies* 2 (June 1985).

Aron, Raymond. *La Révolution introuvable.* Paris: Librairie Arthéme Fayard, 1968.

Aspaturian, Vernon V., Jiri Valenta, and Daivd P. Burke; eds. *Eurocommunism between East and West.* Bloomington: Indiana University Press, 1980.

Assises du Socialisme. *Pour le socialisme.* Paris: Stock, 1974.

Azcarate, Manuel. "L'U.R.S.S. contre nous: Dissidents et Eurocommunistes." *Dialectiques* 24–25 (Autumn 1981).

Bacot, Paul. "Le Front de classe." *Revue Française de Science Politique* 28 (April 1978).

Bahro, Rudolf. *The Alternative in Eastern Europe.* London: Verso, 1981.

Baudouin, Jean. "L'Echec communiste de juin 1981: Recul électoral ou crise hégémonique?" *Pouvoirs* 20 (1982).

———. "Le P.C.F.: Retour a l'archaisme?" *Revue Politique et Parlementaire* (November–December 1980).

———. "Les Phénomènes de contestation au sein du parti communiste français (April 1978–May 1979)." *Revue Française de Science Politique* 30 (February 1980).

Bell, David S. "Eurocommunism: The Revised Standard Version," *Communist Affairs* (April 1982).

————, and Byron Criddle. *The French Socialist Party*. Oxford: Clarendon Press, 1984.

Bérégovoy, Pierre. "Le Front de classe: Force et problémes de la stratégie socialiste." *Le Nouvelle Revue Socialiste* 25 (1977).

Bernstein, Eduard. *Evolutionary Socialism*. New York: Schocken Books, 1978.

Blackmer, Donald L. M. *Unity in Diversity: Italian Communism and the Communist World*. Cambridge, Mass.: M. I. T. Press, 1968.

————, and Sidney Tarrow, eds. *Communism in Italy and France*. Princeton, N. J.: Princeton University Press, 1975.

Boggs, Carl, and David Plotke, eds. *The Politics of Eurocommunism*. Boston: South End Press, 1980.

Boissonnat, Jean. *Les Socialistes face aux patrons*. Paris: L'Expansion/Flammarion, 1977.

Borella, François. *Les Partis politiques dans la France d'aujourd'hui*. Paris: Editions du Seuil, 1973.

Borkenau, Franz. *World Communism: A History of the Communist International*. Ann Arbor: University of Michigan Press, 1962.

Brower, Daniel R. *The New Jacobins*. Ithaca, N. Y.: Cornell University Press, 1968.

Brown, Bernard. *Socialism of a Different Kind*. Westport, Conn.: Greenwood Press, 1982.

————, ed. *Eurocommunism and Eurosocialism*. New York: Cyrco Press, 1979.

Carrillo, Santiago. *Le Communisme malgré tout*. Interviews with Lilly Marcou. Paris: Presses Universitaires de France, 1984.

————. *Eurocommunism and the State*. Westport, Conn.: Lawrence Hill & Company, 1978.

CERES. *Le CERES par lui-meme*. Paris: Christian Bourgeois, 1978.

Charzet, Michel, and Ghislaine Toutain. Le CERES: Un Combat pour le socialisme. Paris: Calmann-Lévy, 1975.

Chevenement, Jean-Pierre. *Les Socialistes, les communistes et les autres*. Paris: Aubier Montaigne, 1977.

Childs, David, ed. *The Changing Face of Western Communism*. London: Croom Helm, 1980.

Claudin, Fernando. *The Communist Movement: From Comintern to Cominform*. New York: Monthly Review Press, 1975.

————. *Eurocommunism and Socialism*. London: New Left Books, 1978.

Dallin, Alexander, ed. *Diversity in International Communism*. New York: Columbia University Press, 1963.

de Ruggiero, Guido. *The History of European Liberalism*. Boston: Beacon Press, 1959.

Djilas, Milovan. *The New Class*. New York: Frederick A. Praeger, 1957.

Duhamel, Oliver, and Henri Weber. *Changer le PC?* Paris: Presses Universitaires de France, 1979.

Duverger, Maurice. *Lettre Ouvert aux socialistes*. Paris: Albin Michel, 1976.

Dux, Dieter. *Ideology in Conflict: Communist Political Theory*. Princeton, N. J.: P. Van Nostrand Company, 1963.

Elleinstein, Jean. *Ils Vous Trompent, Camarades!* Paris: Belford, 1981.

————. *Le P. C.* Paris: Bernard Grasset, 1976.

──────. *The Stalin Phenomenon*. London: Lawrence and Wishart, 1976.

Elliott, Charles F., and Carl A. Linden, eds. *Marxism in the Contemporary West*. Boulder, Colo.: Westview Press, 1980.

Fabre, Jean, François Hincker, and Lucien Seve. *Les Communistes et l'état*. Paris: Editions Sociales, 1977.

Fejto, François. "Les Variations du PCF." *France Forum* (November–December 1981).

Filo della Torre, Paolo, Edward Mortimer, and Jonathan Story, eds. *Eurocommunism: Myth or Reality?* New York: Penguin Books, 1979.

Fiszbin, Henri. *Les Bouches s'ouvrent*. Paris: Bernard Grasset, 1980.

Garraud, Philippe. "Discours, practiques et idéologie dans l'evolution du Parti Socialiste." *Revue Française de Science Politique* 28 (April 1978).

Godson, Roy, and Stephen Hasseler. *Eurocommunism*. New York: St. Martin's Press, 1978.

Griffith, William E., ed. *The European Left: Italy, France, and Spain*. Lexington, Mass.: Lexington Books, 1979.

Hincker, François. "Le Parti communiste au carrefour." *Projet* (January 1982).

──────. *Le Parti communiste au carrefour*. Paris: Albin Michel, 1981.

Ingrao, Pietro. *La Politique en grand et en petit*. Paris: François Maspero, 1979.

Jaurés, Jean. *Studies in Socialism*. London: Independent Labour Party, 1906.

Jenson, Jane, and George Ross. *The View from Inside*. Berkeley: University of California Press, 1984.

Johnson, Richard. *The French Communist Party versus the Students*. New Haven, Conn.: Yale University Press, 1972.

Johnson, R. W. *The Long March of the French Left*. New York: St. Martin's Press, 1981.

Kaplan, Morton A., ed. *The Many Faces of Communism*. London: Collier Macmillan Publishers, 1978.

Kautsky, John H. "Karl Kautsky and Eurocommunism." *Studies in Comparative Communism* 14 (Spring 1981).

Kautsky, Karl. *Bolshevism at a Deadlock*. London: George Allen & Unwin, 1931.

──────. *The Dictatorship of the Proletariat*. Manchester: National Labour Press, 1920.

──────. *The Labour Revolution*. New York: The Dial Press, 1925.

──────. *Terrorism and Communism*. London: National Labour Press, 1920.

Kindersley, Richard, ed. *In Search of Eurocommunism*. New York: St. Martin's Press, 1981.

Kriegel, Annie. *Eurocommunism: A New Kind of Communism?* Stanford, Calif.: Hoover Institution Press, 1978.

──────. *The French Communists*. Chicago: University of Chicago Press, 1968.

──────, ed. *Le Congrés de Tours*. Paris: René Julliard, 1964.

Lange, Peter, and Maurizio Vannicelli. *The Communist Parties of Italy, France, and Spain: Postwar Change and Continuity*. London: George Allen & Unwin, 1981.

Lauber, Volkmar. *The Political Economy of France: From Pompidou to Mitterrand*. New York: Praeger Publishers, 1983.

Laurens, André, and Thierry Pfister. *Les Nouveaux Communistes*. Paris: Stock, 1973.

Lavau, Georges. *A Quoi Sert le Parti communiste français?* Paris: Librairie Arthéme Fayard, 1981.

———. "Eurocommunism: Four Years On." *European Journal of Political Research* 7 (December 1979).

Lavau, Georges. "Le Parti communiste: Un Congrés de survie." *Revue Politique et Parlementaire* 914 (January–February 1985).

Lenin, V. I. *The Lenin Anthology*. Robert C. Tucker, ed. New York: W. W. Norton & Co., 1975.

———. *What Is to Be Done?* New York: International Publishers, 1969.

Lieber, Nancy. "Ideology and Tactics of the French Socialist Party." *Government and Opposition* (Autumn 1977).

Luxemburg, Rosa. *Rosa Luxemburg Speaks*. Mary-Alice Waters, ed. New York: Pathfinder Press, 1970.

———. *The Russian Revolution and Leninism or Marxism?* Bertram D. Wolfe, ed. Ann Arbor: University of Michigan Press, 1961.

Machin, Howard, ed. *National Communism in Western Europe: A Third Way for Socialism?* London: Methuen, 1983.

McInnes, Neil. *Euro-Communism*. Beverly Hills, Calif.: Sage Publications, 1976.

Mandrin, Jacques. [Pierre Guidoni and Didier Motchane]. *Le Socialisme et la France*. Paris: Le Sycamore, 1983.

Marcou, Lilly, ed.. *L'U.R.S.S.: vue de gauche*. Paris: Presses Universitaires de France, 1982.

Marx, Karl, and Friedrich Engels. *The Marx-Engels Reader*. Robert C. Tucker, ed. New York: W. W. Norton & Co., 1972.

Marzani, Carl, *The Promise of Eurocommunism*. Westport, Conn.: Lawrence Hill & Company, 1980.

Middlemas, Keith. *Power and the Party: Changing Faces of Communism in Western Europe*. London: André Deutsch, 1980.

Mitterrand, François. *La Paille et le grain*. Paris: Flammarion, 1975.

Mujal-León, Eusebio. *Communism and Political Change in Spain*. Bloomington: Indiana University Press, 1983.

Napolitano, Giorgio, and Eric J. Hobsbaum. *The Italian Road to Socialism*. Westport, Conn.: Lawrence Hill & Co., 1977.

National Negotiating Committee of Solidarity Draft Program. *Socialist Review* 58 (September–October 1981).

Parti Socialiste Français. *Le Projet socialiste pour la France des années 80*. Paris: Club Socialiste du Livre, 1980.

Platon, François. "Les Communistes au gouvernement: Une Experience complexe et contradictoire," *Revue Politique et Parlementaire* 914 (January–February 1985).

Ranney, Austin, and Giovanni Sartori. *Eurocommunism: The Italian Case*. Washington, D. C.: American Enterprise Institute for Public Policy Research, 1978.

Rieber, Alfred J. *Stalin and the French Communist Party, 1941–1947*. New York: Columbia University Press, 1963.

Robrieux, Philippe. *L'Histoire intérieur du parti communiste*, 1972–1983, vol. 3. Paris: Fayard, 1982.

Rocard, Michel. "Entretien avec Michel Rocard." *Dialectiques* 31 (Winter 1981).

——. *Parler vrai*. Paris: Editions du Seuil, 1979.

Rony, Jean. *Trente ans du parti*. Paris: Christian Bourgeois, 1978.

Ross, George. *Workers and Communists in France*. Berkeley: University of California Press, 1982.

——, and Jane Jenson. "Conflicting Currents in the PCF." *The Socialist Register* (1979). Ralph Miliband and John Saville, eds. London: The Merlin Press.

——. "Strategies in Conflict: The Twenty-third Congress of the French Communist Party." *Socialist Review* (November–December 1979).

——. "The Unchartered Waters of De-Stalinization: The Uneven Evolution of the Parti Communiste Français." *Politics and Society* 9 (1980).

Rossi, A. [Angelo Tasca]. *A Communist Party in Action*. New Haven, Conn.: Yale University Press, 1949.

Roucaute, Yves. *Le PCF et les sommets de l'état: De 1945 à nos jours*. Paris: Presses Universitaires de France, 1981.

Sassoon, Donald. *The Strategy of the Italian Communist Party*. London: Frances Pinter, 1981.

——, ed. *The Italian Communists Speak for Themselves*. Nottingham: Spokesman, 1978.

Schwab, George, ed. *Eurocommunism: The Ideological and Political-Theorectical Foundations*. Westport, Conn.: Greenwood Press, 1981.

Serfaty, Simon, and Lawrence Gray, eds. *The Italian Communist Party: Yesterday, Today, and Tomorrow*. Westport, Conn.: Greenwood Press, 1980.

Souvarine, Boris. *Stalin*. New York: Longmans, Green & Co., 1939.

Starr, Richard F. ed. *Yearbook on International Communism*. Stanford: Hoover Institute Press, 1979.

Stiefbold, Annette Eisenberg. *The French Communist Party in Transition*. New York: Praeger Publishers, 1977.

Szajkowski, Bogdan. "Roots of Eurocommunism." *Contemporary Crisis* 3 (July 1979).

Tartakowsky, Danielle. *Une Histoire du PCF*. Paris: The Presses Universitaires de France, 1982.

Tiersky, Ronald. *French Communism, 1920–1972*. New York: Columbia University Press, 1974.

Tokes, Rudolf, ed. *Eurocommunism and Détente*. New York: New York University Press, 1978.

Trotsky, Leon. *The Basic Writings of Trotsky*. Irving Howe, ed. New York: Schocken Books, 1976.

——. *Dictatorship vs. Democracy*. New York: Workers Party of America, 1922.

——. *The Revolution Betrayed*. New York: International Publishers, 1970.

——. *The Russian Revolution*. Garden City, N. Y.: Doubleday & Company, 1959.

Urban, G. R., ed. *Eurocommunism*. New York: Universe Books, 1978.

Voslensky, Michael. *La Nomenklatura*. Paris: Pierre Belfond, 1980.

Wall, Irwin. *French Communism in the Era of Stalin*. Westport, Conn.: Greenwood Press, 1983.

Weber, Henri, ed. *Le Parti communiste italien: Aux Sources de l'Euro-Communisme*. Paris: Christian Bourgeois, 1977.

Whetten, Lawarence L. *New International Communism*. Lexington, Mass.: D. C. Heath and Company, 1982.

———, ed. *The Present State of Communist Internationalism*. Lexington, Mass.: Lexington Books, 1983.

Williams, Stuart, ed. *Socialism in France: From Jaurès to Mitterrand*. London: Frances Pinter, 1983.

Wohl, Robert. *French Communism in the Making, 1914–1924*. Stanford, Calif.: Stanford University Press, 1966.

Zimble, Brian L. "Partners or Prisoners? Relations between the PCF and CPSU (1977–1983)." *Studies in Comparative Communism* (Spring 1984).

INTERVIEWS

Anderlini, Luigi. May 24, 1982, Rome, Italy.

Elantkowski, Jean Philippe. June 22, 1982, Paris, France.

Elleinstein, Jean. April 26, 1982, Paris, France.

Fiszbin, Henri. May 6, 1982, Paris, France.

Hincker, François. April 19, 1982, Paris, France.

Marcou, Lilly. April 20, 1982, Paris, France.

Martelli, Roger. May 13, 1982, Paris, France.

Rony, Jean. May 27, 1982, Paris, France.

Tartakowsky, Danielle. April 28, 1982, Paris, France.

Index

About the Author

ARMEN ANTONIAN is currently working in private industry. He holds a Ph.D. from the University of California at Riverside. He has had an article, coauthored by Irwin Wall, in *Political Studies* and he delivered a paper at a French history conference.